FUNDAMENTALS, HARMONY, and MUSICIANSHIP

BROWN

MUSIC SERIES

Edited by FREDERICK W. WESTPHAL, PH.D.
Sacramento State College, Sacramento, California

FUNDAMENTALS, HARMONY, and MUSICIANSHIP

MARVIN S. THOSTENSON, Ph.D
Assistant Professor of Music

The State University of Iowa
Iowa City, Iowa

WM. C. BROWN COMPANY PUBLISHERS
135 SOUTH LOCUST STREET • DUBUQUE, IOWA

Manufactured by WM. C. BROWN CO. INC., Dubuque, Iowa
Printed in U. S. A.

PREFACE

An individual who is broadly proficient in his chosen field of endeavor has learned to use the fundamental tools of his craft effectively. The music student, as a beginner, must acquire the skills and basic knowledge which are his fundamental tools. When, as a more advanced student, he has assimilated this knowledge and skill, he must then use it to further his understanding and appreciation of music and to develop his musicianship. With this as his background he is able to realize in his musical activities a truly satisfying experience.

The general purpose of this book with its accompanying manual then, is to present the necessary basic concepts of music fundamentals and harmony which will support more advanced theoretical instruction and to suggest experiences for the development of musicianship which will aid the student in attaining this type of background. This general purpose can be refined by stating that the author has endeavored to make available in an integrated manner, within the scope of a textbook and supplementary manual, sufficient content to provide the basic concepts of fundamentals, harmony, and musicianship necessary for the beginning music major, and to provide the opportunity to stress certain correlated aspects of music study.

The writing of this material is the result of the author's many years of teaching experience with music students. This experience has proven that proficiency in basic knowledge cannot simply be assumed. There is need for ground work. If proficiency has been attained in an area little difficulty will be encountered in demonstrating competence; if difficulty is encountered, proficiency should be acquired.

The work presented in this course has been used, in whole or in part, as the foundation of the undergraduate music theory program at the State University of Iowa for some years. Many sections of the material also have been tested through usage at several other colleges. The course is designed to be completed in two, or if desired, three semesters depending on the ability of a given class. Sufficient material has been included to assure satisfactory competence with average student ability. Whether more or less emphasis is needed in a particular situa-

v

tion must be determined by the instructor to suit his specific class and to make provision for individual differences among students. The creative aspects of many assignments will stimulate the more advanced student. The supplementary units covering the elementary principles of "'Acoustics" and of "Vocal and Instrumental Transposition" offer related material of value to the music student.

In the first two units of FUNDAMENTALS, HARMONY, AND MUSICIANSHIP, emphasis is placed only on fundamentals and musicianship. The units from the third on consist of material selected from each of the three categories. The subject matter is presented in such order as to provide continuity from unit to unit. At the same time relationships among the three categories within a given unit are so correlated as to achieve integration of fundamentals, harmony, rhythm, sight singing, keyboard emphasis, and dictation.

The course of study begins with the rudiments of music—clefs, scales, intervals, manuscript writing, and rhythm. The introduction of these rudiments is the main concern of the first five units and is continued until completed in the twelfth unit. The writer has observed that many undergraduate and even graduate students desirous of studying in various areas of music are handicapped by lack of preparation in basic music theory. By presenting certain fundamentals in such a manner that they are learned to the level of skills, much of this difficulty can be alleviated. For example, as a skill, scale knowledge becomes a *functional tool* for thinking easily within a given key. A thorough knowledge of the fundamentals opens the way to a more comprehensive understanding of music. Fundamental concepts provide the essential, factual, unchanging information which is the means for thinking, studying, and learning harmony, counterpoint, and analysis. Further, the application of this knowledge is the foundation for developing musicianship.

The study of harmony begins in unit three with the construction of triads, and increases in importance until it becomes the principal concern of the last five units. It is predicated upon the inclusion of a minimum number of rules with constant emphasis upon using the developing ear as the ultimate guide to musical effectiveness. Certain chordal concepts are studied as fundamental theory skills to assure proficiency in their spelling, thus making this knowledge readily available for harmonic and analytical use and thought. Excerpts from music literature are used as the basis for many assignments, and also to illustrate the application of harmonic principles. Emphasis on harmonic and non-harmonic analysis is an integral part of the approach to a thorough harmonic understanding used in this text and manual.

The areas of musicianship—pitch ear training, rhythm ear training, sight singing, keyboard emphasis, and the several types of dictation—receive continuing consideration throughout. The selection of the sight singing and melodic dictation examples has been made with the added aim of giving illustration to certain elementary aspects of musical form. To develop musicianship, a five-fold approach to musical awareness—spelling, singing, playing, recognizing, and hearing—is used whenever practical to afford the variety of experience needed. Many fundamental concepts, whose spelling is learned through theory skills, are given additional emphasis as keyboard skills, and are further strengthened by ear training practice. This practice includes the use of the voice in singing, and the use of the ear in recognizing and hearing. The sight singing exercises provide opportunity for application of the student's knowledge of pitch and rhythm, while the dictation sections offer the opportunity to demonstrate and develop individual competence in applying certain fundamental harmonic or rhythmic principles learned.

A few general statements and suggestions are relevant.

1. Musical terms of special importance, or those needing further clarification, are marked with an asterisk in the unit or assignment in which they are first significantly used. These terms are defined in a "Glossary of Musical Terms" following the units as "Appendix A."

2. Appendix B contains four sections. Of these, each of three outline summaries coordinates, under a single subject heading, related aspects of harmonic study which have been presented. These outline summaries of chords, cadences, and non-harmonic tones will be found helpful for giving an over-all orientation for purposes of unity, integration, and review. A fourth outline summarizes standards for student self-evaluation in the performance of basic skills.

3. The "Suggestions for Study," often given for fundamental and harmonic concepts newly introduced are, in certain instances, practically in the nature of assignments and may be used in this way.

4. The "Satisfactory Attainment" suggested to indicate proficiency in the learning of skills is *minimal*. Three levels of attainment are outlined in the Appendix.

5. No extreme ranges are found in the sight singing material. It is advantageous, however, to acquire experience in reading notation at various levels in each of the clefs used, employing octave transpositions as needed. Since this is obviously the technique of the conductor in studying his score it is worth emulating. Note these suggestions concerning the ranges used:

   a. the range covered in the treble clef is from g to f^2.

   b. the range covered in the bass clef is from G to e^1.

   c. sounds beyond the range of a particular voice should be transposed an octave up or down as momentarily needed.

6. No expression marks are used in the music from the Baroque period in accordance with the general practice of the time. However, always incorporate expressiveness in sight singing as an important phase of the development of musicianship.

7. The exercises in Pitch and Rhythm Ear Training, Pitch Skills, Pitch and Rhythm Achievement, or Melodic Dictation may be performed by the students on their respective instruments for class or other dictation practice.

8. Dictation exercises for individual and class use are incorporated in the "Musicianship" section of each textbook unit, together with suggestions for testing and evaluation.

9. An analytical "Table of Contents" and an "Index of Musical Illustrations" are included to further the usefulness of the text.

10. The supplementary "Workbook" includes two principal sections. They are:

    a. flash card sets referred to in the textbook

    b. work sheets covering the assignments in fundamentals, harmony, and analysis.

11. A condensed "Table of Contents" is included in the Workbook.

12. The "Rhythm Skills" found in the accompanying manual may be performed on the instrument of the student's choice, if this is preferred to vocal performance.

In conclusion, the basic philosophy underlying the relatively detailed organization and presentation of the substance of this course is that, once the student has mastered the fundamental tools of his craft, he can give to the more creative aspects of music the recognition and attention they rightly deserve. The skills emphasized are not an end in themselves. Rather, an importance is placed on these skills in order to make them so functional that they can be useful, with a minimum of effort, in ultimate effective and creative expression which is both stimulating and satisfying.

Inherent in the procedures advocated is student knowledge of the reasons for the learning of basic skills and their application to the theoretical and practical aspects of music. The teacher will assure that the learning of skills is accompanied by such instruction as will motivate the student to want to acquire basic knowledge as an important step towards better realizing his potential.

As author, I wish to thank Professor Himie Voxman, Head, Department of Music, and Professor Thomas Turner, Chairman of the Theory Area, Department of Music, both of the State University of Iowa, for fostering a professional climate which stimulates study, experimentation, and research. I am indebted to Professor Richard Hervig, also of the Department of Music, the State University of Iowa, for his many constructive and helpful criticisms. Our acknowledgements extend to the many teachers and graduate students from a number of places who have contributed valuable suggestions, and to the many students who have used these materials during the period of their development.

Permission has been requested and granted for the use of music known to be under the protection of a current copyright; any error in this regard is wholly inadvertent.

Finally, I want to thank my wife, Josephine, whose discerning encouragement and devoted assistance throughout the entire project have been indispensable.

Marvin S. Thostenson
Iowa City
April, 1963

CONTENTS

UNIT THREE

Fundamentals

Musicianship

UNIT FOUR

Fundamentals

Musicianship

UNIT FIVE

Harmony

Fundamentals

Musicianship

UNIT SIX

Harmony

Fundamentals

UNIT SEVEN

UNIT EIGHT

UNIT NINE

UNIT ELEVEN

UNIT TWELVE

SUPPLEMENTARY UNIT TWO

Vocal and Instrumental Transposition

Appendix A—Glossary of Musical Terms

Appendix B—Outline Summaries

FUNDAMENTALS, HARMONY, and MUSICIANSHIP

UNIT 1

I. CLEFS

The method used today for the notation of musical pitch became evident about the year 1000 A.D. Since that time a number of clefs*, known collectively as the "C," "F," and "G" clefs, have been used for notating music. Originally, when notes* higher or lower than those which could be accomodated on the staff of a given clef were needed, a different clef was used. During the past three hundred years this practice has changed. We now use ledger lines* and two clefs—the treble, known as the violin or "G" clef, and the bass, which is the most common of the "F" clefs. These two clefs, either singly or in combination, are used by all voices and by most instruments. Exceptions are the viola, which uses the alto, the most common "C" clef, and the bassoon and trombone, which often use another "C" clef, the tenor, for high notes. A knowledge of these five clefs—the treble, bass, alto, tenor, and soprano—will assist in the development of musicianship, will aid in acquiring proficiency in transposition, and will facilitate the study of scores from earlier periods of music history.

A standard system for identifying the pitch level of each note in each of the clefs is suggested. In this system a given pitch level (middle C, for instance, as "c¹") is identified by the same letter symbol, regardless of the clef in which it is written. *e.g.*:

POSITIVE IDENTIFICATION OF PITCH ON THE GREAT STAFF*

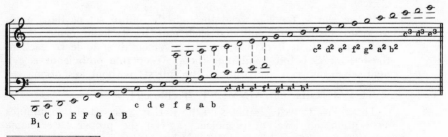

---

*Words marked with an asterisk are defined in the Glossary of Musical Terms.

1

RELATIVE PITCH ORIENTATION IN THE FIVE CLEFS
(middle C and the five lines of each staff)

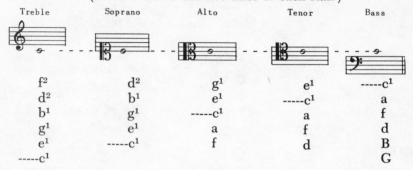

Treble	Soprano	Alto	Tenor	Bass
f^2	d^2	g^1	e^1	-----c^1
d^2	b^1	e^1	-----c^1	a
b^1	g^1	-----c^1	a	f
g^1	e^1	a	f	d
e^1	-----c^1	f	d	B
-----c^1				G

A. The treble clef (*Theory Skill #1*)

Knowledge of the treble and bass clefs is fundamental for any serious study of music. In the treble clef, an acquaintance with the notes extending from f below the staff to e^3 above the staff is sufficient. The four areas are detailed.

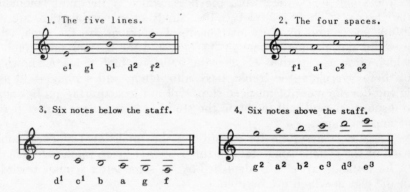

1. The five lines.

e^1 g^1 b^1 d^2 f^2

2. The four spaces.

f^1 a^1 c^2 e^2

3. Six notes below the staff.

d^1 c^1 b a g f

4. Six notes above the staff.

g^2 a^2 b^2 c^3 d^3 e^3

SUGGESTIONS FOR STUDY (Use Flash Card Set #1—"Treble Clef.")

If the clef is familiar, read through the entire set of flash cards to assure facility in identifying each note by its letter name. If the clef is unfamiliar, it may be more convenient first to learn each of the four areas before combining them. Acceptable proficiency is evident when one can read through the full set without hesitation.

SATISFACTORY ATTAINMENT: Treble clef.

The ability to write 24 notes on the staff in a period of two minutes as a minimum level of proficiency, given the proper letter name identification for each item. Use whole notes.

e.g.: Record the following pitches on the treble clef staff:

—g	—a²	—d³
—c²	—b¹	—e¹
—d¹	—f	—g²

A method of evaluating the attainment in theory skills is found in the Appendix under "Suggested Standards for Proficiency in Skills."

B. The bass clef (*Theory Skill #2*)

An acquaintance with the notes from B_1 below the staff to f^1 above the staff is adequate.

SUGGESTIONS FOR STUDY (Use Flash Card Set #2—"Bass Clef.")

Use the techniques described under treble clef, working for similar proficiency.

SATISFACTORY ATTAINMENT: Bass clef.

The ability to complete a test comparable to that suggested for the treble clef.

II. MAJOR SCALES

The C major or diatonic scale*, C, D, E, F, G, A, B, and C, played on the white keys of the piano is familiar. The placement of a sharp sign* before a note (or after its letter name) raises the pitch of the note one-half step. This procedure applied to the C major scale produces the C♯ major scale. Since each of the seven different tones is sharped, the C♯ major scale must contain seven sharps in its key signature.* Sing and play these two major scales, each on its tonic* pitch, and note that the whole and half step patterns are identical, except for the pitch level. Starting with the tonic degree of the C♯ major scale and following the procedure outlined one can readily write the 15 major scales. Notice that the tonic degrees of the successive scales follow the circle of fifths.*

A. The circle of 15 major scales. (*Theory Skill #3*)

1. Write the C♯ major scale in evenly-spaced letter names.

| (7♯) | C♯ | D♯ | E♯ | F♯ | G♯ | A♯ | B♯ | C♯ |

2. Each new scale begins on the 4th tone of the previous one. In each scale the 4th tone is lowered. Therefore, the rule is, UP FOUR, AND LOWER THE FOURTH.

| (6♯) | F♯ | G♯ | A♯ | B | C♯ | D♯ | E♯ | F♯ |

3. Continue applying this rule until no sharps remain.

(5♯)	B	C♯	D♯	E	F♯	G♯	A♯	B
(4♯)	E	F♯	G♯	A	B	C♯	D♯	E
(3♯)	A	B	C♯	D	E	F♯	G♯	A
(2♯)	D	E	F♯	G	A	B	C♯	D
(1♯)	G	A	B	C	D	E	F♯	G
(none)	C	D	E	F	G	A	B	C

4. Continue to apply the same rule, noting that the altered note requires a flat* from this point onward.

(1♭)	F	G	A	B♭	C	D	E	F
(2♭)	B♭	C	D	E♭	F	G	A	B♭
(3♭)	E♭	F	G	A♭	B♭	C	D	E♭
(4♭)	A♭	B♭	C	D♭	E♭	F	G	A♭
(5♭)	D♭	E♭	F	G♭	A♭	B♭	C	D♭
(6♭)	G♭	A♭	B♭	C♭	D♭	E♭	F	G♭
(7♭)	C♭	D♭	E♭	F♭	G♭	A♭	B♭	C♭

SUGGESTIONS FOR STUDY: Observe carefully the whole and half step structure of the major scales. Note that the first four and the last four notes of each scale contain the same pattern of whole and half steps, namely, whole, whole, and half. These four tone groups are called tetrachords, and this particular one, the major tetrachord.*

Practice reciting the circle of 15 major scales in letter names. Doing so in one minute is superior attainment.

Practice reciting the 15 major scales in random order. For this purpose use the 15 cards marked "M" (for major) in the "21 Tones," Flash Card Set #3. The same standard applies.

SATISFACTORY ATTAINMENT: The ability to write the 15 major scales in letter names in a period of three minutes, following the circle of fifths from C♯ through C♭. This attainment level, and that mentioned for each theory skill, is an acceptable minimum. Further information on evaluation and higher levels of attainment can be found under "Suggested Standards for Proficiency in Skills" in the Appendix.

III. RHYTHM

To describe music in simple terms is difficult but, from the stand-point of rhythm*, music can be viewed as an ever-changing complex of sound and silence. At one moment every voice of the score may be sounding; at another some may be silent while others are sounding. The variety of combinations is almost infinite. Inadequate as this description may be, it does suggest one essential fact, namely, that music occupies space in time. Stated in a related manner, music consists of a series of impressions made up of combinations of sound and silence following one after the other in point of time. The relation of these successive impressions to each other and to the passage of time is a phase of rhythm which requires continuing study.

In this unit it is desirable to attain an understanding and working knowledge of four aspects of rhythm, namely: notes and rests, duple and triple organization, meter, and the pulse unit.

A. Notes and Rests

Music is written by means of a series of standard symbols, whose placement on the staff and shape or form determine the pitch and the duration of the tone represented. Since the beginning of the Baroque Period (circa 1600) note and rest* values have remained essentially unchanged. Several notes and their equivalent rests which found constant use during the Ars Nova (1300-1450) and the Renaissance (1450-1600) periods have virtually disappeared from modern notation. These are the breve*, longa, and the maxima, respectively two, four, and eight times the value of the whole note. The notes and rests in current use are listed with their American and English names.

Simple Note	Simple Rest	American Name	English Name
o	▬	whole note (rest)	semi-breve
♩ ρ	▬	half note (rest)	minim
♩ ♩	𝄽	quarter note (rest)	crotchet
♪ ♪	𝄾	eighth note (rest)	quaver
♪ ♪	𝄿	sixteenth note (rest)	semi-quaver
♪ ♪	𝅀	thirty-second note (rest)	demi-semi-quaver
♪ ♪	𝅁	sixty-fourth note (rest)	hemi-demi-semi-quaver

A dot placed after any simple note, or rest, increases its value by one-half. Hence, a dotted note has a value one-and-one-half times that of the simple note.

A double dot placed after any simple note, or rest, increases its value by one-and-three-quarters times. The first dot increases the value by one-half, and the second dot adds one-half the value of the first dot, hence, the total double-dotted note value becomes one-and-three-quarters times that of the simple note's value.

B. Duple and Triple Organization of Pulses

Sing a steady succession of tones on the neutral syllable "la." (La la la la la, etc.) If no attempt is made to sing any "la" louder than any other, the mind will tend to organize the tones in groups of two, three, or perhaps four—the latter really as two groups of two. Should the mind's grouping be in two's, one would hear la la la la la, etc. This rhythmic grouping of tones or pulses in two's is duple organization.*

Should the mind have heard the succession of tones in groups of three, one would hear la la la la, etc. This rhythmic grouping of pulses in three's is triple organization.*

C. Meter

Meter* is the basic pattern of organization and accent used in each measure* of a musical composition. The type of pattern is designated by the numerator* and the denominator* of the meter signature.* The beginning of each measure is given a primary accent; its termination is indicated by a bar line.*

D. The Pulse Unit

Each accented tone sung in determining duple or triple organization indicated the beginning of a pulse unit.* For clarity the pulse unit is often placed in parentheses at the beginning of a musical exercise or illustration. The metronomic tempo* indication, a pulse unit together with a number, often is found as a specific indication of the desired tempo for a musical composition.

1. Meters indicated by a signature whose numerator is 2 or 4

   a. in moderate tempo* the pulse unit is most often the note value indicated by the denominator of the meter signature.

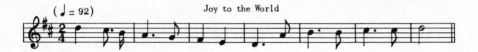

   b. in very slow tempo the pulse unit is often the note whose value is one-half that indicated by the denominator of the given meter signature.

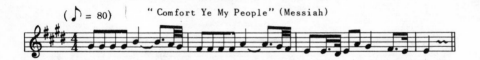

   c. in fast tempo the pulse unit is either the value of the denominator, or, more often, a note twice that value.

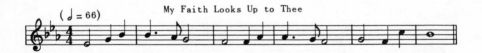

2. Meters indicated by a signature whose numerator is 3, 6, 9, or 12

   a. in moderate tempo (which may vary from quite slow to even fairly fast) the pulse unit can be either the value of the denominator, or a note three times that value.

   (1) the tune *America* is so stately that one feels a pulse on each of its three beats or counts per measure, with a heavier accent on each first beat. Thus the pulse unit is the value of the denominator, since a pulse unit three times this size would lend an uncharacteristic waltz feeling.

Play or sing *America* in two ways, that is, using either
the quarter note or the dotted half note as the pulse
unit. Compare and contrast the effect produced.

(2) the tune *Silent Night* would sound rather plodding
if each of the denominator pulses were given the stress
shown to be appropriate for *America*. Performance
will show that *Silent Night* sounds best when the
pulse unit is a note three times the value indicated by
the denominator. Since the given meter is 6/8, the
pulse unit becomes the dotted quarter note. Always
consider these two possibilities when determining the
pulse unit in a triple meter in moderate tempo.

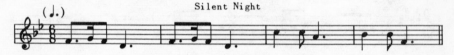

b. in fast tempo the pulse unit is always a note whose value
is three times that indicated by the denominator. This is
characteristic of the waltz, and particularly so of the
scherzo.*

c. in very slow tempo the pulse unit may be the value of the
denominator, or it may be the note whose value is one-
half that indicated by the denominator of the meter signature.

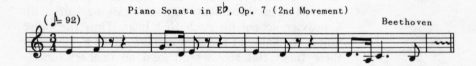

3. Meters indicated by a signature whose numerator is 1, 5, 7, or other less frequently occurring numbers, defy simple categorization. Each of these will be dealt with after the fundamental groupings of two and three are well understood.

4. Summary

Knowledge of what note value to use as a pulse unit in reading and studying music is essential. One must be able to determine the correct value for the pulse unit for any meter at any given tempo. Notice from the following table that each of the meters mentioned may be read from the standpoint of three different pulse units, depending upon whether the tempo is moderate, fast, or very slow.

Meter	*Tempo*	*Pulse Unit*	*Number per measure*	*Performance remark*
4/4	moderate	quarter note	four	"in four"
4/4	fast	half note	two	"in two"
4/4	very slow	eighth note	eight	"in eight"
3/4	moderate	quarter note	three	"in three"
3/4	fast	dotted half note	one	"in one"
3/4	very slow	eighth note	six	"in six"
2/4	moderate	quarter note	two	"in two"
2/4	fast	half note	one	"in one"
2/4	very slow	eighth note	four	"in four"

ASSIGNMENT #1: Basic Rhythmic Principles.

Work Sheet #1 provides space for the written answers and musical examples of this assignment concerning duple and triple organization, meters, and pulse units.

IV. MUSIC MANUSCRIPT WRITING

Most students have had little experience in writing music notation, thus there is need for practice in music manuscript writing. Since the major scales as well as the treble and bass clefs have just been learned, these items, together with the various simple note and rest values, provide logical materials for manuscript practice. To make this project as effective as possible a range is used that is more extensive than the one studied for each clef. The known range is extended through the use of additional ledger lines. A working knowledge of certain symbols used in manuscript notation is necessary background. These symbols are: clef signs, key signatures, note heads, stems, flags, beams, and the double bar.

A. Clef signs
  1. Treble clef

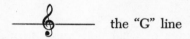 the "G" line

  2. Bass clef

 the "F" line

B. Key signatures
  1. Knowledge of the C♯ major key signature (seven sharps) includes that of any lesser signature. The order in which the sharps occur is F♯, C♯, G♯ D♯, A♯, E♯, and B♯. The order of sharps must be memorized. Each scale uses its respective number of sharps always beginning with F♯.

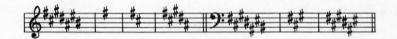

  2. Knowledge of the C♭ major key signature (seven flats), includes that of any lesser signature. The order in which the flats occur is that of the circle of fifths already used in the major scales. It is B♭, E♭, A♭ D♭, G♭, C♭, and F♭, and must must also be memorized. Each scale uses its respective number of flats always beginning with Bb.

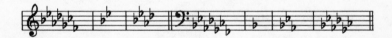

C. Notes
  1. Note heads
    The heads are oval in shape and slightly less than the width of a space on the staff.

Half (♩) and whole (○) note heads can be made with a single movement of the pencil, or with two arcs, as is done with the manuscript pen. For example, the whole note, ○ , consists of ⌒ and ⌣ .

2. Note stems

Stems should be vertical, about three spaces in length, and should extend up or down from the note head respectively as the head is below or above the middle line of the staff. The stem of a note on the middle line may point either up or down. THESE STEM RULES APPLY ONLY TO A SINGLE LINE PART OR SCALE. Downward stems are attached before, and upward stems after the note head.

3. Note flags and beams

Notes of less duration than quarter notes are either given separate flags (♪), or are grouped under one or more common beams (▬ ▬

a. flagged notes are especially useful in vocal music, where it is desirable to show the association of notes with specific syllables of text. The FLAG IS ALWAYS TO THE RIGHT OF THE STEM, regardless of the stem's direction. Single, double, and triple flags indicate respectively, the eighth, sixteenth, and thirty-second note.

b. beams are used to group together two or more notes, using one beam for eighths, two for sixteenths, and so on. In contrast to the thin line which serves well as a stem, a beam should be a broad straight line, usually placed at a slight angle with the staff. The stem direction of a beamed group of notes is that shared by the majority of notes in the group. Since beamed notes are more easily read than flagged notes, it is wise to use beams rather than flags whenever possible.

D. Double bar

The double bar (‖) serves as a practical means of punctuation. It should be placed at the end of each musical exercise, and not necessarily at the far right hand side of the page. Note its use in the foregoing illustrations.

ASSIGNMENT #2: Manuscript writing, rhythm, major scales, clefs.

This assignment, together with needed instructions, is found on Work Sheet #2.

MUSICIANSHIP

The term musicianship° includes various skills which are fundamental in the development of the well-trained musician. These skills include those of ear training—pitch perception, rhythm perception, sight singing, and dictation—and keyboard proficiency.

Each unit's section on "Musicianship" covers some aspect of pitch ear training, rhythm ear training, sight singing, keyboard emphasis, and dictation. "Dictation" is divided into pitch, rhythm, melodic, and harmonic sub-sections. Melodic dictation is not introduced until Unit II, however, and harmonic dictation still later.

Pitch Ear Training

In pitch ear training we shall consider pitch independently of rhythm in order to concentrate upon its unique problems. Each pitch concept studied is also emphasized as a "Theory Skill" and, when practical, as a "Keyboard Skill."

1. Hand singing

Singing from the hand is an easily understood way to begin training the ear. Many scale, arpeggio, and interval patterns can be dictated conveniently from the hand. Henceforth this device, or technique, will be referred to as "handsinging."

a. sing a major scale, associating the numbers 1-8 with the successive degrees of the scale.

b. practice the association of the numbers with the hand as shown following. This is the "keyboard" hand.

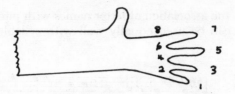

c. use the index finger of the other hand to indicate the desired pattern of pitches, allowing the ends of the fingers of the keyboard hand to represent odd numbers, and the webs, even numbers.

d. practice the following suggested patterns:
   (1) 1 2 1 3 1 4 1 5, etc. (varied intervals)
   (2) 1 3 2 4 3 5 4 6, etc. (intervals in broken thirds)
   (3) 1 1 5 5 6 6 5 4 4, etc. (melody from diatonic scale)
   Invent additional patterns for further practice.

The handsinging range may be somewhat extended. H2 indicates the 2nd scale degree an octave higher. L7 indicates the 7th scale degree an octave lower.

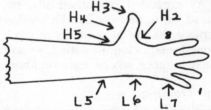

Handsinging in two simple parts is possible by using the thumb and index finger as pointers.

2. The major scales

Ear training exercises which will clarify the relationships among letter names, numbers, and pitches are a logical way to further the understanding of the major scales. Two examples of such exercises are offered. Many more can be devised.

a. the association of letter names with numbers. (This association can be used equally well with syllables.)

b. the association of letter names with pitch. (This association can be used equally well with syllables.)

B ♭ ♭ C   D   E ♭ F   G   A   B ♭

c. sing a part or all of the circle of scales in letter names, starting with any convenient key. Sing each scale within a one octave range, always starting on the tonic degree at the proper pitch.

Letter names and pitch can be associated by using the handsinging technique. The response can be the letter name combined with the pitch, the number with the pitch, or some neutral syllable with the pitch.

As suggested parenthetically, the syllables do, re, mi, fa, so, la, ti, and do, can be used either to supplement or replace the use of numbers in pitch training. This can be done by equating do with 1, re with 2, mi with 3, etc., in each instance where scale numbers have been suggested.

Rhythm Ear Training

Rhythm ear training focuses attention upon those concepts which are necessary to an understanding of rhythm and its performance. In this first unit are given a number of exercises characteristic of three simple meters.*

In order to perform rhythm one must be able to count it. The proficient musician is able mentally to associate the proper count with the rhythm as he reads the notes in performance. It is suggested that the student practice the following steps to promote his rhythmic competence.

Step 1—note the meter, the pulse unit, and set the tempo.

Step 2—"sing-count," that is, use the proper numbers as words for naming each beat when singing the rhythm. If this cannot be done with ease, first write the actual detail of the count below the notes and then practice to gain proficiency.

Step 3—sing the rhythm on the neutral syllable "la" or "ta," counting mentally.

1. Rhythm exercises for group study.
   a. duple organization as found in 2/4 meter.

b. triple organization as found in 3/4 meter.

c. duple organization as found in 4/4 meter.

2. Rhythm skills for individual performance

Some technical aspects of rhythm now have been studied and practiced in class drills. Another approach also will be used: the individual mastery of certain groups of rhythm patterns whose application to music is very general. The rhythms in each set are organized in accordance with some basic rhythmic principle which will be made clear in each instance. Either the "sing-count" or the "neutral syllable" ("la" or ta") methods may be used for the performance of all rhythm skills.

For information concerning the interpretation of satisfactory attainment see "Suggested Standards for Proficiency in Skills" in the Appendix.

  a. Characteristic Rhythms: 4/4 meter (*Rhythm Skill #1*)
    Use Flash Card Set #4 for this skill. The 22 rhythm patterns are selected from those possible, using notes and rests equal to and larger than the denominator, including the use of the tie.*

SATISFACTORY ATTAINMENT: the ability to perform these rhythm patterns in random order at any tempo up to 152 quarter notes per minute.

  b. Characteristic Rhythms: 3/4 meter (*Rhythm Skill #2*)
    Use Flash Card Set #5 for this skill. The 22 rhythm patterns include those based on notes and rests equal to and larger than the denominator, as well as several based upon the dotted quarter and eighth note combination.

SATISFACTORY ATTAINMENT: the ability to perform these rhythm patterns in random order at any tempo up to 152 quarter notes per minute.

Sight Singing

Sight singing is a special type of music reading. It involves the use of several different music skills. There is the need for keeping a rhythmic pulse moving, and this pulse must be organized in terms of the particular note values and meter used. The sequence of changing pitches also must be recognized and superimposed upon the prevailing rhythm pattern at precise moments. In vocal music the words must be properly divided into syllables, each of which must be pronounced at a specific rhythmic moment. It is understandable that the combinations of these patterns can cause difficulty. However, systematic practice in which the student first masters the rhythm, and then the pitch—adding words last—will prove effective in increasing proficiency. The ultimate goal, of course, is to make these separate factors occur as simultaneously as possible. Several specific suggestions for practice follow:

The first essential in sight singing is to deduce certain pertinent INFORMATION about a given selection. A plan is given.

  INFORMATION:
    .... clef; key of .... major (minor); .... meter; begins
    on ....; and on the ....beat
      (degree number or syllable)   (rhythmic position)

Knowing the INFORMATION the student should (as mentioned before) concentrate on the rhythmic problems, learning which rhythms are and which are not characteristic of the given meter. The rhythm of a composition is like a frame, and on this frame "hang" the pitches involved. The pitches can be learned most easily by figuring out their relation, in either numbers or syllables, to whichever major or minor scale is pertinent at the moment. The pitch factor of difficult melodies will need the background of an understanding of the sound of each interval.* This subject will be studied in later units. The addition of words then, to rhythm and pitch, is mainly a matter of additional cencentration, rather than of more difficulty.

To study each of the given musical excerpts effectively, ascertain and apply the pertinent INFORMATION, survey the rhythm and pitch problems, and practice (without instrumental assistance except to establish the pitch level) until each factor is clearly understood. Use as effectively as possible the scale and rhythm knowledge learned thus far.

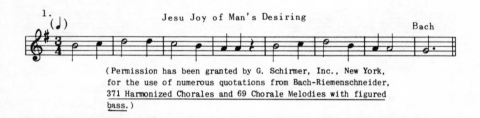

Jesu Joy of Man's Desiring

Bach

(Permission has been granted by G. Schirmer, Inc., New York, for the use of numerous quotations from Bach-Riemenschneider, 371 Harmonized Chorales and 69 Chorale Melodies with figured bass.)

Sonata in C Major, Opus 53

Beethoven

sempre *pp*

Valet will ich dir geben

Bach

Symphony in C Major

4.

Schubert

Symphony No. 34 in C Major, K. 338

5.

Mozart

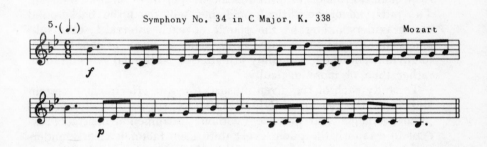

Lohengrin (opera)

6.

Wagner

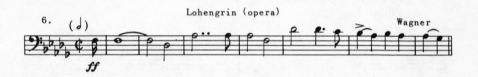

Quam Pulchra Es

7.

Dunstable

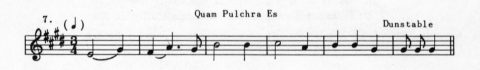

Symphony No. 2 in D Major, Opus 36

8.

Beethoven

Quartet in B♭ Major, K. 589

9.

Mozart

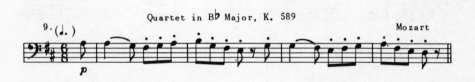

Keyboard Emphasis

A degree of proficiency at the keyboard is almost indispensable for any musician. From the student's standpoint, whenever keyboard practice can strengthen some fundamental of music and thereby make a contribution to his growth, it is serving a useful purpose. In this course opportunity is provided for the development of one or more essential keyboard skills in almost every unit. The first of these skills will be introduced in Unit II. As a prerequisite, non-pianists should demonstrate (1) a knowledge of the natural, flat, and sharp letter names of each of the white and black keys, and, (2) an understanding of the relation of pitch to the keyboard as expressed through the treble and bass clefs.

Dictation

Proficiency in dictation indicates the ability to think pitch and rhythm sounds in terms of their equivalent notation. For dictation practice, students can work together, can listen to materials played in class, or to taped or recorded materials in an ear training (language type) laboratory.

1. Pitch

Throughout these units an unchanging rhythmic value is used for pitch dictation to permit full concentration upon the problem of changing pitch. A suggested procedure for practice of pitch dictation could be:

the key is ....; use .... notes in .... clef; the key tone or tonic degree will be sounded before each exercise; the exercise will be played three times.

For a broad approach to the problems of pitch dictation three types of student responses are pertinent. The *first* and most important type is to record the series of pitches in whole notes on the staff using the clef named. The *second* response, supplementary in nature, would be to record the series of pitches heard in terms of the appropriate scale numbers or sharped or flatted scale numbers, as necessary. For the *third* response, also supplementary in nature, record the series of pitches heard in terms of the appropriate solmization* syllables. The last two types of responses are of value since they readily can be converted into equivalent staff notation.

Pitch Achievement

These exercises are based upon tone patterns found within the major scale. Other practice exercises can be constructed in all major keys.

2. Rhythm

The following procedure and typical examples are suggested for practicing rhythmic dictation.

the meter is ....; no note value smaller than the denominator is used; one measure will be counted aloud before beginning each exercise to set the tempo; the exercise will be played three times. Record the correct succession of rhythmic values.

a. 2 quarter notes in 2/4 meter.

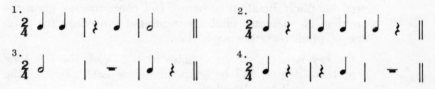

b. 3 quarter notes in 3/4 meter.

c. 4 quarter notes in 4/4 meter.

UNIT 2

I. THE FUNDAMENTAL MELODIC UNIT:

The Major and Minor Second

Examine some composition such as a Bach chorale,* a choral selection, or other piece of musical literature which seems melodious or tuneful. Find two or three examples of a melody,* tune, or theme* of from three to five measures in length. Each of these passages will be constructed of some succession of intervals.* Examine each of these intervals for size, noting how many are small and how many are the larger leaps. Usually more small intervals than large will be found; and more often than not the majority of the small ones are the ordinary whole and half steps.

    A. Enharmonic spellings of the whole and half step intervals.

        Because of the frequency of their occurrence and the ways in which they are used, the whole and half step intervals—technically known as major,* and minor* seconds—may well be called the basic building units of melody. The function of this section is to develop an understanding of and proficiency in the spelling (*i.e.*, using the letter names) of these intervals.

        As an aid to developing this understanding, it should be remembered that the octave can be divided into a chromatic* scale of 12 semitones, but that our system of notation provides for a total of some 35 possible enharmonic* spellings by using each of the natural, sharp, flat, double sharp,* and double flat* letters. Note from the following illustration that each of the 12 tones within the octave can be represented by three letter names except for G♯, whose only enharmonic spelling is A♭.

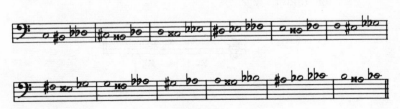

21

B. Combinations of whole and half steps (*Theory Skill #4*).

There are four possible whole and half step movements. Given an initial pitch and moving within this step limitation, the four movements are: a whole step up, a half step up, a half step down, and a whole step down. These basic melodic movements are grouped into four easily sung pairs, each of which is considered separately.

1. whole step up and half step down

Thinking in the C major scale, write the tonic, the supertonic,* and the leading tone* in a five-tone pattern as shown. D is a whole step up, and B a half step down from C.

Following this pattern, a whole and half step combination can be spelled on the tonic degree of each major scale, using only adjacent scale tones.

2. half step up and whole step down

Using the whole and half step pattern learned before, alter the whole step up to a half step up by lowering the upper tone a half step, and extend the half step down to a whole step down by lowering the bottom tone a half step. Thus D becomes D♭ and B becomes B♭.

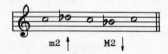

Following this procedure provides a half step up and a whole step down combination from the tonic of each major key.

3. whole step up and whole step down

The whole step up occurs within the scale and was used in "1" before, and the whole step down was obtained by alteration under "2."

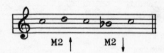

Similar reasoning will produce the whole step up and whole step down on the tonic of each major key.

4. half step up and half step down
   The half step up was obtained by alteration under "2" before, and the half step down occurs within the scale.

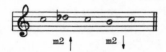

A similar procedure will give the half step up and the half step down from the tonic of each major key.

SUGGESTIONS FOR STUDY: Play and recite each of the four whole and half step patterns just illustrated on the tonic degree of each major scale. Use the 15 flash cards marked "M" in the "21 Tones."

Play and recite each of these whole and half step patterns on the six tones —D♯, E♯, G♯, A♯, B♯, and F♭, the remaining six of the "21 tones." Since these tones occur as tonic degrees only in the advanced keys beyond seven sharps and seven flats, the spellings will include a number of double sharps and double flats.

ASSIGNMENT #3: Practice in writing whole and half steps.

Write these four whole and half step patterns on each of the 21 tones (B♯ through F♭) following the format shown on Work Sheet #3. Four different patterns and 21 tones allow a total of 84 whole and half step combinations to be written.

SATISFACTORY ATTAINMENT: the ability to spell correctly, using alternate treble and bass clefs with whole notes and accidentals, at least 16 whole and half step patterns in five minutes. The format is that of the assignment just completed. However, begin the test on any other note than that on which the assignment was begun, following the 21 tone circle from that point down through the F♭. Then return to B♯ and go through the 21 tone circle again. Continue this procedure for the duration of the test.

II. MAJOR SCALES AND KEYS

A. MAJOR SCALES (*Theory Skill* #5)

Studying the major scales in various ways is one means of stimulating thorough understanding. The major scale sound is familiar, the letter names in each scale have been learned, and the whole and half step and tetrachord structures are known.

Further mastery can be achieved by writing the 15 major scales on the staff. Practice writing the major circle of scales (C♯ through C♭) on alternating treble and bass clefs, two scales to a staff. Also alternate the use of signatures and accidentals with each successive scale. This format is found on Work Sheet #4. For further practice reverse the headings for the signatures and accidentals and again write the major scales as directed above. More practice can be had by beginning on any tone in the 15-tone major circle of keys, and still more practice by arranging the scales in random order.

SATISFACTORY ATTAINMENT: the ability to write at least eight major scales on the staff in five minutes, beginning the test anywhere on the 15-tone major circle from C♯ through C♭.

B. MAJOR KEYS (*Theory Skill* #6)

Using the proper flash cards from the 21 tone set recite the key signatures by looking at the tonic or key side of each card. Recite the tonics or key tones by looking at the signature side of each card. Mix the cards in such a way as to provide for both types of response.

SATISFACTORY ATTAINMENT: the ability to attain a minimum 85 per cent score on a 20-item test whose responses are divided between asking for the key from the signature, and the signature from the key.

III. TRANSPOSITION

Proficiency in changing or transposing music from one key to another is of practical value to any musician. This is particularly true for the vocalist, who often has difficulty finding a composition written in the key which best suits his voice, or for the conductor who suddenly needs a new part. The difficulty of transposition* tends to increase as the interval between the original and the new key becomes larger.

A. *The Principle of Transposition*

Any tone of a musical composition bears an exact interval relationship to the tonic degree of that composition, and this relationship will remain identical in any desired key.

e.g.: 1) A is the 6th degree of the C major scale. Thus, transposed to the key of 3♯s major whose tonic degree is A, the new 6th degree is F♯.

2) E, A, G are the 3rd, 6th, and 5th degrees of the C major scale. In the 4♭ scale whose tonic degree is A♭, these tones become respectively, C, F, and E♭.

B. The following *Rules of Transposition* are extensions of the Principle

  1. transposition up a half step adds seven sharps to a given signature. Thus, in transposing from C to C♯, D♭ to D, E♭ to E, F to F♯, G♭ to G, A♭ to A, and B♭ to B the same letters are read with all inflexion signs raised a half step.

  2. transposition down a half step adds seven flats to a given signature. Thus in transposing from C to C♭, B to B♭, A to A♭ G to G♭, F♯ to F, E to E♭, and D to D♭ the same letters are read with all inflexion signs lowered a half step.

  3. *General Rule of Transposition.*

      a. compute the exact interval between the original tonic and the tonic of the new key, as, for example, two whole steps up from the tonic of C major to the tonic degree of 4♯s major.

      b. maintain this exact interval (even in spelling) between each successive pair of corresponding tones.

  ASSIGNMENT #4: Elementary transposition.
  This assignment is found on Work Sheet #5.

IV. RHYTHM: Characteristics of simple meters with numerators of 2, 3, and 4

The properties which give distinguishing patterns of sound to music written in a certain meter can be called characteristics of that meter. These properties are inherent in the metric organization—duple, triple, compound, or irregular groupings—and this organization is modified by the tempo with its effect upon the size of the unit of pulse.

Broadly speaking, almost any rhythm pattern is possible in any meter, but it may or may not be characteristic of the meter in which it occurs. Here we deal with characteristic groupings, and in this regard several general statements can be made:

  1. the largest note or rest value that can be used in a simple meter (numerator of 2, 3, or 4) is that shown by the meter signature. This note is the sum of the note values comprising a complete measure. *e.g.*:

  2. any simple note, rest, dotted note, or dotted rest value up to that of the meter signature can be used. However, those smaller than the value of the denominator will receive only

cursory attention until the study of "subdivision in rhythm" is introduced.

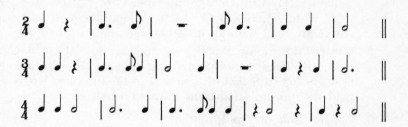

3. duple meter is usually notated to show organization in terms of either two or four denominator pulses. This topic, too, will also receive more attention under "subdivision in rhythm."

4. triple meter is notated to show organization in terms of a group of three denominator pulses.

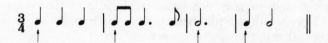

Many rhythm patterns characteristic of duple meter were used in Rhythm Skill #1 (CHARACTERISTIC RHYTHMS: 4/4 meter). These patterns using no value less than the quarter note, give ample illustration of the outlines of 4/4 meter. Reduced to combinations of eighth notes in Rhythm Skill #3 (CHARACTERISTIC RHYTHMS: 4/8 and 2/4 meter), these and similar patterns provide the basic rhythms in 4/8 meter. If the eighth notes are considered to be the first duple subdivision of the denominator quarter note, the same combinations adequately characterize 2/4 meter.

The triple organization of 3/4 meter is shown by the rhythm patterns of Rhythm Skill #2 (CHARACTERISTIC RHYTHMS: 3/4 meter). Here the basic patterns are augmented by some combinations of the dotted quarter and eighth note. Similarly, the same patterns in eighth notes, found in Rhythm Skill #4 (CHARACTERISTIC RHYTHMS: 3/8 meter), outline a solid basis for 3/8 meter. Rhythms Skills #3 and #4 are introduced later in this unit.

As stressed in Unit I, the function of tempo in determining the actual unit of pulse in each given instance is very important. Read again the discussion of the "Pulse Unit." The decision regarding which note value to use as a unit of pulse must be based upon observing the meter, the directions for interpretation (*e.g.,*: Adagio,* Allegro,* Andante,* Largo,* Lento,* Moderato,* Presto*), the metronomic tempo indication, if given (*e.g.:* $\downarrow$ = 76), and the musical style of the composition. These elementary observations are essential for intelligent reading and performance of music. After a basic understanding has been achieved, growth in musicianship will be strengthened by continued study of musical style relative to precise periods of music history, to given composers, and to specific musical compositions.

ASSIGNMENT #5: General rhythm study.

This assignment is found on Work Sheet #6.

MUSICIANSHIP

Pitch Ear Training

1. Review handsinging as described in Unit I. Use the various positions of the hand to call for sound patterns based upon the major scale and the major tetrachord.

2. Acquire proficiency in the recognition* and hearing* of whole and half steps.

   a. sing W up and H down on different beginning pitches, using either the letter names for singspelling, scale numbers, solmization syllables, or the neutral syllable "la."

   b. sing other patterns, such as H up and W down; W up and W down; H up and H down; W down and H up; H down and W up; W down and W up; and H down and H up.

   c. practice playing each of the possible whole and half step patterns on the keyboard or on any other instrument.

   d. listen to the various whole and half step patterns played. Practice recognizing the pattern used. The response, either oral or written, should be such as "(I heard a) W up and a W down," or simply, "W up and W down."

e. given the pitch of the first tone, practice listening to the whole and half step patterns, determining and recording the patterns used, and writing them in correct notation in the assigned clef. *e.g.*:

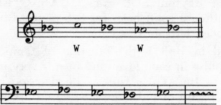

3. Further your proficiency in singing, recognizing, and hearing the major scale.

   a. sing the major scale on any given pitch. Without further given pitch, sing the major scale which can be built upon the second degree of the first one. Next, sing a major scale a half step lower than the last. Sing another major scale a half step below the third scale. The last scale sung should sound at the pitch level of the first scale. This exercise provides practice in shifting from one major key to another either a half or a whole step away. It is important to be able to sense the key tone, or tonic, of each new scale.

   b. sing a major scale when given the pitch of any degree within that scale, *e.g.*: given F♯ as a 3rd degree, then sing the D major scale.

   c. sing several major scales emphasizing the two major tetrachords included in its compass. Given the tonic degree of a major scale, sing only its upper tetrachord. Or given the first tone of the upper tetrachord, that is, the dominant* degree of the scale, sing the entire scale.

   d. devise other procedures for further practice.

Rhythm Ear Training

1. The exercises given are typical of the rhythms found in simple meters. In performing each exercise note the meter, the pulse unit, and set the tempo. Sing the rhythms on "la" or "ta," counting mentally. Whenever problems arise use the "sing-count" technique suggested in Unit I. Notes of the next value smaller than the denominator are counted by inserting "&" to divide the beat.

a. pulse unit is the note value indicated by the denominator of the meter signature.

b. pulse unit is a note value two times that indicated by the denominator.

c. pulse unit note value is three times that indicated by the denominator.

d. pulse unit note value is one-half that indicated by the denominator.

2. Rhythm Skills for individual performance.

Evaluate performance by using the "Suggested Standards" found in the Appendix.

a. Characteristic Rhythms: 4/8 and 2/4 meters, Flash Card Set #6, (*Rhythm Skill #3*)

These 22 rhythm patterns are organized upon the same principle as Rhythm Skill #1. They include the use of the tie. SATISFACTORY ATTAINMENT: the performance of these rhythm patterns in any order and at any tempo up to 176 eighth notes per minute.

    b. Characteristic Rhythms: 3/8 meter, Flash Card Set #7.
(*Rhythm Skill #4*)

        The 22 rhythm patterns are organized upon the principle
used in Rhythm Skill #2, adding combinations of the
dotted eighth and sixteenth note, as well as using the
tie. SATISFACTORY ATTAINMENT: the performance of
these rhythm patterns in any order and at any tempo up
to 176 eighth notes per minute.

Sight Singing: Form Emphasis . . . the phrase

    Achievement in the skill of sight singing is especially dependent
upon the ability to organize simultaneously the pitch and rhythmic
factors of a melodic line. In each melody or tune some combination
of these factors tends to organize it into units known as phrases,*
each of which has its own inner balance. Usually a tune is composed
of two or more phrases. An occasional phrase may be complete in
itself, that is, it has a conclusive (closed or final) quality. More
often, however, a phrase ends in an inconclusive (open) manner
which demands a continuation.

    Practice and study each of the following examples by ascertaining
and applying the pertinent INFORMATION (as outlined in the
first unit), considering the rhythmic and pitch problems, and singing without instrumental assistance. Be sure to note the conclusive
or inconclusive quality of each phrase ending.

1. Symphony in B Minor — Schubert

2. Der Freischutz — Von Weber

3. Concerto No. 5 in E♭ Major, Opus 73 — Beethoven

Symphony No. 1 in B♭, Opus 38

Concerto in D Major, Opus 77 (violin)

Concerto in D Major, Opus 61

Pictures at an Exhibition

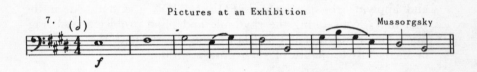

Symphony No. 1 in B♭ Major, Opus 38

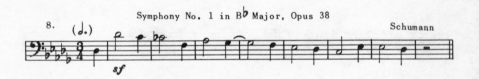

The Little Dustman

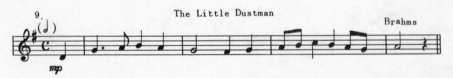

Keyboard Emphasis

Keyboard Skill #1

SATISFACTORY ATTAINMENT: playing the 15 *major scales* at a tempo of at least 120 notes per minute, following the circle of major scales from C♯ through C♭. Use either one or two hands, depending upon your pianistic facility. The evaluation of the performance of keyboard skills is outlined in "Suggested Standards for Proficiency in Skills" in the Appendix.

A *Table of Suggested Fingerings* follows:

Left hand								Scale	Right hand								
3	2	1	4	3	2	1	2 (3)	C♯, D♭	2	3	1	2	3	4	1	2	
4	3	2	1	3	2	1	2 (4)	F♯, G♭	2	3	4	1	2	3	1	2	
4	3	2	1	4	3	2	1	B, C♭	1	2	3	1	2	3	4	5 (1)	
5	4	3	2	1	3	2	1	E	1	2	3	1	2	3	4	5 (1)	
5	4	3	2	1	3	2	1	A	1	2	3	1	2	3	4	5 (1)	
5	4	3	2	1	3	2	1	D	1	2	3	1	2	3	4	5 (1)	
5	4	3	2	1	3	2	1	G	1	2	3	1	2	3	4	5 (1)	
5	4	3	2	1	3	2	1	C	1	2	3	1	2	3	4	5 (1)	
5	4	3	2	1	3	2	1	F	1	2	3	4	1	2	3	4 (1)	
3	2	1	4	3	2	1	2 (3)	B♭	2	1	2	3	1	2	3	4	
3	2	1	4	3	2	1	2 (3)	E♭	2	1	2	3	4	1	2	3	
3	2	1	4	3	2	1	2 (3)	A♭	2	3	1	2	3	1	2	3 (4)	

Dictation

1. Pitch

Certain pitch concepts, such as intervals, triad* qualities, and scale types are sounds which must become very familiar to the music student. These and other sounds are the means by which the musician can think tonal distances, and therefore are an important part of musicianship. To assure competent learning a high standard of SATISFACTORY ATTAINMENT is essential.

A method for determining the PROFICIENCY PERCENT-AGE attained in pitch dictation is given. Reference to this

general method will be made following most pitch skills and
pitch achievement sections. A general standard for evaluating any attained PROFICIENCY PERCENTAGE is outlined
in the Appendix under "Suggested Standards for Proficiency
in Skills."

1. Judge each response as follows:
   a. if both the analysis and spelling are correct the response
       is "C."
   b. if the spelling is incorrect, or is omitted, the response is
       incorrect regardless of the correctness of the analysis and
       is marked "S" to indicate the error in spelling.
   c. if the analysis is incorrect, or is omitted, the response is
       marked "R" to indicate an error in recognition.
2. Compute the PROFICIENCY PERCENTAGE by dividing
   the number of "C" responses by the total number of responses
   in the test. For many pitch skill tests a ten response test is
   convenient.
3. Have the student determine the pattern of error in each pitch
   skill test so he can assess his status. After determining the
   PROFICIENCY PERCENTAGE and counting the number
   of "S" and "R" errors, one of the following statements will
   apply—
   a. if "S" errors predominate there is need for further practice
       of spelling.
   b. if "R" errors predominate there is need for singing, playing
       on one's instrument, and listening to the sound patterns
       involved until they become familiar enough to be easily
       recognized and remembered.

Pitch Skill #1—Hearing Whole and Half Step Patterns
               (the Major and Minor Second)

SATISFACTORY ATTAINMENT: demonstrated ability in hearing the
various whole and half step patterns. Given the initial pitch and the
clef, respond by recognizing, correctly notating, and analyzing each
of five patterns played. Each five-note pattern includes two responses
for purposes of evaluation. *e.g.*:

Pitch Achievement

The following examples of pitch dictation are similar to those
introduced in Unit I. They give practice in hearing and writing pitch

patterns of a general nature based upon the major scale and whole
and half steps. Proficiency in this type of dictation depends largely
on how well the student can correlate his knowledge of the spelling
and his memory of the sound of a given pitch concept.

Compute the PROFICIENCY PERCENTAGE as directed. No
analysis is necessary in this general type of dictation.

1. Rhythmic

Use the dictation procedure of Unit I for the following examples. To compute the PROFICIENCY PERCENTAGE in
this rhythmic dictation, consider each measure to be a response and divide the number of correct responses by the
total number attempted.

a. dictation in which the pulse unit is that indicated by the
value of the denominator.

b. dictation in which the pulse unit is two times that indicated
by the denominator.

    c. dictation in which the pulse unit is three times that in-
        dicated by the denominator.

    d. dictation in which the pulse unit is one-half that indicated
        by the denominator.

2. Melodic

    Hearing a phrase of music immediately suggests the pres-
ence of both vertical (pitch) and horizontal (rhythmic) concepts. The changing melodic line can be recorded as exact
pitches on various degrees of the staff, and the duration of
tone or silence can be represented by note or rest values
within an appropriate meter. For practicing melodic dictation
these directions are suggested:

    a. write in .... clef, using (specify signature or accidentals).
    b. the tonic degree is ....; the meter is ....
    c. the tempo is illustrated, and the phrase is played two to
        four times, depending upon its difficulty.

    A PROFICIENCY PERCENTAGE in melodic dictation can
be computed as follows:

    a. consider each correctly written note to be worth two
        points—one for pitch and one for rhythm.
    b. the number of correct pitches divided by the total num-
        ber of notes gives the PROFICIENCY PERCENTAGE
        in pitch.
    c. the number of correct rhythms divided by the total num-
        ber of notes gives the PROFICIENCY PERCENTAGE in
        rhythm.

d. the sum of the correct pitches and rhythms divided by two times the number of notes gives the over-all PROFICIENCY PERCENTAGE in melodic dictation.

1. Symphony No. 1 in C Minor, Opus 68 — Brahms

2. Clarinet Quintet in A Major, K. 581 — Mozart

3. Symphony No. 2 in D Major, Opus 73 — Brahms

4. Wanderer's Nachtlied, No. 3 — Schubert

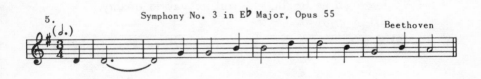

5. Symphony No. 3 in E♭ Major, Opus 55 — Beethoven

6. Prelude and Fugue in C♯ Major (WTC I) — Bach

UNIT 3

I. TRIADS

The triad has long been accepted as the basis of harmonic thinking. It was the French composer and theorist, Jean Philippe Rameau (1683-1764), who codified the principles of tertian harmony* in his work, *Traité d'Harmonie,* first published in the year 1722. Knowledge of the triad and tertian harmony is essential to understanding the language of music.

A. The four triad qualities (*Theory Skill #7*)

There are four forms of the triad*which must become common knowledge to the music student. These four forms, or qualities, considered in conjunction with their sound patterns are: the major, the minor, the diminished, and the augmented. The first step in acquiring this knowledge is to become proficient in spelling the triad forms. This is most easily accomplished by thoroughly learning the major triad.

1. The major triad

A major triad consists of the 1st, 3rd, and 5th degrees of a major scale. In the scale of C major this means that C E G spells a major triad, and similarly, C♯ E♯ G♯ spells a major triad on the tonic degree of the C♯ major scale. The character of the major triad is such that its sound may be described as bright, cheerful, or gay in quality.

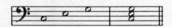 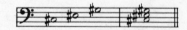

SUGGESTIONS FOR STUDY

1. there are three families of major triads. The "C" family (those on G, C, and F) are either all naturals, like C E G, all sharps, like C♯ E♯ G♯, or all flats, like C♭ E♭ G♭. This family includes nine major triads.

The "A" family (those on E, A, and D) either have a sharp in the middle, like A C♯ E, a double sharp in the

38

middle, like A♯ Cx E♯, or flats at both ends, like A♭ C E♭. This family acounts for nine more major triads.

The remaining three triads are in the "B" family. They are B D♯ F♯, B♯ Dx Fx, and B♭ D F.

2. use the 21 tone flash card set to practice spelling the 21 major triads.

2. The minor triad.

Lowering the 3rd degree of any major triad a half step makes a minor triad. Hence, E G♯ B, a major triad, becomes E G B, a minor triad. The lowered third gives the minor triad a quality of sound which is aptly described as somber, serious, or sad. However, both the major and minor triads have a feeling of stability due to the presence of the perfect fifth interval between their outer voices.

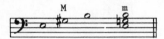
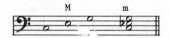

SUGGESTIONS FOR STUDY: Practice spelling the 21 minor triads using the 21 tone flash card set. Remember the comparison between the major and minor triads.

3. The diminished triad.

Lowering the 3rd and 5th degrees of the major triad a half step produces an unstable chord called the diminished triad, because of its lowered fifth interval. On C, C E G becomes C E♭ G♭, or, on C♯, C♯ E♯ G♯ becomes C♯ E G. This triad's quality may be described as tense; its close knit minor third intervals seem to demand a resolution.* This tension is one of the fundamental forces of tertian harmony.

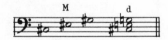

SUGGESTIONS FOR STUDY: Practice spelling the 21 diminished triads from the 21 tone flash card set. Remember the comparison between major and diminished triads.

4. The augmented triad.

Raising the 5th degree of any major triad a half step gives an augmented triad. For example, C E G becomes C E G♯, or B D♯ F♯ becomes B D♯ Fx. The raised 5th degree, technically called the interval of an augmented 5th, imparts to this triad its particular type of instability, the quality of sounding unfinished. Consequently, the augmented triad does not ordinarily conclude a musical selection, but rather, demands a satisfactory continuance.

The necessity for continuance in the diminished and augmented triads can be simply illustrated. Each illustration is intended primarily as an isolated example of satisfactory continuing movement for the benefit of the ear.

a. the diminished triad. Its formation by contracting the intervals of the major triad seems to make further contraction one requirement for satisfactory continuance.

b. the augmented triad. Its formation by enlarging the perfect 5th of the major triad seems to make further expansion one requirement for satisfactory continuance.

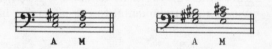

SUGGESTIONS FOR STUDY: Practice spelling the augmented triads from the set of flash cards, remembering the comparison between the major and the augmented triads. There are only 20 augmented triads since the one on B♯ would involve an F triple-sharp which is not used.

ASSIGNMENT #6: Practice in spelling triads.

Write the major, minor, augmented, and diminished triads in eight columns across the page following the 21 tone circle of fifths. (B♯ through F♭). Use Work Sheet #7. The 83 triads in this group (remember the B♯ augmented is impractical) are obtained by following around the 21 tone circle four times. Whenever the B♯ augmented triad occurs in the drill paper or in a test following the circle of fifths write the word "impractical" to account for it.

SATISFACTORY ATTAINMENT: the ability to spell correctly at least 20 major, minor, augmented, and diminished triads in whole notes and accidentals, alternating the use of treble and bass clefs, in a period of five minutes. This test is written exactly like the foregoing assignment, except that the test should start on any other tone than B♯ in the 21 tone circle.

II. THE FOUR BASIC SCALES AND MINOR KEYS

A. The four basic scales

The fundamental difference between a major and a minor scale is found in the lowered 3rd degree of the latter. This difference was experienced when the minor triad was formed by lowering the 3rd degree of the major triad a half step. There are three minor scale forms known as: the natural,* the harmonic,* and the melodic minor.* These four scales—the major and the three variants of minor—constitute the *four basic scales*. Each one is illustrated for sight singing purposes, but only the harmonic minor form will be studied intensively at this time.

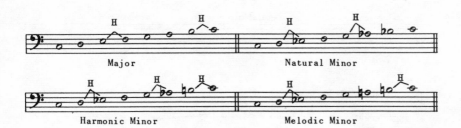

Major   Natural Minor

Harmonic Minor   Melodic Minor

The C major scale needs no key signature, but any minor scale written on C basically requires three flats, those on B♭, E♭, and and A♭. In the natural minor form (to be studied later) all three flats are necessary. In the harmonic minor form the accidental* raising of the 7th degree cancels the effect of the first of the three flats. In the melodic minor form, the accidental raising of the 6th and 7th degrees cancels the effect of two of the three flats. Note this general implication: THE PARALLEL* MINOR SCALE ERECTED UPON THE TONIC OF ANY GIVEN MAJOR SCALE WILL HAVE THREE MORE FLATS, OR THREE LESS SHARPS, THAN THE MAJOR SCALE.

Study the illustrated whole and half step structure of the minor tetrachord* in relation to that of the major tetrachord; that of the Phrygian tetrachord* to that of the major; and that of the harmonic tetrachord* to that of the major.

*a = aug. second

Considered in terms of component tetrachords, the major scale consists of two major tetrachords, disjunct* by a whole step. The minor and Phrygian tetrachords which make up the natural minor scale are also disjunct by a whole step. The harmonic scale consists of the minor and harmonic tetrachords, similarly disjunct. Minor and major tetrachords, the latter becoming Phrygian in the descending form, make up the ascending melodic minor scale. The singing, recognition, and hearing of the four basic scales will be aided by learning the tetrachord structure of each. This structure is illustrated.

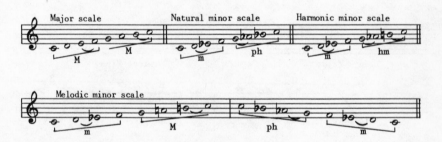

1. The Harmonic Minor Scale (*Theory Skill #8*)

To facilitate study, the harmonic minor scales are written out in letter names. The minor scale relative* to that of C♯ major, seven sharps, is that of A♯ minor beginning on the 6th degree of the former. Thus, the A♯ harmonic minor uses the same notes except that its 7th degree must be raised a half step by using the appropriate accidental.

7♯)   A♯   B♯   C♯   D♯   E♯   F♯   Gx   A♯

Start each new scale on the subdominant,* or 4th degree of the one before, lowering the 6th degree of the new scale permanently, and raising its 7th degree with an accidental.

6♯)	D♯	E♯	F♯	G♯	A♯	B	Cx	D♯
5♯)	G♯	A♯	B	C♯	D♯	E	Fx	G♯
4♯)	C♯	D♯	E	F♯	G♯	A	B♯	C♯
3♯)	F♯	G♯	A	B	C♯	D	E♯	F♯
2♯)	B	C♯	D	E	F♯	G	A♯	B
1♯)	E	F♯	G	A	B	C	D♯	E
none)	A	B	C	D	E	F	G♯	A

Continue, noting that each lowered 6th degree now becomes a flatted tone.

1♭)	D	E	F	G	A	B♭	C♯	D
2♭)	G	A	B♭	C	D	E♭	F♯	G
3♭)	C	D	E♭	F	G	A♭	B	C
4♭)	F	G	A♭	B♭	C	D♭	E	F
5♭)	B♭	C	D♭	E	F	G♭	A	B♭
6♭)	E♭	F	G♭	A♭	B♭	C♭	D	E♭
7♭)	A♭	B♭	C♭	D♭	E♭	F♭	G	A♭

SUGGESTIONS FOR STUDY

1. Use the same type of practice outlined for major scales in Unit I until the letter names are thoroughly familiar. The minor scales must become as familiar as the major scales, since the major and minor modes are equally important, and especially since there are three forms of minor scales.

2. Use the 15 flash cards marked "m" in the "21 Tone" set for reciting the harmonic minor scales in random order. Always note the number of flats or sharps in a given scale and the special effect of the accidental raising of each scale's 7th degree.

3. Practice writing the 15 harmonic minor scales on the staff using treble and bass clefs with either signatures or accidentals. The pattern—similar to that suggested for major scales in Unit II—is found on Work Sheet #8.

SATISFACTORY ATTAINMENT: the ability to write at least eight designated harmonic minor scales on the staff in five minutes, using alternating signatures and accidentals for each successive scale, and alternating treble and bass clefs for each two scales.

B. The Minor Keys and Signatures (*Theory Skill* #9)

Knowledge of the major and minor keys and signatures is an essential aspect of music fundamentals. The major keys were studied in Unit II; in this unit the minor keys are to be learned. Later, opportunity will be given to demonstrate proficiency in both the major and minor keys.

In studying the minor keys it is well to remember that their signatures are independent of the various changes required to form the three types of minor scales. Keeping this point in mind, simple memorization is the easiest manner of learning the 15 minor keys and their signatures. The 15 cards marked "m" (for minor) in the "21 Tones" flash cards will provide a means for practicing. Recite the signatures by looking at the tonic side, and the keys by looking at the signature side of the cards.

SATISFACTORY ATTAINMENT: the ability to show competence in a 20-item test (minimum 85 per cent score) whose responses are divided between asking for the key from the signature, and asking for the signature from the key.

III. THE ALTO CLEF (Theory Skill #10)

The alto clef is the most important member of the family of C clefs, which also includes the soprano, mezzo-soprano, tenor, and baritone clefs. Of these, the alto and tenor clefs are used most frequently, with the soprano, mezzo-soprano, and baritone clefs being less significant. The latter, with middle C on its top staff line, perhaps more often is found in its equivalent form in the F clefs, that is, the clef in which F is the middle line of the staff. Knowledge of the alto clef is a prerequisite to acquaintance with musical literature using the viola. This literature includes such important compositions as the symphony, string quartet, and other chamber music. The C clef sign changes its position in accordance with the location of middle C. The sound notated in the following illustrations is always middle C.

The areas of the alto clef are shown. The range needed in this clef is less than that for the treble or the bass clef, extending from the viola's lowest note, c, below the staff, to the e^2 above the staff.

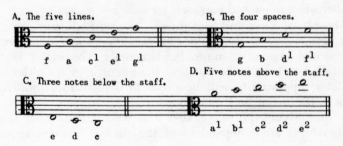

The placement of the flat and sharp signatures on the alto clef staff is relatively identical to that used in both the treble and the bass clef.

SUGGESTIONS FOR STUDY: The ideas suggested for studying treble clef (Unit I) apply equally well to the alto clef. Practice for the same degree of proficiency. Flash Card Set #8 is provided.

SATISFACTORY ATTAINMENT: Alto clef.

The ability to use the alto clef in alternation with the treble and the bass clef in selected theory skills, beginning with those found in Unit IV.

IV. RHYTHM

Characteristics of compound meters with numerators of 6, 9, and 12.

In the simple meters the rhythmic organization is either all duple or all triple. Meters with a numerator larger than 4 are called compound meters* because their rhythmic organization is complex. A meter with a numerator of 6 contains both duple and triple characteristics. To illustrate, a march in 6/8 meter has two beats per measure, like 2/4 meter. However, each of the two 6/8 march beats contains three, rather than two, lesser pulses.

Meters with a numerator of 9 or 12 consist of three or four groups of triple pulses per measure. Whenever the numerator is 9 the meter is triple, both in regard to the organization of the small pulses shown by the denominator value and the number of pulse groups. A numerator of 12 gives an effect like that of a duple numerator of 4, but with each of the four beats divided into triple pulse groups; hence, it is clearly a compound meter.

Four general statements will detail certain characteristics of triple meter:

1. the largest note value that can be used in a triple meter is that shown by the meter signature fraction. This note is the sum of one or more groups of triple pulses in each measure.

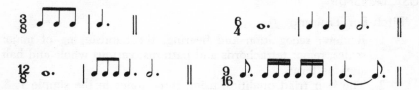

2. the largest simple note or rest value written *as such* in any triple meter is that which is two times the value of the denominator, unless the use of cross-rhythm* (to be studied later) is intended. *e.g.*: in 6/8 meter the largest simple note usable is the quarter note, since its value is less than that of the dotted quarter note, the characteristic triple pulse group.

3. durations longer than twice the value of the denominator are often desirable, but are notated in terms of the characteristic triple grouping unless the effect of cross-rhythm is desired. *e.g.*: the half note, as such, is not characteristic of 6/8 meter since its size obscures triple grouping in terms of dotted quarter values. The value of the half note, therefore, is expressed in equivalent notation characteristic of this meter.

4. dotted notes equal to and larger than the denominator are used in such manner as to lie within, or be in agreement with, the characteristic triple grouping.

ASSIGNMENT #7: Writing characteristic notation and original rhythmic phrases.

This assignment is found on Work Sheet #9.

MUSICIANSHIP

Pitch Ear Training

1. Review: recognition and hearing; the handsinging of major scales; major tetrachords and patterns; various whole and half step patterns.
2. The four triad qualities, using three tones in the simple 1, 3, 5 position.

    a. singspell the major triad on various beginning pitches.

    b. singspell each triad quality in relation to the major. Always do the major triad first. Use any of the 21 tones as the lower note.

    c. singspell the four triad qualities on the same pitch, following the suggested pattern.

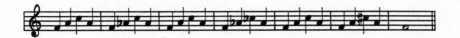

    d. singspell each triad type in sequence but on different pitches for each triad quality.

    e. practice recognizing the four triad qualities.

    f. given the letter name of the lowest tone, practice hearing (or taking dictation) of the four triad qualities. The response may be oral—naming the quality and spelling the triad, or written—recording the quality and accordingly notating the pitches in the assigned clef.

3. The harmonic minor scale.

    a. sing each of the four basic scales illustrated earlier in this unit. Use either numbers, syllables, or the neutral "la." Contrast each minor form with the major scale and with each of the other minor forms.

    b. sing and singspell each of the four basic scales taking care to emphasize their tetrachord structure.

    c. play the 15 harmonic minor scales on the keyboard or on some other instrument.

    d. practice recognizing the four basic scales by the pattern of tetrachords each one contains. (M, M plus M; nm, m plus ph; hm, m plus hm; and mm, m plus M).

    e. practice recognizing each of the four basic scales by the distinctive quality of each.

    f. practice hearing and analyzing the major and harmonic minor scales in dictation, recording the quality and ac-

cordingly notating each in the assigned clef, given the
letter name of the tonic degree.

e.g.:

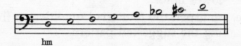

hm

Rhythm Ear Training

1. Practice each of the given examples of triple meter. Note the
meter; note the pulse unit suggested by the descriptive word
or metronomic tempo marking in relation to the given meter;
set the tempo. Sing "la" or "ta," using the sing-count technique
for solving any rhythmic problems encountered.

a. simple meters, numerator of 3.

b. compound meters, numerator of 6.

c. compound meters, numerator of 9.

1. [musical notation, 9/8, ♩. = 72]

2. [musical notation, 9/8, Allegro]

3. [musical notation, 9/16, ♪ = 144]

d. compound meters, numerator of 12.

1. [musical notation, 12/8, ♩. = 100]

2. [musical notation, 12/8, Andante]

3. [musical notation, 12/16, Allegro]

2. Rhythm Skills for individual performance

Evaluate the performance of each skill in the manner outlined in the Appendix.

a. Characteristic Rhythms: 6/4 meter, Flash Card Set #9. (*Rhythm Skill #5*).

SATISFACTORY ATTAINMENT: the performance of these patterns in a steady rhythm, in any order and at any tempo up to 176 quarter notes per minute.

b. Characteristic Rhythms: 9/8 meter, Flash Card Set #10. (*Rhythm Skill #6*).

SATISFACTORY ATTAINMENT: the performance of these patterns in a steady rhythm, in any order and at any tempo up to 176 eighth notes per minute.

Sight Singing: Form Emphasis. . . additional open and closed
phrases

Refer to Unit I for suggestions on giving INFORMATION, on the
study of rhythmic and pitch problems and the combination of these
factors as they pertain to sight singing. After reviewing this material,
study and practice the musical excerpts. Again note which phrases
show conclusive and which inconclusive endings.

5. (♪) St. Matthew Passion Bach

6. ♩.= 108 Album for the Young, Opus 68 Schumann

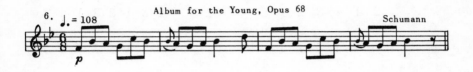

p

7. (♩) Chorale in A Minor (organ) Franck

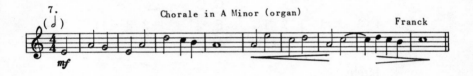

mf

8. (♩.) Symphony No. 4 in D Minor, Opus 120 Schumann

p < > *dolce*

Keyboard Emphasis

Evaluate the performance of these skills in terms of the "Suggested Standards" found in the Appendix.

Keyboard Skill #2—SATISFACTORY ATTAINMENT: the ability to play the major, minor, diminished, and augmented triads on the tonic degree of each of the 15 major scales.

Keyboard Skill #3—SATISFACTORY ATTAINMENT: the ability to play the 15 harmonic minor scales at a tempo of at least 120 notes per minute, following the circle of harmonic minor scales from A♯ through A♭. Use either one or two hands, depending upon current pianistic facility.

Suggested fingerings: (those given in parentheses are needed when continuing into the second octave.)

Left hand	Scale	Right hand
2 1 3 2 1 4 3 2	A♯, B♭	2 1 2 3 1 2 3 4
2 1 4 3 2 1 3 2	D♯, E♭	2 1 2 3 4 1 2 3
3 2 1 4 3 2 1 2 (3)	G♯, A♭	2 3 1 2 3 1 2 3
3 2 1 4 3 2 1 2 (3)	C♯	2 3 1 2 3 1 2 3
4 3 2 1 3 2 1 2 (4)	F♯	2 3 1 2 3 1 2 3
4 3 2 1 4 3 2 1	B	1 2 3 1 2 3 4 5 (1)
5 4 3 2 1 3 2 1	E, A, D, G, C	1 2 3 1 2 3 4 5 (1)
5 4 3 2 1 3 2 1	F	1 2 3 4 1 2 3 4 (1)

Dictation

1. Pitch

Pitch Skill #2—Hearing the Four Triad Qualities.

SATISFACTORY ATTAINMENT: demonstrated competence in hearing the four triad qualities in dictation. Given the initial pitch and clef, respond by correctly recognizing and notating each of ten triads played. *e.g.:*

Each triad and its analysis is considered to be one response for purposes of evaluation. Using the method outlined in Unit II, compute the PROFICIENCY PERCENTAGE, analyze the pattern of error, and evaluate using the SUGGESTED STANDARDS.

Pitch Achievement

These dictation exercises involve the recognition of various step, scale, and triad patterns. Compute the PROFICIENCY PERCENTAGE by dividing the number of correctly notated pitches by the number attempted. Evaluate in terms of the SUGGESTED STANDARDS.

2. Rhythmic

The suggested exercises give practice in recognizing rhythms in several triple and compound meters at various tempi. Compute the PROFICIENCY PERCENTAGE by dividing the number of correctly notated measures by the number of measures attempted.

3. Melodic

Notating a dictated melody involves the evaluation of both rhythmic and pitch concepts. A very useful form of melodic dictation practice is that of recording in correct notation a tune that is common knowledge. The required thinking in tones is a basic tool of the composer, the conductor, the music teacher, and indeed of any observing musician. For practice in melodic dictation—

a. write a familiar tune in notation which is correct in relation both to pitch and to rhythm. Choose any but the most usual key, using it either with key signature or with accidentals.

b. take dictation of such phrases as illustrated, using the procedure outlined in Unit II.

UNIT 4

I. THE DEGREES OF THE SCALE

    A. Functional names of the degrees.

        A knowledge of the names given to the degrees of the diatonic scale, several of which already have been mentioned, helps provide the vocabulary necessary to an intelligent discussion of harmony. The seven degrees with their functional names are listed. Note that each degree is assigned a Roman numeral corresponding with its location in the diatonic scale.

      1.

Degree	*Functional name*	*Symbol*
1st	tonic	I
2nd	supertonic	II
3rd	mediant*	III
4th	subdominant	IV
5th	dominant	V
6th	submediant*	VI
7th	leading tone	VII

      2. To facilitate and increase the understanding of harmony, it is suggested that the Roman numerals be adapted to indicate triad quality, *e.g.*:

        a. major quality—use the ordinary "capitalized" Roman numeral.

        b. minor quality—use the "uncapitalized" Roman numeral, such as "iii" for mediant.

        c. augmented quality—use the major symbol, but add a small plus at the upper right, like "III⁺," for the augmented mediant.

        d. diminished quality—use the minor symbol, but add a small zero at the upper right, like "vii⁰," for the diminished leading tone triad.

    B. Tensions and the various degrees.

        The fact that the major scale includes two half steps together with the five whole steps in its range is productive of many tensions.* That these half steps lie between the 3rd and 4th, and the 7th and 8th degrees of the major scale produces the tensions associated with the major mode.* An elementary exploration of the more obvious tensions found in the major mode can now follow the learning of the functional degree names. For tonal orientation play the C major scale, up and down, before playing each of the following examples.

1. Interval tensions—major mode.

a. play the C–C octave. The playing of this octave is static, or unproductive of tension other than that of pitch level. This indicates that the tonic degree is stable, or in simple words, home base.

b. play the perfect fifth, G–C, the dominant degree followed by the tonic degree. Experimentation with other scale tones moving by leap to the tonic will show this particular leap to be the most convincing. The compelling naturalness of the movement from the dominant to the tonic degree is the basis for the cadence*, which, in this instance, is an authentic cadence.* Quite aptly, the dominant tone (and triad) governs both the major and the minor modes.

c. play the perfect fourth, C–F, the tonic degree followed by the subdominant degree. Then play the inversion of this interval, that is, C, the upper tonic degree, down to F, the subdominant degree. The second interval is a convincing perfect fifth, just like the illustration used in example "b." Therefore, the intervals of a perfect fourth up and a perfect fifth down can be considered as almost equally effective.

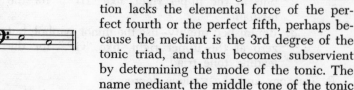

d. play the major third, E–C, the mediant followed by the tonic degree. This combination lacks the elemental force of the perfect fourth or the perfect fifth, perhaps because the mediant is the 3rd degree of the tonic triad, and thus becomes subservient by determining the mode of the tonic. The name mediant, the middle tone of the tonic triad, is logical.

e. play the minor third, A–C, the submediant
    degree followed by the tonic degree. This
    combination also seems weak, probably be-
    cause the submediant degree becomes sub-
    servient by determining the mode of the
    subdominant triad. Thus the term, submedi-
    ant, is logical, since it denotes the middle
    tone of the subdominant triad underneath
    the tonic in the same fashion that mediant
    denotes the middle tone of the tonic triad.

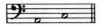

f. play the major second, D–C, the supertonic
    degree followed by the tonic degree. This
    motion gives a melodic effect since it is
    stepwise, and at the same time is logical
    and satisfying. The name, supertonic, de-
    scribes the melodic effect properly, but
    such a name as "pre-dominant" would more
    adequately describe the supertonic's har-
    monic desire to move a perfect fourth up
    to the dominant degree.

g. play the minor second, B–C, the leading
    tone degree followed by the tonic degree.
    Again the stepwise movement has melodic
    significance. Since the movement is that of
    a half step to the tonic, it is even more
    satisfying than that from the supertonic.
    It is possible that the insistent logic of the
    leading tone arises from the fact that it is
    the 3rd degree of the dominant chord,
    whose leap to the tonic was the most na-
    tural sounding of the several scale tone
    leaps, excluding that of the static octave.

2. Relation of each functional degree to the tonic as illustrated
    on the staff.

The tonic, subdominant, and dominant degrees are described as tonal* since their primary function becomes that of defining the tonality.* The mediant, submediant, and the leading tone are known as modal degrees.* This follows, since their inflexion determines whether the mode is major or minor. The supertonic degree remains unchanged in the major and minor mode, but is lowered a half step in the Phrygian church mode. For this reason it is called modal.

C. The Primary Triads (*Theory Skill* # 11)

The preceding discussion has dealt with each degree of the scale and its relation to the tonic degree. Our discussion continues with consideration of the three primary triads* (interchangeably called the three principal triads), those built upon the tonic, subdominant, and dominant degrees of the scale. These three degrees were mentioned as being the tonal degrees, that is, those responsible for determining the tonality. In a later unit the triads found upon the other scale degrees will be studied.

1. Three primary triads: the major mode.

If a triad based upon the available tones of the major scale were erected upon each degree of the major scale, major triads would be found to exist only upon the three tonal degrees, the tonic, subdominant, and dominant. Consideration of the tension of various degrees in relation to the tonic showed the movement from dominant to tonic, V I, to be completely satisfying. This triad root* movement is that of the authentic cadence mentioned earlier. In fact, it can be said that the movement of one triad root to another by the drop of a fifth within the key (or the equivalent upward fourth within the key) is the basic progression* of tertian harmony.

In applying the dominant-tonic relation (harmony's basic progression) other associations within the circle of fifths can be noted: 1) the progression of dominant to tonic follows the circle of fifths TO the tonic, while 2) the progression of tonic to subdominant follows the circle of fifths AWAY from the tonic.

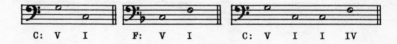

C: V   I   F: V   I   C: V   I   I   IV

The inherent logic of the basic harmonic progression is illustrated by playing the following form of the full cadence,* I IV V I. This cadence will be studied in the next unit.

The major mode always will be heard when the three principal triads, the tonic, subdominant, and dominant, are major in quality. These triads are always built upon the three tonal degrees, those which establish the tonality.

SUGGESTIONS FOR STUDY: The spelling of major triads is already familiar. Now the problem is that of spelling triads major in quality upon the tonic, subdominant, and dominant degrees in each key. Facility can be gained through practicing this type of spelling, that is, spelling major triads upon the 1st, 4th, and 5th degrees of each major scale. Use the 15 flash cards marked "M" in the 21 tone set to suggest the succession of keys.

ASSIGNMENT #8 (Part I): Primary triads—major

Notate and analyze the three primary triads, I IV, V, I for each major key following the major circle of fifths from C♯ through C♭. Alternate the use of signature and accidentals, as well as the use of treble, bass, and alto clefs with each key. Use whole notes. The assignment begins as shown. Use Work Sheet #10.

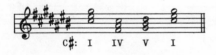

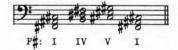

SATISFACTORY ATTAINMENT: the ability to notate and analyze the three primary triads in eight or more major keys in five minutes, alternating the use of signatures and accidentals, and the use of treble, bass, and alto clefs in any order. Use whole notes.

2. Three primary triads: the minor mode*—harmonic (*Theory Skill #12*)

In the major mode the primary triads were major in quality. The harmonic minor scale has a lowered 3rd degree which assures a minor tonic triad. The subdominant is also minor because of the lowered 6th degree when compared with the parallel major scale. The accidently raised 7th degree, the leading tone, gives the harmonic minor a major dominant triad. Thus, the three principal triads of the harmonic minor scale of the minor mode are a minor tonic, a minor subdominant, and a major dominant as shown for the key of E minor.

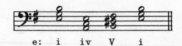

SUGGESTIONS FOR STUDY: Facility in spelling the three primary triads in the harmonic form of the minor mode can be gained by spelling the minor tonic, the minor subdominant, and the major dominant triads built upon the 1st, 4th, and 5th degrees of each scale. Use the 15 flash cards marked "m" in the 21 tones to suggest the sequence of keys. Note the difference in the quality pattern of the major and harmonic form of the minor mode.

ASSIGNMENT #8 (Part II): Primary triads—minor (harmonic)

Notate and analyze the three principal triads, i iv, V, i for each harmonic minor key following the minor circle of fifths from A♯ through A♭. Alternate the use of signature and accidentals, as well as the use of treble, bass, and alto clefs. Use whole notes. The assignment begins as shown. Use Work Sheet #10.

SATISFACTORY ATTAINMENT: the ability to notate and analyze the three primary triads of the harmonic form of the minor mode in eight or more keys in five minutes, alternating in any order the use of key signatures and accidentals, and the use of the treble, bass, and alto clefs. Use whole notes.

II. SCALES: Major and Minor Keys (Theory Skill #13)

In dealing with music of the Baroque, Classical, and Romantic eras, the question of key usually can be resolved by checking the key signature against the initial and final harmonies. For instance, if the signature is four flats, both A♭ major and F minor are possible keys, and the check against the final harmony should clearly establish one or the other. However, should the final harmony be found to be a major chord occurring as the final tonic of what is otherwise a minor tonality, the illustration is that of the "Picardy third,"* a frequently used harmonic concept characteristic of the Baroque period.

> SUGGESTIONS FOR STUDY: To assure proficiency in the major and minor keys, become thoroughly familiar with the following information: (for practice, use all the cards marked "M" and "m" in the 21 tones.)
>
> 1. the number of flats or sharps in any given major or minor key.
> 2. the major and minor keys associated with any given key signature.
> 3. the relative major of any minor key; the relative minor of any major key. (Remember there is no change of signature between relative keys.)
> 4. the parallel major to any given minor key; the parallel minor to any major key. (Remember that a parallel minor key will always have three less sharps or three more flats than the major key on the same tonic degree.)
>
> SATISFACTORY ATTAINMENT: Major and minor keys
>
> The ability to attain a minimum of an 85 per cent score on a 20-item test covering each aspect of the foregoing information.

III. INTERVALS

The study of intervals will be presented in several stages, each based upon the major scale. This approach allows the student to develop a clear understanding through singing, writing, playing, recognizing, and hearing the various interval types. All logical spellings of the 12 simple interval* sounds within the octave will be studied.

A. The major* and perfect* intervals, up (*Theory Skill* #14)

1. The intervals formed between the 1st, or tonic degree, and the 1st, 4th, 5th, and 8th degrees of any major scale are called respectively, the perfect unison, perfect fourth, perfect fifth, and perfect octave.

D: P 1   P 4   P 5   P 8

2. The intervals formed betwen the 1st degree and the 2nd, 3rd, 6th, and 7th degrees of any major scale are called respectively, the major second, major third, major sixth, and major seventh.

D: M 2   M 3   M 6   M 7

This means that a perfect 5th on D must be the interval from D up to A, the 5th tone of the 2 sharp major scale. Approached in the opposite manner, the interval from B to G♯ must be a major 6th, since B and G♯ are respectively the 1st and 6th tones of the 5 sharp major scale. It is obvious that the prerequisite to an understanding of intervals is a working knowledge of the major scales.

3. The following chart will be of help in the singing, recognition, and hearing of the major and perfect intervals up.

Major and Perfect Intervals Up

Scale degrees	Name	Symbol	Ear Training device
1 - 1	perfect unison	P 1	—none needed.
1 - 2	major second	M 2	—fundamental melodic unit, studied in Unit II.
1 - 3	major third	M 3	—1st and 3rd degrees of the major triad, or the song, "Old Black Jo."
1 - 4	perfect fourth	P 4	—the song "Because."
1 - 5	perfect fifth	P 5	—The tune "Twinkle, Twinkle Little Star."
1 - 6	major sixth	M 6	—the song, "My Bonnie . . ."
1 - 7	major seventh	M 7	—sing up an octave and down a half step, or down a half step and up an octave.
1 - 8	perfect octave	P 8	—none needed.

SUGGESTIONS FOR STUDY:

1. Recite in letter names the major and perfect intervals up based upon the tonic degree of each major scale. Use the 15 flash cards marked "M" in the set of 21 tones.

2. Recite the major and perfect intervals up based on the remaining six cards in the 21 tone set, namely, D♯, E♯, G♯, A♯, B♯, and F♭. Use the comparison method of transposition; for example, base the spellings on D♯ on those known to be correct for D.

D: M 3   D♯: M 3   D: P 5   D♯: P 5   D: M 6   D♯: M 6

3. Play and spell the M and P intervals up, basing them upon each degree of the C chromatic scale and its enharmonic spellings. Nine degrees permit two spellings (C♯ and D♭, D♯ and E♭, E and F♭, E♯ and F, F♯ and G♭, G♯ and A♭, A♯ and B♭, B♯ and C, and B and C♭).

ASSIGNMENT #9: Writing the major and perfect intervals up.

Write the M3, P4, P5, M6, and M7 up in five columns across the page following the 21 tone circle of fifths (B♯ through F♭), using properly stemmed half notes and accidentals. Work Sheet #11 is provided for this purpose. There are 105 intervals in the group obtained by following through the 21 tone circle five times. The major second is not included in this assignment, nor in the following proficiency test, since it was studied in an earlier assignment. However, it is included in the hearing test for these intervals.

SATISFACTORY ATTAINMENT: the ability to spell correctly at least 20 major and perfect intervals up, using alternate treble, bass, and alto clefs, and whole notes and accidentals, in a period of five minutes. The proficiency test is written just like the assignment, except that the test should start on any other tone than B♯, the first tone of the 21 tone circle.

IV. RHYTHM: Irregular meters, numerators of 1, 5, 7, and 8.

The use of irregular meters* with the numerators 1, 5, 7, and 8, is relatively infrequent in the music written between 1700 and 1900, the period of music with which many people are most familiar. Their use is much more frequent, however, in the music of the twentieth century. Using such numerators is rapidly becoming a common practice characteristic of the rhythmic freedom of the present day. Because of the diversity of the numerators and their rhythmic implications, each will be considered independently.

A. Meters whose numerators are "1."

Theoretically, any numerator can be used over any possible denominator. From previous units it becomes apparent that when meters with numerators of 2 or 3 are performed rapidly, the effect is that of using one pulse per measure. Hence, two-two, two-four, three-four, or three-eight meters become respectively, 1/1, 1/2, 1/dotted half note, and 1/dotted quarter note meters. Returning to the use of a real "1" in the numerator and remembering that successions of single pulses tend to be heard as groups of two or three, it becomes evident that the use of a "1" meter for more than a measure or two would possibly result in a "paper rhythm," meaning rhythm which does not sound like it is notated to sound.

An experiment with one-beat measures is offered. Pulsate in groups of two—duple organization—for one or more measures, occasionally interpolating a single unit pulse *e.g.:*

```
1 2 1 2 1 1 2 1 2 1 2 1 1 2 1 2 1 2 1 1 2 1
>   >   > >   >   >   > >   >   >   > >   >
```

The effect is quite appealing, due partly to the shift of accent (comparable to a change in marching step) resulting from the two successive "1" pulses. Next pulsate in groups of three, likewise interpolating an occasional single unit pulse, *e.g.:*

```
1 2 3 1 2 3 1 1 2 3 1 2 3 1 1 2 3 1 1 2 3 1
>       >     > >       >     > >       >
```

Again the over-all rhythmic conflicts produce an interesting effect.

A rhythmic "jar" like the foregoing is used by Stravinsky in the opening measures of the *Symphony of Psalms* where he interpolates a single measure of 1/4 into a section whose prevailing meter is 2/4. In this instance the effect is that of a stop, or cadence, after which the music immediately continues. The rhythm pattern shown below is that of the example quoted, measures 7 through 9.

This example suggests that the use of "1" as a real numerator is effective when it acts as a momentary contrast to some other prevailing meter.

B. The use of "5" as a numerator.

The use of 5 as a numerator probably began, as far as traditional harmony and music literature are concerned, during the nineteenth century as a natural result of inquisitive minds seeking for special musical effects. Many of the composers of the century display much subtlety of rhythmic grouping under conventional meter signatures. However, the conscious use of a 5 meter throughout a movement represented a step forward rhythmically. The "Andante con Grazia" from Tschaikovsky's *Symphony No. 6 in B Minor* is a fine illustration of the use of this less usual meter.

$$\frac{5}{4} \quad \text{♩ ♩ | ♩ ♩ ♩ | ♩ ♩ | ♩ ♩ ♩} \quad = \frac{2+3}{4}$$

Reiterating the tendency to divide non-stressed pulses into groups of either two or three, it is quite natural to suggest that five-four meter would be performed either as a 2 plus 3 over 4, or as a 3 plus 2 over 4. Experimentation with the two groupings may indicate that the former seems more smooth, but the suggestion should be made that each measure must be considered in terms of its musical content and its position within the phrase. This should not rule out the possibility of such combinations as 2 plus 1 plus 2, and 1 plus 2 plus 2, all over 4, or whatever denominator is indicated. Several such examples, together with suggestions for performance, are given in the section devoted to "Musicianship."

C. The use of "7" as a numerator.

The suggestions made concerning 5 as a numerator readily can be extended for the numerator 7. Confronted with a 7 in the numerator, the question arises as to which of the several groupings of seven pulses would be applicable and appropriate. If one studies the music involved, the natural grouping will become evident, and there is little doubt but that this grouping will include some possible combination of 2, 3, or 4 pulses. The seventh measure of "The People that Walked in Darkness" from Peter Mennin's *Christmas Story* illustrates the point.

have seen   a great light.

In the Mennin example the grouping of pulses is 2 plus 3 plus 2 over 4. Several other groupings are listed following with the suggestion that each be practiced in order to obtain more familiarity with irregular rhythm patterns which create cross-rhythms. Think in terms of a denominator of either a quarter note or an eighth note with each combination.

4 plus 3	4 plus 2 plus 1	2 plus 4 plus 1
3 plus 4	4 plus 1 plus 2	2 plus 2 plus 2 plus 1
2 plus 2 plus 3	1 plus 2 plus 4	2 plus 2 plus 1 plus 2
2 plus 3 plus 2	1 plus 4 plus 2	2 plus 1 plus 2 plus 2
3 plus 2 plus 2	2 plus 1 plus 4	1 plus 2 plus 2 plus 2

D. The use of "8" as a numerator.

The number 8 as a numerator in its own right is of rather infrequent occurrence, but it can result from a subdivided 4/4, or even 2/2 meter. The use of this numerator in ordinary duple organization involves no new problem. As a compound meter it lends itself to many interesting possibilities in irregular groupings, however, several of which present noteworthy cross-rhythmic conflicts. Three of these are shown following; the student should devise many more. Practice each one, thinking in a denominator of either a quarter note or an eighth note.

3 plus 3 plus 2   3 plus 2 plus 3   2 plus 3 plus 3

ASSIGNMENT #10: Irregular Meters—rhythmic phrases and musical examples.

This assignment is found on Work Sheet #12.

MUSICIANSHIP

Pitch Ear Training

1. Review: the singing, recognition and hearing of whole and half steps and combinations of them; the four basic major and minor scales and their component tetrachords; and the four triad qualities.

2. Functional degree names.
   a. given the pitch of the tonic degree of a major scale,
      1) sing the name and pitch of another functional degree indicated by a handsinging sign.

> 2) sing "la" on the correct pitch for any functional degree requested by name.
> 3) respond to the sound of any of the scale tones by saying the functional name and appropriate numeral.
> *b.* given the pitch of the tonic degree of a harmonic minor scale, respond as indicated under "a."

3. The major and harmonic cadence patterns.

This pitch pattern is a melodic version of one form of the full cadence. Learning to hear this cadence pattern in major and in the variant forms of minor will be a pitch skill in a later unit. Becoming familiar with each new cadence pattern will provide some background in the elementary sounds of harmonic dictation.

4. The major and perfect intervals up.

The singing, recognizing, and hearing of intervals is one of the more difficult achievements of ear training. Achievement will be facilitated by concentrated and systematic drill in the pertinent problems.

a. sing any of the M and P intervals up in response to a handsign, given the pitch of the lower tone.

b. respond by singing "la" on the correct pitch, given the lower tone and the interval name.

c. recognize by naming each interval sounded on the keyboard. Each interval should be studied as a melodic sound (as two successive tones), and as a harmonic sound (as two tones sounded simultaneously).

d. given the letter name of the lower tone, practice the hearing or dictation of the major and perfect intervals up. The response may be oral—naming the interval and spelling it, or written—recording the interval name and accordingly notating the pitches in the assigned clef. *e.g.*:

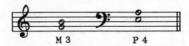

Rhythm Ear Training

1. In the study and practice of the following exercises note each change of meter, its pulse unit, and set the tempo. Sing "la" or "ta" as neutral syllables, or use the sing-count technique to solve problems.

    a. changing meters.

    b. numerator of "5."

    c. numerator of "7."

   d. numerator of "8" (non-duple)

  2. Rhythm Skills for individual performance.

   See the SUGGESTED STANDARDS in the Appendix for evaluating the performance of these skills.

   a. Characteristic Rhythms: 5/4 meter, Flash Card Set #11, (*Rhythm Skill #7*)

    SATISFACTORY ATTAINMENT: the performance of these rhythms in any order and at any tempo up to 176 quarter notes per minute.

   b. Characteristic Rhythms: 7/8 meter, Flash Card Set #12, (*Rhythm Skill #8*)

    SATISFACTORY ATTAINMENT: the performance of these rhythms in any order and at any tempo up to 176 eighth notes per minute.

Sight Singing: Form Emphasis . . . the structure of the phrase

  A phrase is often unified through the repetition of a figure derived from the distinctive use of some pitch or rhythm pattern, or a combination of both. The use of such patterns, or motives,* is an important technique for maintaining a basic unity throughout a phrase. In special instances the repeated figure forms a sequence.* Each of these is also a means by which phrases can be lengthened, or to use the technical term, extended. In music of the present day further variety is often achieved in phrases through the use of irregular meters, as well as by shifting from one meter to another within a musical thought.

  Use the ideas suggested for studying the following excerpts. Also analyze their structure, that is, determine by study and discussion what makes one phrase different from another.

Sonata in D Major, Opus 10, No. 3

6. Largo   Beethoven

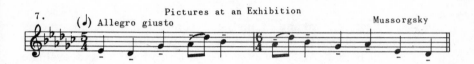

Pictures at an Exhibition

7.   (♩) Allegro giusto   Mussorgsky

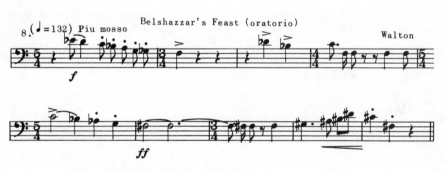

Belshazzar's Feast (oratorio)

8. (♩=132) Piu mosso   Walton

(Copyright 1931 by the Oxford University Press, London.   Quoted
by permission of the Oxford University Press.)

Keyboard Emphasis

Evaluate performance using the SUGGESTED STANDARDS in the Appendix.

Keyboard Skill #4—SATISFACTORY ATTAINMENT: the ability to play the tonic, subdominant, and dominant triads in the 15 major keys. Either hand or both may be used.

Keyboard Skill #5—SATISFACTORY ATTAINMENT: the ability to play the tonic, subdominant, and dominant triads in the 15 minor keys (the harmonic minor scale as the basis). Either hand or both may be used.

Dictation

1. Pitch

   Pitch Skill #3—Hearing the Major and Perfect Intervals, Up.

   SATISFACTORY ATTAINMENT: demonstrated competence in hearing the major and perfect intervals up. Given the pitch and clef of the lower note, respond by correctly recognizing and notating each of 10 intervals played. *e.g.*:

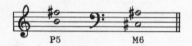

   Each interval and its analysis is considered to be one response for purposes of evaluation. Compute the PROFICIENCY PERCENTAGE, analyze the pattern of error, and evaluate using the SUGGESTED STANDARDS.

Pitch Achievement

   These dictation exercises involve scale, interval, and triad patterns. Compute the PROFICIENCY PERCENTAGE by dividing the number of correctly notated pitches by the number attempted. Evaluate by using the SUGGESTED STANDARDS.

2. Rhythmic

   The suggested exercises give practice in recognizing rhythms written in irregular meters and in using irregular groupings of pulses. Compute the PROFICIENCY PERCENTAGE and evaluate.

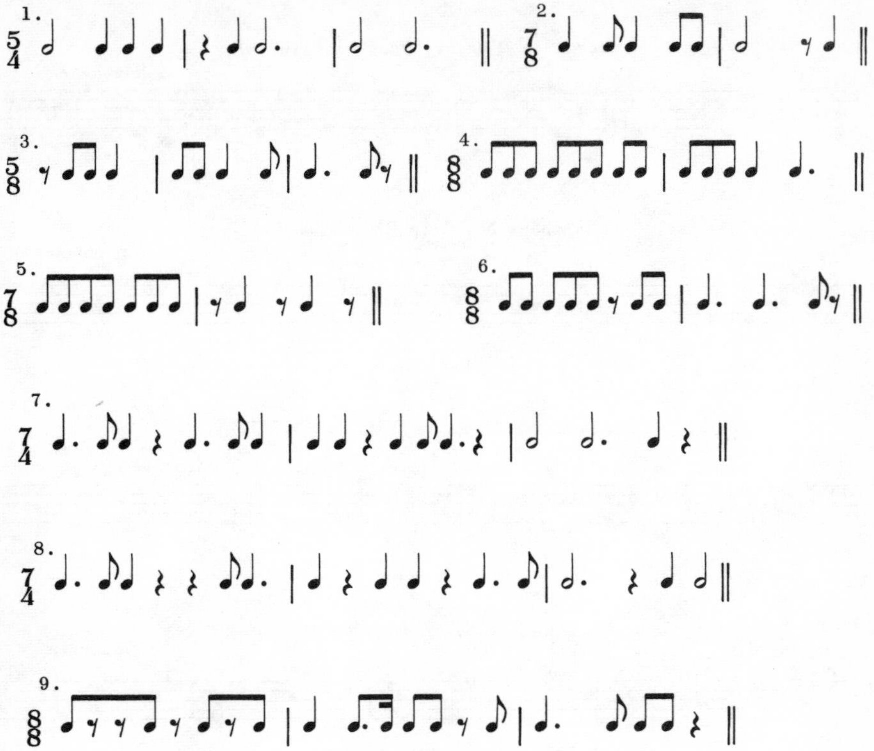

3. Melodic

Compute the PROFICIENCY PERCENTAGE and evaluate in the manner outlined in Unit II.

a. write any familiar tune in correct musical notation in the key of either two flats or two sharps. Use a logical meter and rhythm, and either key signature or accidentals.

b. practice taking dictation of such phrases as are illustrated. Outside the classroom this can be done as a cooperative venture among two or more students, or by listening to tapes prepared for the purpose.

Sometime She Would?

Farnaby

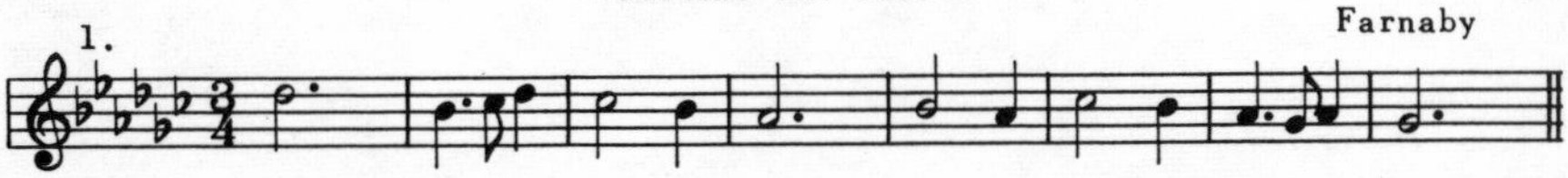

Concerto in D Major, Opus 61 (violin)

Beethoven

Symphony No. 1 in B♭, Opus 38

Schumann

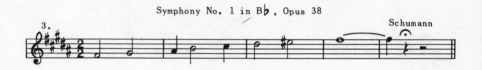

Prelude and Fugue in D Major (WTC I)

Bach

Concert No. 8 in G Major

Couperin

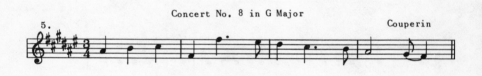

Mount of Olives (oratorio)

Beethoven

UNIT 5

HARMONY

I. INTRODUCTION—spacing and voice range; closed positions; open positions.

Harmony* is the element which provides appropriately organized sound within a musical composition. The organization of this sound may be as apparent as that of a melody in a simple chordal setting, or as complex as the less apparent, but equally important and effective, harmonic logic expressed or implied in a polyphonic composition.

The inexperienced student will first write harmony with the root of each chord in the bass voice, but, as confidence and experience increase, progressions including chords with their root in any upper voice will be used. According to one school of thought, four voices, expressed or implied, provide for much of the Western music of the past three centuries. The voice names are those derived from choral usage, namely, bass, tenor, alto, and soprano. The soprano and alto voices are notated in the treble clef; the tenor and bass voices normally are written in the bass clef. These two staffs used together form the great staff, and are joined by a common brace ({).

(In some choral music the tenor part may be written in the treble clef, but is understood to sound an octave lower than notated. Another often found variation is that of indicating this type of treble clef with a C clef sign. More recent and desirable is a trend to use the treble clef with an "8" below it to designate the downward transposition of an octave. Note the illustrations.)

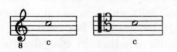

Triads are composed of three tones, but harmonic practice often requires the sounding of four parts. This poses the problem of distributing the three triad tones among four voices. This problem must be considered in its various aspects, namely spacing,* voice distribution,* and the two general types of chord distribution known as closed* and open* position.

75

A. Spacing

Spacing is the term used when speaking of the intervallic distance between pairs of adjacent voices. In four part harmony the interval between the soprano and alto and the alto and tenor voices is traditionally limited to an octave, but the interval between the tenor and bass voices can be extended to approximately an octave and a fifth. (See compound interval.*)

When writing harmony, a decision must be made regarding the range of each voice or part. Further, the student must remain aware of this range throughout the harmonization. Since choral music is just one of the areas for studying harmony, it is unwise to limit the usable range to only that which can be encompassed by the human voice for which a given part is named. For study purposes the illustrated ranges are suggested. Be sure to keep within the range logical for each voice in a given instance, whether the harmonization is intended to be vocal or instrumental in conception.

SUGGESTED RANGES FOR THE FOUR VOICES

B. Voice distribution

Harmony is written in closed position, open position, or in a combination of the two. The difference between the two types of position exists in the spacing used within and between each of the two upper pairs of adjacent voices. It is pertinent to remember that the interval or spacing between the tenor and bass voices remains the same whether in closed or open position. When the upper three voices, considered as a unit, lie within an octave, the chord* is said to be in a closed position. In the initial stages of study it is most logical to double the root of each chord. (See doubling*). This is shown in the following explanation of the closed and open positions.

C. Closed chord positions (*Theory Skill* #15)

1. Major mode

In the chord shown, the tenor and bass voices share the same pitch, the 1st degree, and the three upper voices, the tenor, alto, and soprano, sound adjacent tones of the F major triad, namely, the 1st, 3rd, and 5th degrees, neatly contained within an octave. This chord illustrates the most compact distribution of voices possible in the closed position. If the tenor, alto, and soprano voices are moved upward on the triad tones, maintaining the three adjacent chord tone relationship, five more closed positions are possible within the maximum spacing allowed between the tenor and bass voices. The Roman/Arabic analysis is shown below each chord posi.-tion.

$$F: \quad I^5 \quad I^8 \quad I^3 \quad I^5 \quad I^8 \quad I^3$$

These chord positions are combinations of tones which appear very frequently in music. They should be memorized as a prerequisite to the study of actual chord progressions, which are, in their turn, the essence of harmonic study.

SUGGESTIONS FOR STUDY

Practice playing the group of six closed positions in the various major keys. The root is in the bass voice of each chord, but note carefully the distribution of the doubled root, the third, and the fifth of each chord in the three upper voices. Becoming aware of this feeling for hearing the root, third, and fifth at will is important in achieving good intonation° in any performing group.

ASSIGNMENT #11 (Part I): Closed positions, major mode.

Write in four voices, using whole notes, and alternating between key signatures and accidentals, the six closed positions of each major sharp key and of C major. Work Sheet #13 is provided.

When necessary, transpose the *entire chord position* up or down
an octave in order to stay within the suggested voice ranges.

2. Minor mode

Remember that the spelling of major and minor triads differs only in the lowered 3rd degree of the latter. Consequently, the problems of spacing and voice distribution of closed
chord positions in the minor mode are the same as those of
the major mode. In the illustration note that the last two
closed positions have been transposed down an octave to place
them within an easier range.

f: i5   i8   i3   i5   i8   i3

SUGGESTIONS FOR STUDY

Practice playing the group of six closed positions in the various
minor keys. Note the similar voicing of each chord in the minor
mode in relation to that of the corresponding one in the major
mode. Also note, however, the difference in sonority* between
the minor and major chord positions.

ASSIGNMENT #11 (Part II): Closed positions, minor mode.

Write the six closed positions in A minor and in each of the
minor flat keys as described under part one of the assignment.
The reverse side of Work Sheet #13 provides sufficient space.

SATISFACTORY ATTAINMENT: the ability to notate at least
16 closed chord positions in five minutes, alternating between
given major and minor keys after completing each set of six
positions.

D. Open chord positions (*Theory Skill #16*)

1. Major mode

When the span of the three upper voices covers an interval
of more than an octave, the chord is in open position. These
open positions occur so frequently in music that they merit
considerable study. Their usefulness lies in adding brilliance
to a chord. As a first step in writing the six open chord positions, write the tenor and bass voices as illustrated. They are
identical in both the open and the closed positions.

The voicings of closed position cannot be maintained in open position. Rather, within and between each of the two pairs of upper voices a chord tone is omitted, thus giving each open chord position a wider distribution of its component intervals. Study the following illustration.

By following a similar pattern five more open chord positions can be written without exceeding the interval of a twelfth between the tenor and bass voices.

SUGGESTIONS FOR STUDY

Play the six open positions in several major keys. Note that the intervals separating the pairs of upper voices in each chord are larger in open position than in closed position. Continue to develop an awareness for the location of the root, the doubled root, the third, and the fifth of each chord.

ASSIGNMENT #12 (Part I): Open position, major mode.

Write the six open positions of C major and each of the major flat keys in whole notes, alternating the use of key signatures and accidentals. Work Sheet #14 is available.

2. Minor mode

The primary difference between major and minor chord positions is that of spelling. This is already familiar to the student, and consequently it is unnecessary to show each step in writing the open positions of a minor chord. The six positions are illustrated.

f: i³   i⁵   i⁸   i³   i⁵   i⁸

SUGGESTIONS FOR STUDY

Play the six open positions in various minor keys, comparing their sound with each of the previous sets of closed and open positions. Note the dark, sad, or somber sound of the minor mode in contrast to the bright, gay sound of the major mode.

ASSIGNMENT #12 (Part II): Open positions, minor mode.

Write the six open positions in A minor and in each of the minor sharp keys as described under part one of this assignment. Use Work Sheet #14.

SATISFACTORY ATTAINMENT: the ability to notate correctly at least 16 open chord positions in five minutes, alternating between given major and minor keys after completing each set of six positions.

FUNDAMENTALS

I. SCALES: The Natural Minor (Theory Skill #17)

The four basic scales were explained and compared in Unit III. Particular attention was devoted to the harmonic minor form. The natural minor form is less complex than the harmonic because the accidentally raised 7th degree of the latter is unnecessary. Thus, no problem need arise in writing the 15 natural minor scales. Begin with the seven sharp natural minor scale on A♯. Observe the sequence of whole and half steps.

7♯   A♯   B♯   C♯   D♯   E♯   F♯   G♯   A♯

As in the major scales, each new minor scale begins on the 4th degree of the preceding one, and the 6th degree of each new scale is permanently lowered one-half step.

6♯	D♯	E♯	F♯	G♯	A♯	B	C♯	D♯
5♯	G♯	A♯	B	C♯	D♯	E	F♯	G♯
4♯	C♯	D♯	E	F♯	G♯	A	B	C♯
3♯	F♯	G♯	A	B	C♯	D	E	F♯
2♯	B	C♯	D	E	F♯	G	A	B
1♯	E	F♯	G	A	B	C	D	E
none	A	B	C	D	E	F	G	A
1♭	D	E	F	G	A	B♭	C	D
2♭	G	A	B♭	C	D	E♭	F	G
3♭	C	D	E♭	F	G	A♭	B♭	C
4♭	F	G	A♭	B♭	C	D♭	E♭	F
5♭	B♭	C	D♭	E♭	F	G♭	A♭	B♭
6♭	E♭	F	G♭	A♭	B♭	C♭	D♭	E♭
7♭	A♭	B♭	C♭	D♭	E♭	F♭	G♭	A♭

SUGGESTIONS FOR STUDY

1. Follow the suggestions given for studying major scales in Unit I.
2. Note that the natural minor scale consists of a minor tetrachord and a Phrygian tetrachord disjunct by a whole step. Practice spelling, playing, and singspelling the natural minor scales using the tetrachord principle of construction.
3. Practice reciting the natural minor scales from the 15 cards marked "m" in the set of "21 Tones."
4. Practice writing the 15 natural minor scales on the staff alternating the use of treble, bass, and alto clefs, as well as the use of signatures and accidentals within each clef. Work Sheet #15 is provided.

SATISFACTORY ATTAINMENT: the ability to notate correctly, using whole notes, at least eight natural minor scales in five minutes. Alternate the use of treble, bass, and alto clefs, and the use of signatures and accidentals, as shown on Work Sheet #9.

II. INTERVALS: Minor and Perfect, Down (Theory Skill #18)

As stated before, each category of intervals is explained by reference to the major scale. The intervals formed between the 8th, or upper tonic degree of the major scale, and the 8th, 5th, 4th, and 1st degrees are all perfect. They are the perfect unison, perfect fourth, perfect fifth, and perfect octave, down.

P1 P4 P5 P8

The intervals formed between the 8th degree and the 7th, 6th, 3rd, and 2nd degrees are minor intervals.* They are the minor second, minor third, minor sixth, and minor seventh, down.

m2   m3   m6   m7

Thus, a perfect fifth down from D must be G, since G is the tone found by counting five steps down the D major scale from D. Or, a minor third down from B must be G♯, since G♯ is the tone found by counting three steps down the B major scale from B.

SUGGESTIONS FOR STUDY

1. The accompanying chart will be found helpful in singing, recognizing, and hearing the minor and perfect intervals down.

Scale degrees	Name	Symbol	Ear training device
8-8	perfect unison	P 1	—none needed
8-7	minor second	m 2	—half step, fundamental unit studied in Unit II.
8-6	minor third	m 3	—"Caisson Song."
8-5	perfect fourth	P 4	—"I've Been Workin' . . ."
8-4	perfect fifth	P 5	—the first to the third note of "Star Spangled Banner."
8-3	minor sixth	m 6	—sing down a major triad, namely, <u>8</u> 5 <u>3</u> 1
8-2	minor seventh	m 7	—"None But the Lonely Heart" by Tschaikovsky, or the leap at the end of Berlin's "White Christmas."
8-1	perfect octave	P 8	—if necessary, sing down a major scale.

2. Practice reciting in letter names the minor and perfect intervals down, thinking from the upper tonic degree of each major scale.

3. Practice reciting the same intervals based upon the other possible degree names—D♯, E♯, G♯, A♯, B♯, and F♭.

ASSIGNMENT #13: Writing the minor and perfect intervals down.

Write the m3, P4, P5, m6, and m7 down in five columns across the page, following the 21 tone circle (B♯ through F♭). Alternate the treble, bass, and alto clefs on successive staffs using accidentals and half notes, stemming the upper and lower tones of each interval up and down respectively. There are 105 intervals in this group, obtained by following through the 21 tone circle five times. The minor second is not considered in this assignment nor in the SATISFACTORY ATTAINMENT since it was studied as a fundamental melodic concept together with the major second in Unit II. It is, however, included in the hearing test for these intervals. Use Work Sheet #16 for this assignment.

SATISFACTORY ATTAINMENT: the ability to spell correctly at least 20 minor and perfect intervals down in five minutes. This test is written in the same manner as the assignment, except that it should begin on any tone of the 21 tone circle other than B♯.

III. RHYTHM: Duple subdivision of the denominator

In previous units considerable emphasis has been given to the pulse unit and its relation to tempo and meter, as well as to the respective functions of the denominator and numerator. The current subject— duple subdivision*—has been mentioned briefly in connection with the size of the pulse unit in very slow tempi, and also in studying the characteristics of simple meters.

Each simple note, considered in the order of decreasing size, is the duple subdivision of the one that precedes it. Thus, the whole note divides into two half notes, and the latter in turn divides into two quarter notes. Since note values the size of the denominator and larger have been the concern of the units dealing with characteristics of simple and compound meters, attention is now focused on note values smaller than the denominator. These smaller note values are known as subdivisions, and can conveniently be divided into those of the first, second, and third orders.

A. Subdivisions of the first order

Any note or rest of the denomination next smaller than the indicated denominator is a subdivision of the *first* order. These notes occur naturally in pairs, but may be used otherwise as well. The main problem is that of keeping the notation characteristic of the meter in which it occurs. Two examples are given.

B. Subdivisions of the second order

Any note or rest of the second denomination smaller than the given denominator is a subdivision of the *second* order. These notes occur naturally in groups of four, but may also be used in other ways. Again, the problem is that of keeping the notation characteristic of the meter in which it occurs. Two examples will lend illustration.

(musical notation in 3/4 time)

(musical notation in 4/4 time)

C. Subdivisions of the third order

Any note or rest of the third denomination smaller than the denominator indicated is a subdivision of the *third* order. These notes occur naturally in groups of eight, but also are used in other ways. Note that the third subdivision is not always practical, or necessary, especially if it involves values smaller than the thirty-second note. As before, the problem is that of maintaining the character of the meter in which the notation is used. Two examples are given.

(musical notation in 3/2 time)

(musical notation in 3/4 time)

D. Uncharacteristic notation

It is not usual for a short note to be followed by a note value so long as to destroy the characteristic groupings of a particular meter. In general, the characteristic groupings of the common duple meters equal the value of the quarter note. This is true as well in a triple meter such as 3/4, but the characteristic groupings of triple meters with smaller denominators equal three times the denominator value. This does not place any restriction on the actual duration of a sound, but suggests that a duration longer than a characteristic grouping must be divided into two or more equivalent tied note values. Study the following examples for illustration of this point.

Incorrect notation	Corrected notation
(musical notation 3/4)	*(musical notation 3/4)*
(musical notation 4/4)	*(musical notation 4/4)*
(musical notation 6/8)	*(musical notation 6/8)*

Other examples for study and performance of duple subdivision in the various meters will be found in the musicianship
section of this unit. Two rhythm skills to demonstrate competence
in individual performance are also included.

ASSIGNMENT #14: Rhythmic writing using duple subdivisions.
This assignment is found on Work Sheet #17.

MUSICIANSHIP

Pitch Ear Training

1. Review: singing, recognizing, and hearing the four triad qualities; the four basic major and minor scales and their component tetrachords; the major, and harmonic minor cadence
   patterns. The natural minor cadence pattern is illustrated.
   Compare it with that of the harmonic minor and major.

2. The minor and perfect intervals, down.
   a. given the pitch and letter name of the upper degree, sing
      numbers, syllables, "la," or singspell each of the minor
      and perfect intervals down in response to a handsign.
   b. given any tone of the C chromatic scale and the interval
      name, respond by singing "la" on the correct pitch.
   c. practice recognizing intervals sung or played on any in-
      strument by responding with the interval name, spoken
      or written. Interval recognition must be practiced both
      melodically (one tone played after the other) and har-
      monically (both tones played at once). Melodic intervals
      are much easier for most students to recognize. For this
      reason harmonic intervals must be considered to be the
      main challenge.
   d. given the letter name of the upper tone, practice hearing
      in dictation the minor and perfect intervals down. The
      response may be oral—naming the interval and spelling it—
      or written—recording the interval name and accordingly
      notating the pitches in the assigned clef. *e.g.*:

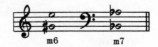

3. The closed chord positions of the major and minor triad.

Although both the closed and open positions have been studied as theory skills in this unit, only the closed positions are given consideration as a pitch skill at this time.

The root of each chord is in the bass voice; therefore, the problem is that of recognizing the presence of the root, third, or fifth in the soprano voice, each in relation to the root in the bass voice. In its simplest form this amounts to recognizing, respectively, a perfect octave, a major or minor third, or a perfect fifth in the outer voices, usually with an octave span added to the simple interval named. The problem of separating two voices—even the outer ones—from the rest of the texture* is difficult for many students because of the masking* effect produced by the composite of tones. Systematic, purposeful drill over a period of time will make the positions familiar enough to eliminate much of the difficulty.

The examples illustrate two approaches to the problem of isolating the outer voices, and suggest a technique useful for separating any given voice from a musical texture.

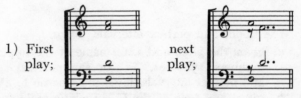

1) First   next
   play;   play;

play first chord again; repeat as desired.

2) the second approch is that of playing the four tones of the chord simultaneously—releasing the two inner voices after an eighth note's duration. In both instances the outer voices are placed in relief in relation to the entire chord.

A single chord can be either the tonic or that of any other functional degree. For simplicity we shall assume that each chord position is based upon a tonic triad, either in the major mode or the minor mode. Therefore, one recommended recognition response is that of identifying each chord by the Roman numeral "I" or "i" for, respectively, major or minor chords, together with the appropriate Arabic numeral for the soprano voice. The major Roman/Arabic symbols are thus, I^8, I^3, I^5, and those for minor are i^8, i^3, and i^5.

Another type of response is that of identifying the numerical composite of tones used in the manner illustrated, thinking from the bass tone upwards.

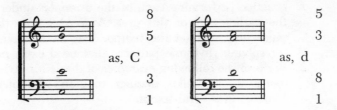

as, C

as, d

a. practice playing and recognizing each of the six closed positions in major as a distinct composite of tones.

b. practice the six closed positions of a minor chord in the same way.

c. practice the closed positions of either the major or minor mode, the added difficulty being that of differentiating between the modes.

d. given the letter name and clef location of the tonic degree, practice hearing the closed positions of the major and minor modes. Record the Roman/Arabic symbol as evidence of recognition, and notate the chord position on the bass and treble clefs.

Rhythm Ear Training

The sing-count technique can be useful for the understanding and performance of subdivisions because it helps to illustrate various rhythmic problems. Learn to use the following illustrations for singing-the-count.

— first duple subdivision of the denominator (1 &)

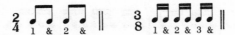

— second duple subdivision of the denominator (1 e & a)

— third duple subdivision of the denominator (1 ta e ta & ta a ta)

1. Practice performing each of the examples under "Rhythm" in the earlier part of this unit. ALWAYS note the meter, the pulse unit, and set the tempo. Use the sing-count technique for solving rhythmic patterns that need extra practice.
2. Perform the following examples of duple subdivision in various meters in a similaɪ manner to gain additional experience. Practice in several tempi.

3. Rhythm skills for individual performance.
   Evaluate performance in the usual manner.
   a. Characteristic First and Second Duple Subdivisions: 3/4 meter, Flash Card Set #13. (*Rhythm Skill # 9*)

SATISFACTORY ATTAINMENT: the performance of these rhythms in any order and at any tempo up to 120 quarter notes per minute.

b. Characteristic First, Second, and Third Duple Subdivisions: 2/4 meter, Flash Card Set #14. (*Rhythm Skill #10*)

SATISFACTORY ATTAINMENT: the performance of these rhythms in any order and at any tempo up to 88 quarter notes per minute.

Sight Singing: Formal Emphasis . . . two phrase sentences.

The sentence consisting of two phrases, either similar or dissimilar, is the one most common in music. Similar phrases may differ only in their cadence, or they may have only an initial motive in common. Such pairs often are called antecedent* and consequent* phrases. Phrases that are dissimilar may differ in length as well as in their rhythmic and melodic makeup. Analyze each of the following examples with the thought of discerning the items just mentioned. The examples vary in mode, meter, use of rhythmic subdivisions and intervals, as well as in their phrase structure and form. Again, the techniques outlined in previous units will be helpful for practice and study.

1. Sonata in C Major, Opus 2, No. 3 — Beethoven

2. Merry Wives of Windsor — Nicolai

3. Album for the Young, Opus 68 — Schumann

4. Sonata in E♭ Major — Haydn

5. The Bellringer's Daughter — Loewe

6. Sonata in E Major, Opus 14, No. 1 — Beethoven

7. Mount of Olives (oratorio) — Beethoven

The Barber of Seville

8.   Rossini

Symphony in F Minor (Farewell)

9.   Haydn

Keyboard Emphasis

Evaluate each keyboard skill in the usual manner, as shown in the SUGGESTED STANDARDS.

Keyboard Skill #6

SATISFACTORY ATTAINMENT: the ability to play the six closed positions of the tonic chord in any four major and also in any four minor keys.

Dictation

1. Pitch

   Pitch Skill #4—Hearing Minor and Perfect Intervals, Down.

   SATISFACTORY ATTAINMENT: demonstrating competence in hearing the minor and perfect intervals down. Given the pitch of the upper tone and the clef, respond by correctly recognizing and notating each of 10 intervals played. *e.g.*:

   Each interval and its analysis is considered to be one response. Compute the PROFICIENCY PERCENTAGE, analyze the pattern of error, and evaluate.

Pitch Skill #5—Hearing Closed Chord Positions in Major and Minor.

SATISFACTORY ATTAINMENT: demonstrated competence in hearing the closed chord positions of major and minor quality. Given the pitch and the location of the bass voice, respond with the correct recognition and notation for each of five examples. *e.g.*:

A: I⁸

e♭: i⁵

For purposes of evaluation, each chord and its analysis are separate responses to allow for the fact that each Roman/Arabic combination, such as "i⁵," can be correctly spelled in several ways. Thus each analysis is marked either "C" or "R," and each spelling either "C" or "S." Incorporate this variation in using the SUGGESTED STANDARDS. Compute the PROFICIENCY PERCENTAGE and evaluate.

Pitch Achievement

These dictations give practice in recognizing a succession of intervals which do not necessarily remain in the key indicated by the beginning note or pattern.

The beginning note is given and the entire line is played slowly without pausing between tones. The response may be either in music notation—with all enharmonic spellings acceptable —or in interval names without notation. Both types of response should be practiced. As before, the PROFICIENCY PERCENTAGE is found by dividing the number of correct responses by the number in the test.

2. Rhythmic

This dictation involves recognizing how first and second duple subdivisions sound in certain simple and compound meters. For purposes of evaluation it is suggested that each exercise be scored at one point per pulse unit. Following this suggestion compute the PROFICIENCY PERCENTAGE as shown before.

3. Melodic

a. think of a motive for a two phrase sentence; decide its mode, its key, its meter, and express it in music notation using either a key signature or accidentals. Consider whether its two phrases need to be similar or dissimilar to express your ideas most musically.

b. practice taking dictation of such phrases as suggested. Compute the PROFICIENCY PERCENTAGE in the usual manner.

Suite No. 4 in D Minor

Handel

1.

Symphony No. 4 in E Minor, Opus 98

Brahms

2.

4. Harmonic

Practice recognizing the tonic, subdominant, and dominant triads in the major and harmonic minor modes. The key is announced and the tonic degree is sounded. The response may be as follows:

a. recognize the sound and record only the appropriate Roman symbol for the functional degree name of the triad sounded. The PROFICIENCY PERCENTAGE is computed by dividing the number of correct responses by the total number of responses in the test.

b. recognize the sound; record the appropriate Roman symbol, and correctly notate the triad in the assigned clef. Consider the notation together with the analysis as one response for computing the PROFICIENCY PERCENTAGE.

UNIT 6

HARMONY

I. THE STRICT CONNECTIONS OF THE PRIMARY TRIADS

As one undertakes the actual writing and analysis of harmony, the background knowledge which has been gained in clefs, triads, and their qualities, and in the distribution of voices in closed and open positions, acquires a new meaning. An understanding of these fundamentals will now be assumed. Inasmuch as the three primary triads are the crux of traditional harmony, the several means of connecting these chords will be our first area of harmonic exploration.

The student will find it helpful, as each new topic is introduced, to refer to the outline summary of "Chords" found in the Appendix. This outline will show him how the concept currently being considered fits into the over-all study of harmony.

Any two chords whose roots are a fifth apart, such as the dominant and the tonic, or the tonic and the subdominant, have one common tone.* It will be recalled that the subdominant and dominant chords have no common tone, since they are built upon adjacent degrees of the scale. Many details of importance in harmonic connection are outlined:

A. Strict connection of chords having *one* common tone. (V I; I IV; I V; IV I)

1. Given a bass root moving an interval of either a fourth or a fifth, up or down,

   a. use any desired position, either closed or open, for the first chord,

   b. hold over or repeat the common tone in whatever voice it occurs, and,

   c. move the remaining two voices each one step in the same direction, either up or down as is appropriate for spelling the second chord.

2. Chord connections involving a bass movement of a perfect fifth down, or its inversion,* a perfect fourth up, are the *basic* harmonic movements in music. The root movements of

95

these connections follow the circle of downward fifths, and may thus be described as progressive.*

3. Chord connections involving the inverse bass movement, namely, a perfect fifth up or the equivalent perfect fourth down, follow the ascending circle of fifths. Since the harmonic function of these connections is often that of building or sustaining tension, they are called retrogressive.*

B. Strict connection of chords that have *no* common tone. (IV V; V IV)

There is a feeling of contrast between two chords whose bass roots are one degree apart because they have no common tone. The traditional method of connecting chords having no common tone is that of using contrary motion.*

Given a bass root moving the interval of a second either up or down, use any position, closed or open, for the first chord. Move the three upper voices of the first chord in contrary motion to the direction of the bass root movement, seeking the nearest chord tones of the second chord. One voice will need to move a third, and the other two will need to move only a second. Examples of this type of connection are shown.

$$c: \text{IV}^3 \quad \text{V}^8 \qquad c: \text{IV}^5 \quad \text{V}^3 \qquad c: \text{V}^5 \quad \text{IV}^8 \qquad c: \text{V}^3 \quad \text{IV}^5$$

C. Strict connections of the primary triads in cadences.

It is quite appropriate that the progressive connection, V I, in which the bass root motion is from the dominant to the tonic degree, is known as the authentic cadence and similarly, that the retrogressive connection, IV I, is known as the plagal cadence. It is desirable to emphasize that the cadence names are descriptively appropriate only when these chord progressions are the means of bringing about a stop, or punctuation, in a phrase, sentence, section,* or movement* of a musical composition.

The principles of harmonic connection just discussed can be learned in a practical way by writing musical illustrations of several types of cadences. In the accompanying chart, four cadence formulae are symbolized. Study their appearance and use in the given excerpts.

Cadence Name	*Cadence Formula*	*Remarks*
authentic	....V I	....final or conclusive in effect; often used to close any type of section
plagal*	....IV I	....fairly conclusive, but not as much so as the authentic cadence; often used as the added "Amen" to a hymn
half*	.....any, then V	....inconclusive, hence the name
full	.....IV V I	....conclusive; perhaps least used of the various full cadence formulae.

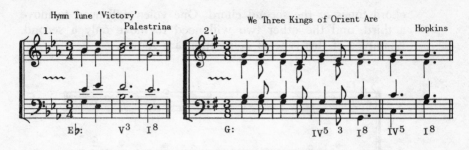

ASSIGNMENT #15: Writing strict harmonic connections using the three primary triads in cadence formulae.

This assignment is found on Work Sheet #18.

D. Strict connection in harmonizing a bass line or a melody.

Harmonizing a melody, or indeed, composing a melodic line which enhances a given succession of bass root progressions, is a matter of developing such an intensive acquaintance with the character and harmonic function* of musical sounds that the intellect and the ear will be able to cooperate effectively. Proficiency must be gained in harmonizing both bass lines and melodies using the three primary triads.

ASSIGNMENT #16: Harmonizing a Given Bass Line—primary triads, strict connections, changes of position.

This assignment, together with appropriate instructions, is found on Work Sheet #19.

FUNDAMENTALS

I. TETRACHORDS

Several diatonic four tone patterns known as tetrachords have already become familiar in sound. Since these tetrachords are readily combined in easily discerned pairs to form the major, the three forms of minor, and the modal scales, it is important to become proficient in their spelling. The basic tetrachord is that built on the first four tones of the major scale, and for that reason it is known as the major tetrachord. The spelling of the major tetrachord, plus the minor, Phrygian, harmonic and Lydian* will be explained.

Five tetrachord forms (*Theory Skill* #19)

1. the major

    The first four notes of the C major scale form the successive intervals of a whole step, another whole step, and a half step, or technically, two major seconds followed by a minor second.

2. the minor

    Lowering the 3rd degree of the major tetrachord changes its interval sequence to a major second followed by a minor second, and then by a major second. This pattern is invariably found as the first four notes of either the natural, harmonic, or melodic minor scales.

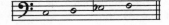

3. the Phrygian

    Lowering the 2nd and 3rd degrees of the major tetrachord produces the interval sequence of a minor second followed by two major seconds. This tetrachord is given its name because its interval pattern is found in the first four notes of the Phrygian mode.

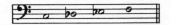

4. the Lydian

    Raising the 4th degree of the major tetrachord produces an interval sequence consisting of three successive major seconds. This tetrachord is given its name because its interval pattern is found in the first four notes of the Lydian mode.

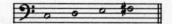

5. the harmonic

   Lowering the 2nd degree of the major tetrachord produces
an interval sequence consisting of a minor second, an augmented (half step larger than a major) second, and a minor
second. This tetrachord is given its name because its interval
pattern is that which gives the characteristic sound to the
upper four tones of the harmonic minor scale.

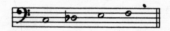

SUGGESTIONS FOR STUDY
1. Play each of the five types of tetrachords, beginning on the first
   note of each major scale.
2. Practice singspelling each of the five types of tetrachords on
   each of the 21 tones.

ASSIGNMENT #17: Spelling the five tetrachords.

   Write the tetrachords in five columns across the page following
the circle of fifths from B♯ through F♭, using eighth notes four to
a beam. Alternate the use of treble, bass, and alto clefs on successive staffs. Follow along the 21 tone circle five times to obtain
the 105 possible tetrachords. Use Work Sheet #20.

SATISFACTORY ATTAINMENT: the ability to spell correctly at
least 16 tetrachords in five minutes. The test is written in the
same manner as the foregoing assignment, except that the starting note in the circle of fifths should be any other than B♯.

II. INTERVALS: Minor, Perfect, Augmented Fourth, and Diminished
     Fifth, Up (Theory Skill #20)

   It is known that a minor second is a half step smaller than a major
second. Hence, by analogy, each of the minor intervals is a half step
less in compass than its major counterpart. For instance, a minor sixth
above B must be G, since the interval B–G♯ is the major sixth found on
the 1st degree of the B major scale. Or, the interval E to D must be

a minor seventh, since a major seventh based on the 1st degree of the
E major scale includes the tones E and D♯.

Since the perfect intervals are familiar they are included on the
given chart for reference and comparison. The addition of one interval—
the tritone*—completes the 12 simple interval sounds which can be found
in each octave. The tritone may be spelled either as an augmented or
raised perfect fourth, or as a diminished or lowered perfect fifth. The
example is based on the D major scale.

M2   m2   M3 m3   P4 A4   P5 d5   M6 m6   M7 m7

SUGGESTIONS FOR STUDY

1. The chart will be helpful for singing, recognizing, and hearing the minor,
   perfect, augmented fourth, and diminished fifth intervals up.

Scale degrees	Name	Symbol	Ear training device
1-1	perfect unison	P 1	—none needed
1-lowered 2	minor second	m 2	—half step; foundamental unit studied in Unit II
1-lowered 3	minor third	m 3	—first interval of Brahms' "Lullaby;" first interval in "Let Me Call You Sweetheart."
1-4	perfect fourth	P 4	—first interval of "Because."
1-raised 4	augmented fourth	A 4	—the tritone's unusual sound seldom, if ever, is used to begin a familiar tune. Think a P4 and raise it a half step.
1-lowered 5	diminished fifth	d 5	—the same remark applies. Think a P5 and lower it a half step.
1-5	perfect fifth	P 5	—first leap in "Twinkle, Twinkle."
1-lowered 6	minor sixth	m 6	—first and third notes of "Let Me Call You Sweetheart;" first interval of "Go Down Moses."
1-lowered 7	minor seventh	m 7	—first and fourth notes of theme, "Introduction" to *Lohengrin*, 3rd act.
1-8	perfect octave	P 8	—"Somewhere Over the Rainbow."

2. Practice reciting in letter names the minor 2nd, 3rd, 6th, 7th, augmented
   4th, and diminished 5th intervals based on each of the 21 tones.
3. Practice singspelling each of the same intervals based upon any of the
   21 tones.

ASSIGNMENT #18: Writing the minor, augmented fourth, and diminished fifth intervals up.

Write the m3, A4, d5, m6, and m7 up in five columns across the page, following the 21 tone circle (B♯ through F♭). Use the treble, bass, and alto clefs alternately on successive staffs. Use accidentals and flagged eighth notes, stemming the lower and upper tones of each interval down and up respectively. There are 105 intervals in this group, obtained by following through the 21 tone circle five times. Since the m2, P4, P5, and P8 are familiar, they are included only in the hearing test for these intervals. Work Sheet #21 is provided.

SATISFACTORY ATTAINMENT: the ability to spell correctly at least 20 of the foregoing intervals in five minutes. The test should be written using whole notes and accidentals and should begin on any tone of the 21 tone circle except B♯; otherwise there is no change from the plan described in the assignment.

III. TENOR CLEF (Theory Skill #21)

The range of notes to be learned in tenor clef (the C clef whose middle C is found on the fourth line of the staff) extends two octaves

up from the note c below the staff.

c   c2

The four areas—

1. The five lines

d   f   a   c1 e1

2. The four spaces

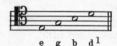

e   g   b   d1

3. One note below the staff

c

4. Five notes above the staff

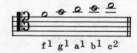

f1 g1 a1 b1 c2

The placement of the seven sharp and seven flat signatures on the tenor clef staff is shown. Note how the placement of the seven sharp signs differs from that of treble clef, for instance.

SUGGESTIONS FOR STUDY

Using Flash Card Set #15 (Tenor Clef), apply the techniques described under treble clef in Unit I. Work for similar proficiency.

SATISFACTORY ATTAINMENT: sufficient understanding and proficiency in the tenor clef so that it can be used in alternation with the treble, bass, and alto clefs in selected theory skills, beginning with those found in Unit VII.

IV. RHYTHM: Triple subdivisions

The use of subdivisions of the denominator and lesser note values adds much interesting variety to the rhythmic effect of a meter without disrupting the characteristic patterns of that meter. This is true of triple* as well as of duple subdivision. That a simple note divides into a duplet* of the next smaller note value is well understood; that any duplet may be replaced by a triplet of the same denomination and same over-all rhythmic value is the important factor in triple subdivision.

Many subdivisions of the simple and dotted notes larger than the denominator have been encountered in studying characteristics of the several types of meter. In this unit, those larger subdivisions which remain characteristic of triple subdivision will be used without further mention. However, those which disrupt the prevailing meter, such as triple subdivision of the whole note in 4/4 and duple subdivision of the dotted half note in 3/4, along with others, will be dealt with in the next two units.

The table outlines the information essential to an understanding of triple subdivisions:

The two examples illustrate the use of duple and triple subdivisions in one duple and in one triple meter. Further examples for performance, as well as rhythm skills for demonstrating individual proficiency, are to be found in the section on "Musicianship."

ASSIGNMENT #19: Subdivisions in rhythm and melody.
This assignment is found on Work Sheet #22.

MUSICIANSHIP

Pitch Ear Training

1. Review: practice singing (when possible), recognizing the sound, and hearing in dictation the five tetrachords; the major and perfect intervals up and the minor and perfect intervals down; the six closed positions of a major and minor chord.

2. Minor, perfect, and tritone intervals, up.

   a. given the pitch of the lower tone, sing the m2, m3, P4, A4, P5, d5, m6, and m7 in response to the interval name.

   b. given the pitch of the lower tone, sing each of the afore-named intervals from that tone.

   c. practice recognizing the sound of intervals played melodically and also harmonically, each as a separate type of pitch concept. Respond by saying or writing the name of the interval.

   d. given the pitch of the lower tone, practice hearing the minor, perfect, and tritone intervals up. The response may be oral—naming the interval and spelling it, or written—recording the interval's name and accordingly notating its pitches in the assigned clef. *e.g.*:

3. The open chord positions of the major and minor triad.

   Although the sound of the open positions is different from that of the closed positions, there is no new problem involved. Again, the bass and soprano voices must be isolated from the composite texture. Deduce which one of the three major or three minor Roman/Arabic symbols is appropriate in each given instance. Use the techniques shown under closed positions in Unit V. The Roman/Arabic and numerical composite responses are illustrated.

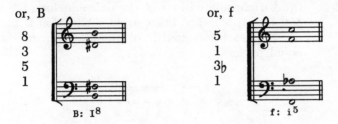

   a. practice playing and recognizing the six open positions of a major chord.

   b. practice playing and recognizing the six open positions of a minor chord.

   c. practice distinguishing and recognizing the open positions of either a major or a minor chord.

   d. given the letter name and clef location of the tonic degree, practice hearing the open positions of the major and minor modes, recording the Roman/Arabic symbol as evidence of recognition, and notating the chord position on the great staff.

Rhythm Ear Training

   The sing-count technique again can be useful for understanding and performing the triple subdivisions because it helps to illustrate various rhythmic problems. Learn to use the following illustrations for singing-the-count.

   —first triple subdivision of the denominator (1 ti te).

— second triple subdivision of the denominator (1 ti te &
ti te). Notice that the second triple subdivision is based
upon dividing each half of the denominator value into
three equal pulses.

— third triple subdivisions of the denominator (1 ti te e ti te
& ti te a ti te). The third triple subdivision is based upon
dividing each one-fourth of the denominator into three
equal pulses.

1. Practice performing each of the two examples under "Rhythm"
   in the earlier section of the unit. Always note the meter, the
   pulse unit, and set the tempo. Use the sing-count technique
   for solving rhythmic patterns that prove to be difficult.
2. Perform the following examples of triple subdivisions in
   various meters in a similar manner to gain additional experience.

6. 𝄵 [rhythm notation]

7. 𝄵 [rhythm notation]

8. 𝄵 [rhythm notation]

9. 𝄵 [rhythm notation]

3. Rhythm Skills for individual performance.

Evaluate the performance of each skill in the manner previously suggested.

a. Triple Subdivisions of the Denominator 3/4 meter, Flash Card Set #16. (*Rhythm Skill #11*)

SATISFACTORY ATTAINMENT: the performance of these rhythms in any order and at any tempo up to 72 quarter notes per minute.

b. Triple Subdivisions of the Denominator: 2/4 meter, Flash Card Set #17. (*Rhythm Skill #12*)

SATISFACTORY ATTAINMENT: the performance of these rhythms in any order and at any tempo up to 72 quarter notes per minute.

Sight Singing: FORM EMPHASIS—sentences with more than two phrases

At times a composer feels that more than two phrases are necessary to give desirable length, balance, and contrast to a musical sentence. Practice singing the given excerpts, and do further study using the suggestions previously given. Note the meter, the rhythmic subdivisions, and the use of motives. Determine by their sound and use of scale tones which of the following examples seems to close with an authentic cadence.

Symphony No. 4 in D Minor, Opus 120

Schumann

Concerto in E Minor, Opus 64 (violin) — Mendelssohn

Symphony No. 8 in F Major, Opus 93 — Beethoven

Mass in B Minor — Bach

St. Matthew Passion — Bach

Double Concerto in A minor, Opus 102 (violin and cello)

Brahms

Sonata in C Minor, Opus 13

Beethoven

Keyboard Emphasis

Evaluate each skill performance as described previously.

Keyboard Skill #7

SATISFACTORY ATTAINMENT: the ability to play the six open positions of the tonic chord in any four major and in any four minor keys.

Dictation

1. Pitch

   Pitch Skill #6—Hearing the Minor, Perfect, Augmented Fourth, and Diminished Fifth Intervals, Up.

   SATISFACTORY ATTAINMENT: demonstrated competence in hearing the minor, perfect, augmented fourth and diminished fifth intervals up. Given the pitch and the clef of the lower tone, respond by correctly recognizing and notating each of the ten intervals played. Each interval and its analysis is considered to be one response. Compute the PROFICIENCY PERCENTAGE, analyze, and evaluate.

Pitch Skill #7—Hearing Open Position Chords in Major and Minor.

SATISFACTORY ATTAINMENT: demonstrated competence in hearing the open chord positions in major and minor. Given the pitch and the location of the bass voice, respond with the correct recognition and notation for each of five examples. *e.g.*:

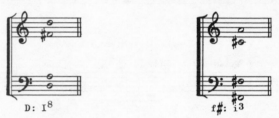

For evaluation mark each chord and its analysis separately, since a given analysis is correct for more than one chord spelling. Mark each analysis either "C" or "R," and each spelling either "C" or "S." Then compute the PROFICIENCY PERCENTAGE, analyzing the pattern of error and evaluating.

Pitch Achievement

The given dictations consist of a succession of intervals related to more than the scale suggested by the first several notes. These include various step, tetrachord, scale, and triad patterns. The beginning tone is given and the entire line is played slowly—about three seconds duration—without pausing between tones. Responses in interval names and in music notation—with enharmonic spellings acceptable—should both be practiced. The PROFICIENCY PERCENTAGE is found by dividing the number of correct responses by the number in the test.

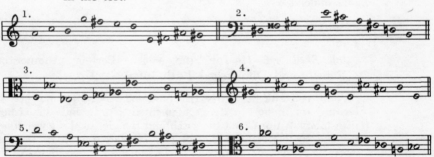

2. Rhythmic

These dictations give practice in recognizing the sounds of first and second triple subdivisions in various simple and compound meters. For purposes of evaluation it is suggested that each denominator value be given one point; for example, in 3/16 meter, three points per measure. Compute the PROFICIENCY PERCENTAGE.

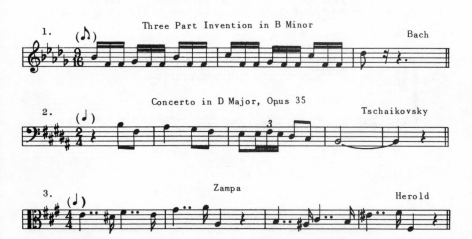

3. Melodic

Each of these melodic dictations is one phrase in length. In each instance take note of the rhythmic and pitch problems involved. Compute the PROFICIENCY PERCENTAGE.

Three Part Invention in B Minor

Bach

Concerto in D Major, Opus 35

Tschaikovsky

Zampa

Herold

4. Harmonic

Discerning the voice distribution of chords is not an easy task. A very analytical type of listening which includes sensitivity to the degrees of the scale, an awareness of interval sizes and distances, and the ability to isolate tones partly masked by others is required.

a. practice taking dictation in arpeggiated (see arpeggio*) chords in various closed and open positions. Write the response in notation on the great staff using Roman/Arabic symbols for the analysis. Compute the PROFICIENCY PERCENTAGE as shown for Pitch Skill #5, Unit V.

b. practice taking dictation in non-arpeggiated chords in various closed and open positions. Respond and compute

the PROFICIENCY PERCENTAGE as suggested under
"a."

UNIT 7

HARMONY

I. FREE CONNECTIONS OF THE PRIMARY TRIADS

The adjectives "strict" and "free," when applied to chord connections, permit a simple classification for certain types of voice movements which occur frequently in harmonic progressions. They are encountered constantly in harmony using the primary and secondary triads.* Free connections are an important means of achieving variety where the continued use of strict connections could lead to monotony. These free chord connections can best be understood in relation to the strict connections using the smallest possible voice movements. Such strict connections were studied in the previous unit. A brief review will serve as an introduction to our study of free connections.

A. Strict connections.

    1. When chords have one common tone the bass movement will be a fourth or a fifth, up or down. The connection is completed by holding the common tone and allowing the other voices to move by step, either both up or both down. This connection applies to I IV, I V, V I, IV I. Note that this type of connection remains either closed or open, depending upon the position of the first chord.

    2. When chords have no common tone the bass movement will be a second, up or down, as is appropriate. To complete this connection, move the upper three voices in contrary motion to that of the bass, with two voices moving by step and one by a third. In the primary triads this connection applies only to IV V, and V IV. Note that this type of connection remains either closed or open, depending upon the position of the first chord.

B. Free connections.

    1. Two successive chords with roots a fourth or a fifth apart.
        a. in the movements I IV, IV I, I V, and V I hold the common tone in one voice, but allow the voice sounding the

114

3rd in the first chord to sound the 3rd of the second chord also. The remaining voice will move by step. The effect of this connection is that of changing from closed to open position, or vice versa. If the 3rd of the chord is in the soprano voice the first chord may be in either closed or open position, but when the 5th is in the soprano voice the first chord *must* be in open position. Several illustrations of this "step-leap" technique are given.

b. given the same basic movements, move the upper three voices in contrary motion to the bass, rather than holding the common tone. In this connection—as in the strict connections—no change of position type will occur. The analysis is given.

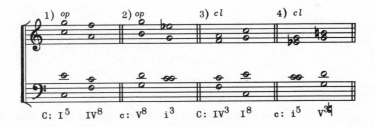

When the 5th is in the soprano of a closed position chord, another contrary motion movement is possible. In this instance two voices move up and two move down, resulting in a change of position from closed to open. Note the consecutive fifths* by contrary motion which are found in the outer voices. Some theorists do not favor the use of such fifths, but they are quite common in music literature. Occasional usage is acceptable if it produces the desired sonority. The analysis is given.

C: I^5 IV^5 c: V^5 i^5

2. Two successive chords with roots a second apart.

    a. the no-common tone connection pertinent now is that between the subdominant and dominant chords. Most IV V connection should be done employing strict contrary motion, but where freedom is possible it is encouraged. Since there is no common tone, the main possibilities are for the upper three voices to move by contrary motion other than by the shortest distance, or the use of a special contrary motion in which two voices move up and two move down. Note that the latter movement effects a change from closed to open position. *e.g.*:

c: iv^8 $v^{3\natural}$ C: V^8 IV^5

    b. another much used connection of the same chords is the unique one in which a subdominant chord in the CLOSED position of the 3rd moves to the dominant in the OPEN position of the 3rd. *e.g.*:

C: IV^3 V^3

3. Freedom in doubling.

Thus far the doubling of the root of the triad has been taken for granted in each explanation and example. There are, however, many instances in which the effect of the voice lines will be enhanced by some other type of doubling. Usually we consider doubling the root, but if it becomes apparent that a doubled 5th, a tripled root and no 5th, or a doubled 3rd will produce a more melodic line, then the musical consideration should predominate. Freedom in doubling, therefore, can be considered to be a *second* technique whose function is predominantly contrapuntal,* that is, concerned with melodic line more than with harmonic connection. The *first* such technique was mentioned in Unit VI and concerned the use of more than one position of the same chord over a held bass tone. Here again the effect produced enhances the melodic line. It will be well to remember that the additional freedom imposes additional responsibility, since doubling other than the root seems to facilitate the formation of consecutive fifths and octaves, while at the same time permitting the musical mind a welcome latitude.

II. ALTERED CHORDS—the Picardy third.

A characteristic of music written during the Baroque period is that of frequent use of the Picardy third. The real meaning of the word "Picardy" in this connection is not clear and perhaps not too important, but it does provide a colorful name for the harmonic device. The Picardy third is an accidental raised or major 3rd degree used in the minor scale to give a major quality to the final cadential tonic chord in the minor mode. Clearly, the composer, in using the Picardy third, was applying the principle that the harmonic material of one mode (major or minor) can, if suitable and desirable, be used in the opposite mode. The practical result was that the minor tonic chord was made major in quality by alteration of its 3rd degree. The last two bars of a Bach chorale* provide an example.

Freuet euch, ihr Christen alle

(Picardy third)

ASSIGNMENT #20: Free connection of I, IV, and V chords.

This assignment, together with necessary explanations, is found on Work Sheet #23.

ASSIGNMENT #21: Part writing* in harmony—free connections of I, IV, and V chords in major and minor modes.

This assignment, together with the necessary explanations, is found on Work Sheet #24.

III. NON-HARMONIC TONES: returning — unaccented and accented; returning six-four dissonance.

The study of non-harmonic tones is begun in this unit with the discussion concerning the returning tone. At points throughout the remainder of this manual, each of the other non-harmonic tones will be given similar consideration. A brief outline summary of "Non-harmonic Tones" is found in the Appendix. The student is urged to refer to this summary in his study of each of the non-harmonic tones.

The harmonic connections studied have included bass movements of seconds, fourths, and fifths. Most of the voice leading in the upper three parts can be described by the terms "common tone," "step-movement," "step-leap," and "contrary motion." It is obvious that all notes written in connecting chords, either on the basis of one common tone or no common tones—and either strict or free—must be notes essential to the harmony. It therefore follows that non-harmonic tones,* or various ornamental tones,* are dissonances* which cannot be accounted for as members of the chords with which they are associated. Rather, any given non-harmonic tone can be accounted for as the momentary replacement of either the root, third, or fifth of a chord. It is important that the study of these non-harmonic tones takes into account the problem of harmonic rhythm. Harmonic rhythm*—first discussed in Unit VI—is again mentioned with some emphasis, because many instances will arise in which a given tone is considered "harmonic" or "non-harmonic" depending upon the rhythmic location of each harmonic change.

A. The Returning tone.

The returning tone,* accented and unaccented, is a decoration or embellishment of a single tone. Basically it is a three tone figure, whose first and third tones are the same, and whose second, or auxiliary tone,* is either a half step or a whole step higher or lower. If this embellishing tone coincides rhythmically with a change of harmony, with a reiteration of a given harmony, or with a strong beat, it is said to be accented. Examples of each type of returning tone, accented and unaccented, are given.

1. —the *unaccented* returning tone.

Note that it is always dissonant to the *first* chord if a change of harmony occurs.

2. —the *accented* returning tone.

Note that it is always dissonant to the *second* chord if a change of harmony occurs.

A study of the foregoing examples shows that the returning tone may be the embellishment of any single tone or of more than one tone of a given chord, or it may decorate the common tone between any two chords having such a tone. Note that a returning tone is not possible between the subdominant and dominant triad chords, since they have no common tone.

3. The six-four dissonance* is one of the more important considerations of harmonic and non-harmonic practice. This dissonance often will be found as a decoration of the dominant chord in final cadences, and less often as a decoration of the tonic and other chords. Perhaps the most logical description is that which considers the six-four dissonance an embellishment of a root position chord. Study the example.

Note 1: The root of "1" is the C in the bass voice.

Note 2: The root of "2" is the G in the bass voice.

Note 3: The root of "3" is also the G in the bass voice, and the C and E in the tenor and alto voices are the dissonant 4th and 6th degrees temporarily replacing the 3rd and 5th degrees, B and D, which follow.

Playing each illustration will be helpful. The single chord of "1" and of "2" sound stable, each taken separately, but in "3" the dissonant 6th and 4th degrees above the bass root, G, must move to the 5th and 3rd degrees to achieve stability. In fact, the alto E and the tenor C are literally impelled by the G in the bass voice to become members of the G chord. This horizontal 6 to 5 movement in one of three upper voices, and a similar 4 to 3 movement in another, are the essence of the resolution of the unstable six-four dissonance.

At times 6-5 and 4-3 movements above a bass root take place under circumstances utilizing the characteristic effect of the returning tone. For example, in illustration "4" the returning six-four dissonance decorates an authentic cadence. The returning six-four dissonance in "5" serves to embellish the final tonic chord, giving a sound which is almost that of the plagal cadence.

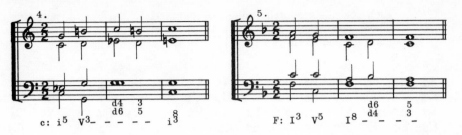

c: i⁵ V³– – – – i³   F: I³ V⁵ I⁸ – – – –

Note: In illustration "5" the tonic chord of the penultimate measure
is analyzed as a I⁸ on the first beat. On the second half note
beat the important change is the use of the six-four dissonance,
followed by its resolution to five-three as shown in the last
measure.

The motions which can now be incorporated with the individual voice lines through the use of the returning tone provide another important means of acquiring the technique of
contrapuntal writing. This is especially true when the motions
introduced result from a discreet and thoughtful understanding of the sound and effect of the non-harmonic tones used.

ASSIGNMENT #22: Non-harmonic tones—the returning tone, including its use in the six-four dissonance.

This assignment, together with necessary explanations, is found
on Work Sheet #25.

FUNDAMENTALS

I. MINOR SCALES

Each of the three forms of the minor scale has been discussed in
relation to the major scale pattern and in relation to its tetrachord structure. Only the melodic minor scale form requires further study. Concerning the minor scales, it should be understood that music written in
the minor mode is seldom based exclusively upon one form of minor
scale. More frequently, the characteristics of all the minor scale forms
are discernible in varying degrees, each contributing something to the
composite of qualities known as the minor mode.

The melodic minor scale (*Theory Skill #22*)

A simple description of the melodic minor scale is that its ascending form sounds like a major scale spelled with a lowered 3rd degree,
and that its descending form is identical with the natural minor
scale. Thinking in tetrachords, pairing a minor disjunct by a whole
step with a major completes the ascending scale; whereas, in the
descending form the upper tetrachord must be spelled Phrygian to
account for the lowering of the 6th and 7th degrees of the scale.

For the melodic minor scale, think each of the natural minor scales
following the circle of fifths from A♯ through A♭, but in writing

each scale, accidentally raise the 6th and 7th degrees a half step. These accidentals apply only to the ascending pattern, since the natural minor form is retained in the descending scale pattern.

A♯	B♯	C♯	D♯	E♯	Fx	Gx	A♯	G♯	F♯	E♯	D♯	C♯	B♯	A♯
D♯	E♯	F♯	G♯	A♯	B♯	Cx	D♯	C♯	B	A♯	G♯	F♯	E♯	D♯
G♯	A♯	B	C♯	D♯	E♯	Fx	G♯	F♯	E	D♯	C♯	B	A♯	G♯
C♯	D♯	E	F♯	G♯	A♯	B♯	C♯	B	A	G♯	F♯	E	D♯	C♯
F♯	G♯	A	B	C♯	D♯	E♯	F♯	E	D	C♯	B	A	G♯	F♯
B	C♯	D	E	F♯	G♯	A♯	B	A	G	F♯	E	D	C♯	B
E	F♯	G	A	B	C♯	D♯	E	D	C	B	A	G	F♯	E
A	B	C	D	E	F♯	G♯	A	G	F	E	D	C	B	A
D	E	F	G	A	B	C♯	D	C	B♭	A	G	F	E	D
G	A	B♭	C	D	E	F♯	G	F	E♭	D	C	B♭	A	G
C	D	E♭	F	G	A	B	C	B♭	A♭	G	F	E♭	D	C
F	G	A♭	B♭	C	D	E	F	E♭	D♭	C	B♭	A♭	G	F
B♭	C	D♭	E♭	F	G	A	B♭	A♭	G♭	F	E♭	D♭	C	B♭
E♭	F	G♭	A♭	B♭	C	D	E♭	D♭	C♭	B♭	A♭	G♭	F	E♭
A♭	B♭	C♭	D♭	E♭	F	G	A♭	G♭	F♭	E♭	D♭	C♭	B♭	A♭

SUGGESTIONS FOR STUDY

The suggestions made for studying the harmonic form of the minor scale (Unit III) are both appropriate and adequate for the melodic minor scale. Work Sheet #26 is provided for practice in writing these scales on the staff.

SATISFACTORY ATTAINMENT: the ability to write any six melodic minor scales on the staff in whole notes, alternating the use of signatures and accidentals as well as the treble, bass, alto, and tenor clefs, in a period of five minutes. Write each scale up for one octave, and down through the 5th degree to show the ascending and descending inflexions of the 6th and 7th degree. *e.g.*:

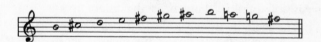

II. FOUR BASIC SCALES (Theory Skill #23)

The major scale, together with the three forms of the minor scale, are the basis of much of the music of the Western hemisphere. The student of music will have no trouble differentiating among the major, the natural minor, the harmonic minor, and the melodic minor scales in terms of either sound or spelling if his understanding and proficiency are thorough.

SUGGESTIONS FOR STUDY

The suggestions referred to for the study of the melodic minor scale are again adequate to insure a good background in scales. Stated briefly, the problem is simply that of knowing (in spelling and characteristic sound) the 15 major scales and the 15 minor scales, the latter each with its three variant forms, making a total of 60 scales. Practice writing these scales using Work Sheet #27.

SATISFACTORY ATTAINMENT: the ability to write on the staff at least eight scales including each of the four types. Use whole notes. Alternate the use of signature and accidentals and the use of treble, bass, alto, and tenor clefs.

III. INTERVALS: Major, Perfect, Augmented Fourth, and Diminished Fifth, Down (Theory Skill #24)

In Unit V it was learned that the intervals of a second, third, sixth, and seventh, measured down from the upper tonic of any major scale, are minor in quality. Major intervals are, of course, a half step larger than minor intervals. By lowering the bottom tone of the minor second, third, sixth, and seventh intervals, therefore, the corresponding major intervals down have been derived. Study the illustrations.

m2 M2   m3 M3   P4 A4   P5 d5   m6 M6   m7 M7

Applying the reasoning just suggested, a major third down from B is G, since B down to G♯ is a minor third; further, F♯ down to A is a major sixth, since F♯ down to A♯ is a minor sixth.

As in Unit VI the perfect intervals are included only for reference and comparison, and the downward tritone is added to complete the 12 simple intervals possible in each octave. Its spelling must be practiced in two ways—as an augmented fourth and as a diminished fifth. It is important to note that the tritone is the only interval having the same span in either its original or inverted form. To illustrate, the perfect fourth inverted becomes a larger interval, the perfect fifth; but the tritone remains a tritone, and changes only its name and spelling from that of an augmented fourth to a diminished fifth, or vice versa.

SUGGESTIONS FOR STUDY

1. The chart will be helpful in singing, recognizing, and hearing the major and perfect intervals down.

Scale degrees	Name	Symbol	Ear training device
8-8	perfect unison	P1	—none needed
8-lowered 7	major second	M2	—whole step; fundamental melodic unit studied in Unit II
8-lowered 6	major third	M3	—"Swing Low, Sweet Chariot"
8-5	perfect fourth	P4	—"Ive Been Work'n . . ."
8-lowered 5	augmented fourth	A4	—think down a perfect fourth, then lower the pitch another half step.
8-raised 4	diminished fifth	d5	—think down a major triad as in "Star Spangled Banner," then raise the pitch one half step.
8-4	perfect fifth	P5	—first and third notes of "Star Spangled Banner"
8-lowered 3	major sixth	M6	—"Nobody Knows . ."
8-lowered 2	major seventh	M7	—think down an octave and up a half step, or up a half step and down an octave.
8-1	perfect octave	P8	—none needed.

2. Practice reciting in letter names the M2, M3, A4, d5, M6, and M7 intervals down based upon the tonic degree of each major scale.
3. Practice reciting these intervals on the remaining six of the 21 tones, namely, D♯, E♯, G♯, A♯, B♯, and F♭. If necessary, use the comparison method of transposition as explained in Unit IV.

ASSIGNMENT #23: Major, Augmented Fourth, and Diminished Fifth Intervals, Down.

Write the M3, A4, d5, M6, and M7 down in five columns across the page following the 21 tone circle (B♯ through F♭). Alternate the use of treble, bass, alto, and tenor clefs on successive staffs, and write in properly flagged sixteenth notes and accidentals. As before, there are 105 intervals in this group, obtained by following through the 21 tone circle five times. As in Unit VI, the M2, P4, P5, and P8 are included only in the hearing test for these intervals. Use Work Sheet #28.

SATISFACTORY ATTAINMENT: the ability to spell correctly at least 20 of these intervals in five minutes. Write the test using whole notes and accidentals, and start on any tone other than B♯.

IV. RHYTHM: Possible subdivisions of simple notes

Rhythmic notation is based on the duple principle that each note value from the largest through the smallest divides into a duplet of the next smaller value. The triple principle is also familiar, namely that any duplet may be replaced by a triplet of pulses of respectively equal total duration. Together, the duple and triple principles explain the subdivision of the simple note value into 2, 3, 4, and 8 pulses. There are several other subdivisions which may occur in music. In this unit the list is extended to include subdivision of the simple note into 5, 7, and 9 equal pulses.

The characteristics of a meter are evident when the sequence of rhythms does not disrupt the organization imposed by the numerator upon the denominator of that meter. Triple subdivisions of notes larger than the denominator always conflict with the organization of a duple meter because they superimpose rhythmic patterns characteristic of some triple meter. Other aspects of these conflicts will be studied and their performance practiced in Unit IX. The subdivision of the half note and the quarter note are outlined, but the same principles may apply to each simple note.

Given simple note—the half note

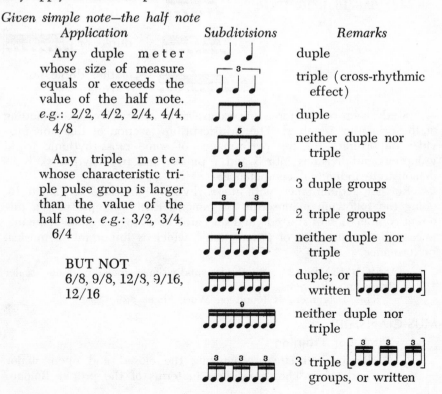

Application	Subdivisions	Remarks
Any duple meter whose size of measure equals or exceeds the value of the half note. *e.g.*: 2/2, 4/2, 2/4, 4/4, 4/8		duple
		triple (cross-rhythmic effect)
		duple
		neither duple nor triple
Any triple meter whose characteristic triple pulse group is larger than the value of the half note. *e.g.*: 3/2, 3/4, 6/4		3 duple groups
		2 triple groups
		neither duple nor triple
BUT NOT 6/8, 9/8, 12/8, 9/16, 12/16		duple; or written
		neither duple nor triple
		3 triple groups, or written

Given simple note—the quarter note

Application	Subdivisions	Remarks
Any duple meter whose size of measure equals or exceeds the value of the quarter note.		duple
		triple (possible cross-rhythmic effect)
		duple
e.g.: 4/16 in addition to those listed above.		neither duple nor triple
Any triple meter whose characteristic triple pulse group is larger than the value of the quarter note.		3 duple groups; or
e.g.: 3/2, 3/4, 6/4, 6/8, 9/8, 12/8		2 triple groups, or
BUT NOT 3/16, 6/16, 9/16, 12/16.		neither duple nor triple
		duple, or
		neither duple nor triple

Study each of the foregoing examples to achieve an understanding of the principles involved. The "Musicianship" section of this unit provides opportunity for the performance of some cross-rhythmic triple groupings, subdivisions into 5 and 7 pulses, and two rhythm skills to demonstrate individual competence.

Further acquaintance with these rhythmic divisions is gained by doing the following manuscript assignment. Each example uses a different combination of slurred* and staccato* notes to give some acquaintance with the problem of articulation,* which is important in musical performance.

ASSIGNMENT #24: Rhythmic subdivisions; melodic minor scale; tenor and alto clefs.

This assignment is found on Work Sheet #29.

MUSICIANSHIP

Pitch Ear Training

1. Review: practice recognizing the closed and open, major and minor chord positions in terms of the proper Roman/

Arabic symbol (I^3, I^5, I^8; i^3, i^5, i^8), and hearing the same in dictation—expressing them in music notation; practice singing, playing, recognizing, and hearing the major, natural minor, harmonic minor, and melodic minor cadence patterns. The melodic minor cadence pattern is illustrated.

2. The four basic scales
    a. sing, singspell, and play each of the four scale types—major, natural, harmonic, and melodic minor—for a given tone.
    b. either sing, or recognize, the upper tetrachord of any of the basic scale types, given the tonic pitch.
    c. either sing, or recognize, the lower tetrachord of any of the basic scale types, given the upper tonic pitch.
    d. either sing, or recognize, any tone of one of the basic scale types, given the lower tonic pitch.
    e. practice hearing and analyzing the four basic scale types, recording the quality and notating each in the assigned clef, given the letter name of the tonic degree.*e.g.*:

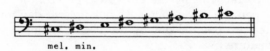

mel. min.

3. The major, perfect, and tritone intervals, down.

    The singing, recognizing, and hearing of intervals makes practical use of one's knowledge of scale patterns, the scale degrees, and the distances between various degree pairs. The student is encouraged to explore these sounds, using both the voice and any instrument.

    a. sing each of the intervals, the M2, M3, P4, A4, P5, d5, M6, M7, and P8 down, in response to the interval name, given the pitch of the upper tone.
    b. sing "la" on the correct pitch, given the upper tone and the interval name.
    c. practice recognizing intervals played or sung melodically.

    d. practice recognizing intervals played harmonically, that is, simultaneously. This type of recognition is more difficult than melodic recognition, but is very important as the basis for recognizing harmonic concepts.

    e. given the letter name of the upper tone, practice hearing the major, perfect, and tritone intervals down. The response may be oral—naming the interval and spelling it, or written—recording the interval name and notating the pitches in the assigned clef.

Rhythm Ear Training

A consideration of all the possible subdivisions of a simple note confronts a musician with several new problems in the performance of rhythm. Odd divisions smaller than the denominator (such as 5 or 7) are not divisible by 2, 3, or 4, and so must be performed more nearly as approximations, rather than with the exactness of the more characteristic subdivisions.

Subdivisions larger than the denominator may make it necessary for the performer to think in the characteristic patterns of a meter different from the one being performed. This he must do by recognizing the cross-rhythmic conflict and superimposing it upon the given meter. In our present day music such conflicts often are pointed out by the use of frequent shifts in the meter signature.

The foregoing half note triplet group can be worked out in exact rhythmic durations by following the sequence of rhythms and reasoning shown.

(accented in fours)  (practice sing-count)

(as if in 3/2 meter)  (second duple subdivisions)

(as if in 3/2 meter)

(as written in 4/4)

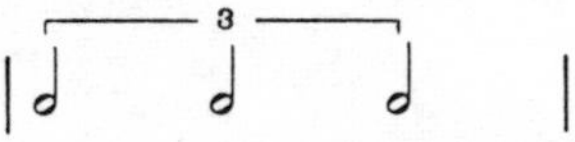

In studying the rhythmic exercises check the meter, determine the pulse unit, note the type of divisions used and set the tempo. Use the sing-count technique to solve performance problems. Sing-count any bracketed group of notes equal to or larger than the denominator as a 1, 2, 3. *e.g.*:

1. Possible divisions of simple notes in various meters.

Special combinations of numbers and syllables have been suggested for denominator subdivisions in 2, 3, 4, 6, and 8, and for the bracketed triple groups equal to and larger than the denominator. It is suggested that groups of five and groups of seven be counted in numbers, maintaining equal duration for each pulse.

4.

5.

6.

7.

8.

9.

2. Rhythm Skills for individual performance.

Evaluate the performance of each rhythm skill in the manner previously suggested.

a. Possible Subdivisions of the Simple Half Note: 4/4 meter, Flash Card Set #18. (*Rhythm Skill #13*)

SATISFACTORY ATTAINMENT: the performance of these rhythms in any order and at any tempo up to 96 quarter notes per minute.

b. Possible Subdivisions of the Simple Half Note: 3/4 meter, Flash Card Set #19. (*Rhythm Skill #14*)

SATISFACTORY ATTAINMENT: the performance of these rhythms in any order and at any tempo up to 96 quarter notes per minute.

Sight Singing. FORM EMPHASIS—Folk Song

Folk songs are songs which belong to the people, either through adoption or because their composers are no longer known. Many have been transmitted by voice, generation after generation, undergoing a type of refinement in the process. Almost every nation—or group of people within a nation—cherishes the folklore and folk song which it holds as a heritage. In many instances it is possible to observe a certain lilt, a rhythmic strength, a typical rhythm, or a melodic twist that seems to be characteristic of the people represented.

In each of the examples—the majority of which are folk songs—note the mode, the meter, the cadences and the grouping of phrases into sentences. Note characteristics which appear to lend a nationalistic flavor to the folk songs.

Lerchengesang, Op. 70, No. 2

Brahms

Keyboard Emphasis
Keyboard Skill #8

SATISFACTORY ATTAINMENT: the ability to play the authentic cadence, (I) V I, using good voice leading at the highest possible level of competence described below.

"Minimum" Level—in any four major and any four (harmonic) minor keys, using the closed positions of the 3rd, the 5th, and the 8th in alternation in the first chord in successive keys.

"Above-average" Level—in any four requested major and any four requested (harmonic) minor keys, using either the closed or open positions of the 3rd, the 5th, and the 8th in alternation in the first chord in successive keys.

"Superior" Level—in any four requested major and four requested (harmonic) minor keys, using either the closed or the open positions of the 3rd, the 5th, or the 8th in the first chord upon request in successive keys.

e.g.:

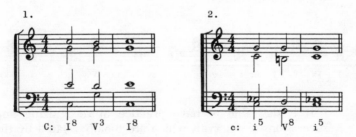

1.

$\text{C: } \text{I}^8 \quad \text{V}^3 \quad \text{I}^8$

2.

$\text{c: } \text{i}^5 \quad \text{V}^8 \quad \text{i}^5$

Dictation
1. Pitch

Pitch Skill #8—Hearing the Four Basic Scales.

SATISFACTORY ATTAINMENT: demonstrated competence in hearing the major, natural, harmonic, and melodic minor scales.

Given the pitch and the clef of the tonic degree, respond by correctly recognizing and notating each of five scales played. *e.g.*:

Each scale and its analysis is considered to be one response. Compute the PROFICIENCY PERCENTAGE and evaluate.

Pitch Skill #9—Hearing the Major, Perfect, Augmented Fourth, and Diminished Fifth Intervals, Down.

SATISFACTORY ATTAINMENT: demonstrated competence in hearing these intervals. Given the clef and pitch of the upper note, respond by correctly recognizing and notating each of ten intervals played. *e.g.*:

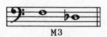

Each interval and its analysis is considered to be one response. Compute the PROFICIENCY PERCENTAGE and evaluate.

Pitch Achievement

The qualities of the three principal triads of the four basic scales are illustrated.

It is desirable to have practice in recognizing and hearing successions of intervals which are tonally related by the tensions found in the three principal triads of the major and minor scales. Listen to each of the following dictations and identify the scale type to which it belongs. The pitch and the clef of the first tone are given. Some examples begin on the tonic, others on the subdominant, and still others on the dominant degree of the scale to which they belong. Respond by notating the pitches heard and placing a Roman numeral beneath each note which begins a new chord. Each note and each numeral constitute separate responses.

e.g.:

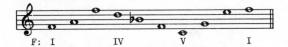

F: I   IV   V   I

Compute the *PROFICIENCY PERCENTAGE* by dividing the number of correct responses by the number attempted.

2. Rhythmic.

The rhythmic dictations give practice in recognizing and hearing several of the possible subdivisions of simple notes in various meters. Consider each pulse unit's value to be one response, and compute the PROFICIENCY PERCENTAGE by dividing the number of correct responses by the number attempted.

3. Melodic.

An excellent index to the status of a student's development in musicianship is his ability to write a familiar tune using the correct pitch and rhythm notation, without the assistance of an intrument.

a. make a list of familiar folk songs, that is, folk songs whose tunes are always in the mind. Keep this list as a source of material for this type of melodic dictation.

b. practice expressing folk songs in music notation. Write each one in a logical meter, but do not write it in the original key—if it is known. Each tune should be notated in a different key, major or minor as necessary, in order to broaden the ability to think in any needed tonality. Compute and compare the PROFICIENCY PERCENT-AGE for a number of tunes.

c. practice taking melodic dictation. The folk songs and themes in this group include from one to three phrases.

First listen to the entire dictation, than concentrate on notating each phrase as it is repeated several times. Compute the PROFICIENCY PERCENTAGE.

4. Harmonic.

    a. practice hearing arpeggiated two-chord progressions such as those illustrated, played in eighth notes in 6/8 meter. The response should be in corresponding melodic notation, together with the Roman/Arabic analysis implied. For purposes of evaluation each eighth note is one point, and the Roman/Arabic symbol is two points, independent of the notation. To find the PROFICIENCY PERCENTAGE divide the number of correct points by the number attempted.

    e.g.:

1.   2.

3.   4.

    b. practice hearing non-arpeggiated two-chord progressions such as are illustrated in order to become more proficient in isolating each voice from its context—at the same time listening to cadence structures, some complete and some incomplete. Recognition of the bass voice will determine the basic function of the root position chords, while recognizing the soprano voice determines the melodic outline and, also, gives a clue to the voice distribution. Recognizing the two middle voices is the final factor in determining whether the chord is closed or open in its distribution. Given the letter name and location of the bass tone of the first chord:

1) respond by writing the Roman/Arabic symbols. Count the Roman and Arabic numbers as separate or independent responses. Determine the PROFICIENCY PERCENTAGE by dividing the number of correct responses by the total number attempted.

2) respond by writing the Roman/Arabic symbol and notating each chord on the great staff. Count each chord and each symbol as separate responses. Determine the PROFICIENCY PERCENTAGE in the usual way.

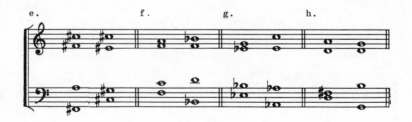

UNIT 8

HARMONY

I. THE FIRST INVERSION

Since the connection of root position chords has been studied it is now logical to consider the use of the first inversion chord. Triads comprise a root, a third, and a fifth. When either the third or the fifth is in the bass voice the chord can be described as an inverted chord.* Further discussion of the use of the 5th degree in the bass voice will be given under "non-harmonic tones" in connection with the continuing consideration of the six-four dissonance. The occurrence of the third, the modal degree of any triad, in the bass voice is descriptive of the first inversion. As is the case with root position chords, the first inversion chord is guided by its nominal root, but this root does not appear in the bass voice. The use of both the root position and first inversion of the primary chords makes all the scale degrees except the second usable in the bass voice, hence allowing that voice a greater degree of freedom.

A. The First inversion of the primary triads in major and minor.

1. Positions.

Since the root is found in one or more of the upper three voices of an inverted chord, the pattern of possible positions is varied. Some positions can be described as closed, others as open, and still others as combining features of both. These are called mixed positions.*

First inversion triads or chords are often referred to as first inversions, or simply as sixth chords.* The last name has its basis in the fact that the interval of a sixth (ignoring added octaves) separates the bass voice from the voice sounding the root, and gives the chord its characteristic sound.

2. Doublings.

The root or the fifth of each chord position can be doubled freely, but some caution must be observed in doubling the 3rd degree. This 3rd degree can be doubled when doing so results in a more melodic and musical voice line. Such a line is most likely to occur if two voices move to or away from a doubled third by contrary motion. See the following excerpt from the Bach chorale for examples.

The doubling to use in any given instance, involving either the fundamental positions or the first inversions, should be that which gives the most effective forward motion to the voices. This is known as good voice leading.

Such factors as changing positions over a static bass, changing chords and chord positions under a held melodic tone, the use of non-harmonic tones, and lastly, a critical choice of doublings, constitute the liberalizing influences which can modify horizontally the connections of vertical harmonies. Always write exercises which seem musical. This process carried to its ultimate perfection is found in the music of every great composer. Even in the Bach chorales, where the melody is pre-existent as well as predominant, the effect of contrapuntal-melodic thinking is constantly evident. In the following example the supertonic triad and the passing tone* are used. Both are explained later in this unit.

Allein Gott in der höh' sei ehr'

Bach

G: I^8 3 IV^6 V^8 (ii^3) I^6 V^5 I^3

(Permission has been granted by G. Schirmer, Inc., New York, for the use of numerous quotations from the Bach-Riemenschneider, *371 Harmonized Chorales and 69 Chorale Melodies with Figured Bass.*)

3. Connections.

   a. when connecting two chords one or both of which are sixth chords, hold over one or more common tones, as seems desirable. In the foregoing chorale excerpt, note the instance in which one common tone is held between two chords, one of which is in the first inversion. Study these given examples also.

   b. freely double either the root or the fifth of the first inversion chord, but less frequently the 3rd degree. This word of caution is given since the 3rd degree, being modal, is the one which determines whether a chord is major or minor in quality. In the foregoing chorale the third is doubled in each of the two first inversion chords. This is true in one instance in the following examples.

   c. note that two or three movements are possible through the use of leaps, especially in the soprano voice, but *not only* in the soprano voice.

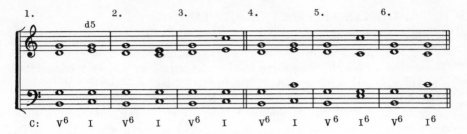

C: V⁶ I V⁶ I V⁶ I V⁶ I V⁶ I⁶ V⁶ I⁶

d. note, also, from many of the foregoing examples, that the remaining voice usually moves by step.

e. avoid the use of consecutive fifths and octaves. However, hidden octaves are quite satisfactory when they occur as the result of using various positions within a given chord. (See the illustrative exercise.)

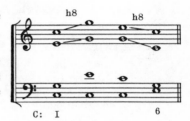

II. ALTERED CHORDS—the minor subdominant chord in the major mode

Composers were not slow to realize that chords which were effective in one mode often could be effective in the opposite mode. In Unit VII the use of the Picardy third was cited as a first illustration of this principle. As another instance, the minor subdominant chord of the minor mode is quite often incorporated into the major mode. This is accomplished by the simple expedient of lowering the 6th degree of the major scale a half step, thus lowering the 3rd degree of the subdominant chord to form a chord minor in quality. Study the example quoted.

Liebestraum

Liszt

Ab: V   I   iv⁶   8   I

III. CADENCES—PERFECT, MASCULINE

Several harmonic progressions used as cadences, or means for closing a phrase, sentence, or other section of music are now well known. Those that end with finality are further described as perfect,° imperfect, masculine,° and feminine. Any *conclusive* cadence is *perfect* if its last two chords are in root position with the root doubled in the soprano voice of the last chord. A cadence whose voice leading differs from that mentioned is imperfect. Further, a conclusive cadence whose final tonic chord occurs on a first beat or on the third beat of a four beat measure is *masculine*. Any deviation from the rhythmic position of the final chord as described is known as feminine. *Perfection* and *rhythmic gender* are important in describing the characteristics of conclusive, but *not* conclusive cadences.

SUGGESTIONS FOR STUDY

1. Practice in harmonizing the figured bass° on the great staff.

    In most instances there are several acceptable solutions for chord connection. Practice realizing (see "realization"°) the suggested chord progressions, making sure to write several versions of at least one exercise. Make them simple. Use only chord tones, writing in whole notes without a meter signature.

    a. I I6 IV IV6 V V6 I—1♯ major, the first chord in closed position. (The subdominant chord may be either major or minor.)

    b. i iv6 V6 i6 V V6 i—2♭ minor, the first chord in open position.

    c. I V6 V I6 V6 IV6 I—2♯ major, the first chord in open position.

    d. i6 i6 iv6 iv6 iv V6 V6 i—2♯ minor, the first chord in closed position.

2. Analyze the harmonic progressions and doublings, and the cadence characteristics—type, perfection and rhythmic gender (when applicable)—used in these examples from the Bach chorales.

Vater unser

Gottes Sohn ist kommen · Bach

Wo soll ich fliehen hin · Bach

ASSIGNMENT #25: Part writing in harmony—free connections of the primary triads including the use of the first inversion chord.

This assignment is found on Work Sheet #30.

IV. NON-HARMONIC TONES: the suspension; the passing tone; related six-four dissonances

A. The accented and unaccented suspension.

The suspension* is a non-harmonic tone of great beauty and abundant usage. It can decorate any step movement between two chords, the downward form being the more common and more appropriate to the name. The upward suspension is often known by another name, the retardation.* Technically, the suspension results from a chord tone's being sustained beyond the point of harmonic change. After the second chord is sounded, the sustained tone of the first chord moves to resolve the suspension. If the suspended tone is sounded again at the moment of harmonic change, the suspension becomes accented. If it is not sounded again, but rather is sustained, it is unaccented. Some theorists call what is here described as an accented suspension, a form of the appoggiatura.

1. These examples include the unaccented (S) and the accented (S') suspension, each in one or more voices, always related to step movements.

2. The next examples show the returning tone and the suspension (S or S') used in several combinations. The student is urged to explore the usage of non-harmonic tones thoroughly. Their use and effectiveness will be limited only by the depth of imagination and musicianship one can apply.

3. Note the use of the unaccented suspension, accented suspension, and the suspension decorated by a returning tone in the Bach chorale. Keeping in mind the analysis provided again analyze the first measure, assuming that the harmonic rhythm does not change. To do so, one must consider the notes occurring within the second beat as being non-harmonic to the tonic chord.

O Wir Armen Sünder

Bach

D: I⁵ V⁶ I ⁶ IV³   I⁵ (ii) I⁶ (ii) V⁵ I⁸

4. Since the accurate analysis of non-harmonic tones is depend-
    ent on knowledge of the harmonic rhythm, it is well to note
    that in the Bach chorales, as well as in much other music,
    the unit of harmonic rhythm is most often the quarter note
    value, but it can be two, three, or four times this value.
    Further, there are times, especially in approaching a cadence
    point, in which harmonic changes occur in eighth note values.
    Such harmonic rhythm is evident in this excerpt.

Ich dank dir, lieber Herre

Bach

b: (vii°) i³ (vii°⁶) i⁶ iv⁶ V 3♯   i⁸

B. The accented and unaccented passing tone.

The passing tone—certainly the most common of all non-harmonic tones—occurs in both unaccented and accented forms,
diatonically as well as chromatically. The diatonic form occurs
very naturally between two chords whenever the interval of a
third exists in a given voice movement. The examples are again
from the Bach chorales. Note the unaccented (P) and accented
forms (P').

Ein feste burg ist unser Gott   Ach was soll ich sünder machen

D: I   VI I^6 vii^{o6} I $(\overset{V}{/}V)$ V   e: i   6   3   iv   VII III

1. The chromatic form can occur whenever the interval of a whole step exists between two chords. Since this happens frequently, the composer must be discriminating in the use of this non-harmonic tone if its effect is to remain significant.

1.   2.   3.   4.

C: I   IV   V   I   I   IV   I   V   I   vi   IV   V

2. Both the diatonic and chromatic forms can occur in any combination over considerable distances. Note how the passing tone becomes an effective technique of composition in the hand of the accomplished composer.

Sonata in A Major, Op. 2, No. 2

Beethoven

Sonata in F Minor, Op. 2, No. 1

Beethoven

C. Six-four dissonance related to the suspension and the passing tone.

The discussion of the six-four dissonance given under the "returning tone" in Unit VII is applicable in principle. The main differences among the various non-harmonic dissonances are found in how they are approached or introduced, but their resolutions are similar. Note how the following six-four dissonances—occurring as a part of the dominant harmony in the cadence—are composed of some combination of non-harmonic tones above a bass root.

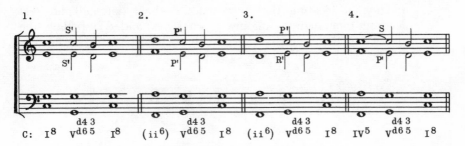

ASSIGNMENT #26: Non-harmonic tones—the suspension, passing tone and related six-four dissonance.

This assignment including analysis and some writing is found on Work Sheet #31.

ASSIGNMENT #26 (Part II): Non-harmonic tones—the six-four dissonance in Bach chorales (Source: Bach-Riemenschneider, 371 *Harmonized Chorales*. G. Schirmer, New York.)

Study the following cadences in the Bach chorales. In each instance, note the type and combinations of non-harmonic tones used as the six-four dissonance over the dominant root, and how each dissonance is resolved.

a. Chorale No. 166, ms. 5 and 6.
b. Chorale No. 171, last two measures.
c. Chorale No. 178, last two measures.
d. Chorale No. 191, ms. 5 and 6.
e. ————, last two measures.
f. Chorale No. 235, ms. 10 and 11.
g. Chorale No. 253, ms. 5 and 6.
h. Chorale No. 262, last two measures.

In the last two illustrations, observe how the dominant root also is involved in a momentary returning dissonance, giving the effect of a "non-harmonic chord," that is, a chord structure whose use is decorative rather than harmonically functional.

FUNDAMENTALS

I. SECONDARY TRIADS

A. Major mode (*Theory Skill #25*)

The triads found on the various degrees of the major scale are the three primary or principal triads (studied in Unit IV), and the four secondary triads* built on the supertonic, mediant, submediant, and leading tone degrees. The quality of each triad is determined by its position within the scale. Since all major, minor, augmented, and diminished triad spellings have already been learned, the remaining problems are those of 1) developing facility in locating the supertonic, mediant, submediant, and leading tone degrees of any given scale, and 2) spelling the quality of the triad associated with each secondary degree.

The triads found in the C major scale are:

Following a similar pattern the triad found upon each degree of any major scale can be written or spelled out, since the degree-quality pattern of a given mode does not change. Thus, the supertonic triad of A major is a B minor triad since the supertonic triad *is* minor in quality, and the supertonic degree *is* B in A major.

The relationship between degree and quality is shown in the table.

Functional name	Abbreviation	Quality	Degree symbol
tonic	T	M	I
supertonic	ST	m	ii
mediant	M	m	iii
subdominant	SD	M	IV
dominant	D	M	V
submediant	SM	m	vi
leading tone	LT	d	vii°

SUGGESTIONS FOR STUDY

1. Learn the degree-quality pattern for the major mode.
2. Spell or write the supertonic triad of each major key from that of C♯ through C♭.
3. Spell in turn the mediant, submediant, and leading tone triads of each major key from C♯ through C♭.
4. The D minor triad is ii in C major. In what key has it a mediant function? In which a submediant function? Why cannot the minor

triad be the leading tone triad in the major mode? Consider other minor triads in a similar fashion.

ASSIGNMENT #27 (Part I): Secondary triads—major mode.

Write the ii, iii, vi, and vii° triads for each major scale following the circle of major keys from C♯ through C♭. Alternate the use of signature and accidentals with each key, and the use of treble, bass, alto, and tenor clefs with successive staffs as started following. Indicate the function of each triad by writing the proper form of the Roman numeral beneath it. The assignment begins as shown. Work Sheet #32 is provided.

C♯:   ii   iii   vi   vii°   F♯:   ii   iii   vi   vii°   B: ii

SATISFACTORY ATTAINMENT: the ability to notate and analyze the four secondary triads in eight or more major keys in five minutes, alternating the use of signatures and accidentals and clefs as done in the assignment. Use whole notes.

B. Harmonic minor mode (*Theory Skill #26*)

The secondary triads of the minor mode are determined by the intervallic differences found within the three minor scale forms. Each variant scale form therefore has its own degree-quality pattern, and this means that the minor mode contains much harmonic potential. For information, reference, and comparison the degree-quality pattern of each of the three minor scale forms is presented in outline form.

The Minor Mode

		Functional Degree Name	Major Mode Quality	Symbol	Natural Scale Quality	Symbol	Harmonic Scale Quality	Symbol	Melodic Scale Quality	Symbol
P R I M A R Y	T R I A D S	Tonic	M	I	m	i	m	i	m	i
		Subdominant	M	IV	m	iv	m	iv	M	IV
		Dominant	M	V	m	v	M	V	M	V
S E C O N D A R Y	T R I A D S	Supertonic	m	ii	d	ii°	d	ii°	m	ii
		Mediant	m	iii	M	III	A	III+	A	III+
		Submediant	m	vi	M	VI	M	VI	d	vi°
		Leading Tone	d	vii°	M	VII	d	vii°	d	vii°

Intensive study is limited to the secondary triads of the harmonic minor scale—the scale form which is basic to harmony in the minor mode. The illustration is in D harmonic minor.

SUGGESTIONS FOR STUDY

1. Learn the degree-quality pattern for each variant form of the minor mode.
2. Spell or write the secondary triads found in each of the harmonic minor scales.
   e.g.: the supertonic-diminished triad of the key of one sharp minor is the F♯ diminished; the mediant-augmented of the key of one flat minor is the F augmented triad; etc.
3. Spell all of the supertonic, mediant, submediant, and leading tone triads for each harmonic minor scale.
4. Compare the secondary harmonic minor triads of a given key with those based upon the natural and melodic variants of the same key.

ASSIGNMENT #27 (Part II): Secondary triads—minor mode (harmonic variant).

Write the ii⁰, III⁺, VI and vii⁰ triads for each harmonic minor scale following the circle of minor keys from A♯ through A♭. Alternate the use of signature and accidentals with each key, and the use of treble, bass, alto, and tenor clefs with successive staffs as shown. Indicate the function of each triad by writing the proper form of the Roman numeral beneath it. Use Work sheet #32.

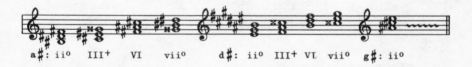

SATISFACTORY ATTAINMENT: the ability to notate and analyze the four secondary triads in eight or more minor keys in five minutes, alternating the use of signatures and accidentals, and clefs as done in the assignment. Use whole notes.

II. SOPRANO CLEF (Theory Skill #27)

The soprano clef* is the last of the five clefs we are to consider. Further proficiency in the five clefs, the treble, bass, alto, tenor, and soprano, will be developed by continual contact with them through writing, singing, and playing. The gamut for the soprano clef, whose first line is middle C, will arbitrarily extend from "a" below the staff to a^2 two octaves higher.

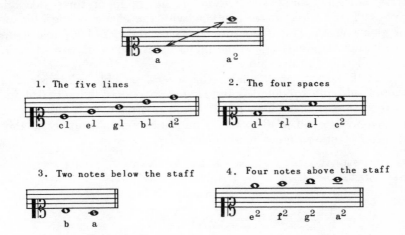

1. The five lines   2. The four spaces

3. Two notes below the staff   4. Four notes above the staff

Note the placement of the seven sharp and the seven flat signatures on the staff in the soprano clef.

SUGGESTIONS FOR STUDY

Practice the soprano clef using the techniques which were suggested for the treble clef in Unit I. Flash Card Set #20 is available.

SATISFACTORY ATTAINMENT: the ability to use the soprano clef in alternation with the treble, bass, alto, and tenor clefs in selected theory skills beginning with those found in Unit IX.

III. RHYTHM: Possible subdivisions of dotted notes in triple meters

Since a dot increases the value of a simple note by one-half, a dotted note naturally divides into three simple notes of the next lesser value. This has become familiar in the group of three denominator pulses characteristic of each triple meter. *e.g.*:

The division of the denominator value and of lesser note values into *two* equal parts is a similar problem in both duple and triple meters. In general, a comparable statement applies to *triple* subdivision. In contrast, however, duple subdivision of the group of three denominator pulses of any triple meter conflicts with the characteristic organization of such a meter. This is because the characteristics of a duple meter are being superimposed on a triple meter. This aspect of cross-rhythm will be studied in the next unit.

In the accompanying table the several possible subdivisions of the dotted half note are detailed and characterized in relation to 3/4 and 6/8 meters. In a similar manner the dotted quarter note is subdivided and related to 3/8 and 6/16 meters. The same principles apply to the subdivision of other dotted note values.

Possible Subdivisions of the Dotted Half Note -- (𝅗𝅥.) -- in 3/4 (and 6/4) Meters

Subdivision	Remarks
2	cross-rhythm
	characteristic triple pulse group
4	cross-rhythm
5	neither duple nor triple, but a combination of both
	duple subdivision
	cross-rhythm (as in 6/8)
7	neither duple nor triple, but a combination of both
8	cross-rhythm
3 3 3	triple subdivision (or nine notes under one beam)

Possible Subdivisions of the Dotted Half Note -- (𝅗𝅥.) -- in 6/8 (9/8 and 12/8) Meters

Subdivision	Remarks
	duple subdivision

cross-rhythm (or ♩ ♪♪♩)

cross-rhythm

neither duple nor triple, but a combination of both

two characteristic triple pulse groups

cross-rhythm (as in 3/4)

neither duple nor triple, but a combination of both

cross-rhythm

first triple subdivision (could also be a group of nine under one double beam)

Possible Subdivisions of the Dotted Quarter Note (♩.) in 3/8 (6/8, 9/8, and 12/8) Meters

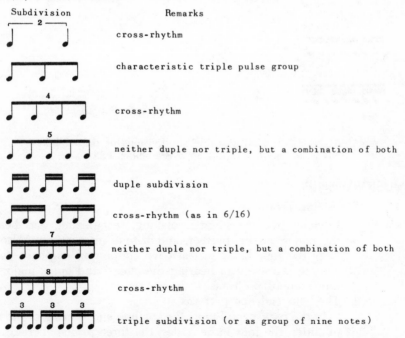

Subdivision	Remarks
	cross-rhythm
	characteristic triple pulse group
	cross-rhythm
	neither duple nor triple, but a combination of both
	duple subdivision
	cross-rhythm (as in 6/16)
	neither duple nor triple, but a combination of both
	cross-rhythm
	triple subdivision (or as group of nine notes)

Possible Subdivisions of the Dotted Quarter Note (♩.) in 6/16 (9/16 and 12/16) Meters

Subdivision	Remarks
♪. ♪.	duple subdivision
♪ ♪ ♪	cross-rhythm (as in 3/8)
♩ ♩ ♩ ♩ (4)	cross-rhythm
♩ ♩ ♩ ♩ ♩ (5)	neither duple nor triple, but a combination of both
♫♫♫ ♫♫♫	two characteristic triple pulse groups
♫♫ ♫♫ ♫♫	cross-rhythm (as in 3/8)
♫♫♫♫♫♫♫ (7)	neither duple nor triple, but a combination of both
♫♫♫♫♫♫♫♫ (8)	cross-rhythm
♫♫♫ ♫♫♫ ♫♫♫ (3 3 3)	first triple subdivision (also can be nine notes under a triple beam)

> ASSIGNMENT #28: Possible subdivisions of dotted notes.
> This assignment is found on Work Sheet #33.

MUSICIANSHIP

Pitch Ear Training

1. Review: practice singing, playing, recognizing, and hearing the major, minor, perfect, and tritone intervals up. Also, review the four basic scales. Give continuing emphasis to becoming proficient in hearing the closed and open, major and minor chord positions.

2. The four cadence patterns.

   In the past several units the spelling and hearing of the triad qualities, the four basic scales, the three principal triads, and the tonic, subdominant, and dominant cadence patterns associated with each scale type have been studied. These cadence patterns now are introduced as a pitch skill, since their recognition and hearing are an asset in learning to recognize cadences.

   a. sing by number the sequence: 1 3 5, 1 3 5, 4 6 8, 4 6 8, 5 7 9, 5 7 9, 8 5 3 1, in thinking of the cadence pattern for each type of scale. Practice each type—major, natural minor, harmonic minor, and melodic minor—beginning on various tonic pitches.

   b. recognize the type of cadence pattern according to the sequence of triad qualities.

   c. recognize the type of cadence pattern according to the type of scale.

   d. practice hearing and analyzing the four cadence patterns, recording the quality and notating each in the assigned clefs when given the location of the tonic degree. Note that these patterns can be notated in any meter whose numerator is "3." *e.g.*: harmonic minor cadence pattern.

3. The nine positions of the major triad.

   In learning to recognize the four triad qualities, the triad position with the root as the lowest and the 5th degree as highest tone became familiar. The study of the closed and the open positions extended familiarity to recognizing the 3rd degree, and the doubled root in the upper voice, still with the 1st degree in the lowest voice. Now the major triad will be studied as three groups of chord positions whose root, 3rd, and 5th degrees can be *either or both* the lower or upper voices. This will include a beginning study of the sound of the first inversion triads, as well as that of the six-four dissonance.

C: 5/1 8/1 3/1   A♭: 8/3 3/3 5/3   F: 3/5 5/5 8/5

   a. play and sing each group of three chord positions. It is suggested that each chord position be learned by the lower and upper degree numbers as identification. *e.g.*: 8/3 for the first inversion with the root in the upper voice, or 3/5 for the second inversion (six-four dissonance) with the 3rd degree in the upper voice.

b. learn the following singing devices which will prove helpful for remembering several of the chord positions. (3' means 3 an octave higher)

1. 5/1—sing 1, 3, 5
2. 8/1—sing 1, 3, 5, 8
3. 3'/1—sing 1, 3, 5, 8, 3'
4. 8/3—sing "Let Me Call You Sweetheart" (first 3 notes)
5. 3'/3—sing "Who's Sorry Now" (first 4 notes)
6. 5'/3—sing (1) 3, 5, 8, 3', 5'
7. 3'/5—sing "Were You There . . ." (first 3 notes)
8. 5'/5—sing "Down by the Old Mill Stream" (first 4 notes)
9. 8'/5—sing (1, 3) 5, 8, 3', 5', 8'

c. practice recognizing each of the nine major chord positions by its numerical label; also by its voice distribution.

d. practice hearing and analyzing the nine chord positions, each in the assigned clef, when given the letter name of the bass tone. This bass tone may or may not be the chord root. *e.g.*:

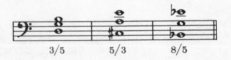

Rhythm Ear Training

In studying the subdivisions of the dotted note one finds that only a few of the possibilities are used with any frequency. Divisions of the dotted note into two, four, five, and seven equal parts are sufficient illustration of the more usual possibilities. It is suggested that the dotted value being divided should be thought of as one broad pulse. Then the mind can concentrate on subdividing that basic pulse into the desired number of divisions. Since all the meters and their characteristic subdivisions have been explained, it is not logical to invent syllables to represent these latest subdivisions. Rather, in dividing a dotted note into five pulses, count out five numbered subdivisions. *e.g.*:

$\frac{3}{4}$ 1 - - | 1 - - | 1 2 3 4 5 | 1 - - | etc.

1. Characteristic subdivisions of the dotted note in simple triple
   meters.

2. Subdivisions of the dotted note in compound triple meters.

3. Rhythm Skills for individual performance.
   Evaluate the performance of each rhythm skill in the usual
   manner.

a. Possible Subdivisions of the Dotted Half Note: 3/4 meter, Flash Card Set #21. (*Rhythm Skill #15*)

SATISFACTORY ATTAINMENT: the performance of these rhythms in any order and at any tempo up to 120 quarter notes per minute.

b. Possible Subdivisions of the Dotted Quarter Note: 6/8 meter, Flash Card Set #22. (*Rhythm Skill #16*)

SATISFACTORY ATTAINMENT: the performance of these rhythms in any order and at any tempo up to 92 dotted notes per minute.

Sight Singing: FORM EMPHASIS—Chorales, Hymn Tunes, and Carols

The chorale is especially important as the basis for the many cantatas and much organ music of the Baroque period, and as a means of expressing worship. The cantatas, the four "Passions," and the wealth of organ music of J. S. Bach draw heavily upon the chorale tradition. The *371 Harmonized Chorales* (Bach-Riemenschneider, G. Schirmer, New York) are a compilation of the chorales the master used in his numerous sacred works. Some are found in different settings and keys, each dictated by the particular situation for which Bach was composing.

Harmonically, the Bach chorales represent a rich selection from the many chordal possibilities of the major-minor modes. Contrapuntally, they show the life-giving forward motion to be derived from thinking each voice melodically within a harmonic framework, and formally, they are generally of a multi-phrase structure. Most of the inner phrases cadence either into areas within the tonic key in the broad sense, or into keys closely related to the tonic. In your study, always note the cadence which closes each phrase, conclusively or otherwise, at or away from the basic key or tonic. The group of keys, or tonal areas,* included in the phrases of each given selection describes its tonal arch.* Note further that an authentic cadence used to lead into a related key must be considered inconclusive relative to the home key.

The Welsh hymn tune* is of the sturdy quality which characterizes the sacred music of that heritage. The old English tune, "Greensleeves," is but one of many lovely tunes found among the carols* of many lands.

It is interesting to note that most *hymn tunes* (the word "hymn" refers to the poetry) are known by a name given them by their composer, arranger, or compiler, and the chorales are usually known by their first line of text.

Lasst uns erfreuen

Geistliche Kirchegesang, 1623

1. (♩)

Dir, dir, Jehovah, will ich singen

Bach

2. (♩♪)

Ich bin, ja Herr, in deiner macht

Bach

3. (♩)

4. (♩) Wachet auf

Nicolai, 1599

5. (♩.) In dulce jubilo

14th Century German

6. (♩.) Greensleeves

Old English Carol

162

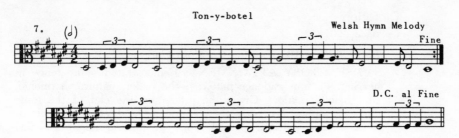

Keyboard Emphasis

Keyboard Skill #9

SATISFACTORY ATTAINMENT: the performance of the plagal cadence, (I) IV I, using acceptable voice leading, at your highest level of competence as outlined in Unit VII under Keyboard Skill #8. *e.g.*:

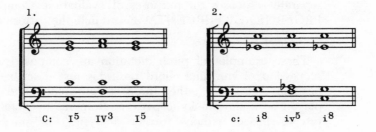

Dictation

1. Pitch.

Pitch Skill # 10—Hearing the Four Cadence Patterns.

SATISFACTORY ATTAINMENT: demonstrated competence in hearing the four cadence patterns: the major, natural, harmonic, and melodic minors. Given the pitch and the clef of the tonic degree, respond by correctly recognizing and notating each of five cadence patterns played. *e.g.:* g: natural minor cadence pattern.

Consider each cadence pattern together with its analysis to be one response. Compute the PROFICIENCY PERCENTAGE, the pattern of error, and evaluate.

Pitch Skill #11—Hearing the Nine Major Chord Positions.

SATISFACTORY ATTAINMENT: demonstrated competence in hearing the nine major chord positions, namely, those in which the root, 3rd, or 5th degree of the triad may be either or both the lowest and highest voice. Given the pitch and the clef of the lowest voice (the root in only three of the nine positions), respond by correctly recognizing and notating each of the five positions played. *e.g.:*

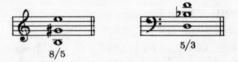

Consider each chord position and its analysis to be two separate responses for purposes of evaluation. Compute the PROFICIENCY PERCENTAGE and note the pattern of error.

Pitch Achievement

These examples of pitch dictation are composed of some succession of the nine chord positions just described. Each position consists of either three or four tones, and will be played as a slow melodic pattern. Respond by notating the pitches heard without further analysis. For purposes of evaluation, each note after the first counts as one response. Compute the PROFICIENCY PERCENTAGE by dividing the number of correct responses by the number attempted.

2. Rhythmic.

The rhythmic dictations give practice in recognizing and hearing several of the possible subdivisions of dotted notes in triple meters. For purposes of evaluation consider each note to be one response. Compute the PROFICIENCY PER- CENTAGE by dividing the number of correct responses by the number attempted.

3. Melodic.

   It is important for the musician to express himself in musical notation which is intended to represent musical thoughts. Since all musicians are familiar with hymns and carols, these can be helpful as source materials.

   a. practice expressing familiar chorales, hymn tunes, and carols in music notation, using other than the usual keys. Compare your version with the original, when available.

   b. compose a hymn tune, a chorale melody, or a carol based on the words and phrase structure found in some selected example. Do not, however, be influenced by the original setting. If you desire, use an original phrase plan.

   c. practice taking melodic dictation. Compute the PROFICIENCY PERCENTAGE in the usual way.

Toulon

Genevan Psalter, 1551

1.

Herr, nun lass uns frieden

Bach

2. (♩)

An wasserflüssen Babylon

Bach

3. (♩)

Passion Chorale

Hassler

4. (♩)

Hilf, Herr Jesu, lass gelingen

Bach

5. (♩.)

4. Harmonic

The recognition of the harmonic function and position of a given chord is emphasized in this series of dictations. Listen to these and similar examples for practice of the recognitions suggested. In each case the key should be given before the example is played.

a. recognize each root position triad, assigning the correct Roman numeral to describe its function, and the correct Arabic numeral to identify the soprano voice and give some information about the chord position.

b. use your developing harmonic and aural skills to recognize the function of each chord and to name the cadence progression. Observe whether each conclusive cadence is perfect or imperfect. Further background information is given under "Cadences" in the Appendix.

c. recognize each first inversion chord by assigning the Arabic numeral "6," without regard to the pitch of the soprano voice. Thus, in contra-distinction to the use of 3, 5, and 8 to identify the exact position of the soprano voice in root position chords, the numeral "6" is used only to indicate that one hears a chord whose 3rd degree is its bass tone. As before, the Roman numerals are used to describe the chord function.

For purposes of evaluation each Roman and each Arabic numeral counts as one response. Each complete recognition of a chord thus counts two points. Compute the PROFICIENCY PERCENTAGE in the usual manner.

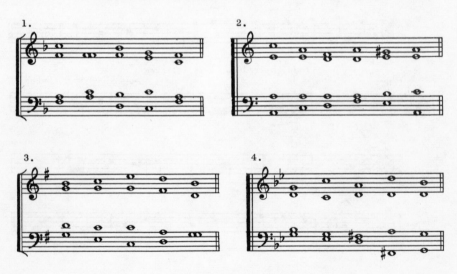

5.

6.

7.

8.

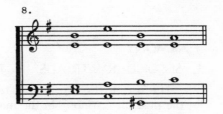

UNIT 9

HARMONY

I. SECONDARY TRIADS IN THE MAJOR AND MINOR MODES

The use of three principal triads makes available only a small part of the possible harmony in the major and minor modes, but, nevertheless, these three triads are a powerful unifying force for determining and maintaining tonality. By including the secondary triads, therefore, the use of a fuller and more varied harmonic vocabulary is made possible. The secondary triads, that is, those triads which are built on the supertonic, mediant, submediant, and leading tone degree in each scale, are so named because their function is subordinate to that of the primary triads. The chord on the leading tone, of diminished quality in both the major and harmonic minor, must be considered in at least two ways, namely, as a secondary triad and as a member of the dominant family. The distinction between these two categories is not always clear. It is clear, however, in the natural minor scale where the quality of the leading tone triad is major, and where its function is strongly secondary to that of the primary triads of the scale.

The many harmonies made possible by the inclusion of the secondary triads will be studied from several points of view. These, stated generally, are as follows:

(1) harmony based on the use of one or more of the one-common-tone chord progressions.

    a. those based on the root movement of a downward fifth (or upward fourth).

    b. those based on the root movement of an upward fifth (or downward fourth).

(2) harmony based on the use of one or more of the no-common-tone chord progressions.

    a. those based on the root movement of an ascending second (but never the descending seventh).

    b. those based on the root movement of a descending second (but never the ascending seventh).

(3) harmony based on the use of one or more of the two-common-tone chord connections.

    a. those based on the root movement of a descending third (or ascending sixth).

    b. those based on the root movement of an ascending third (or descending sixth).

(4) harmony based on a judicious combination of the foregoing techniques.

The suggestions discussed earlier for voice leading in connecting chords having one common tone and those having no common tone remain applicable in principle, but the student is encouraged to search for other possibilities. For instance, since the 3rd degree of the secondary chords—other than that on the leading tone—is the root of one of the primary triads, this degree may be doubled freely, with resulting changes in voice leading. Many examples from the Bach chorales will be found to contain a number of free doublings in both modes. The harmony of the chorales will not be difficult to comprehend if it is thought of as contrapuntal harmony, arising from the use of non-harmonic tones to modify and enliven the vertical harmonies by putting melodic motion into their component voices.

One new technique of chord connection must be studied, namely, that dealing with those chords which include two common tones and whose roots move either a third or a sixth. The simplest voice leading in the instance when a bass tone moves a third or a sixth between root position chords is that of holding the two common tones and moving the remaining voice by step. In a free connection between such chords, one of the two common tones can be held and the remaining two voices moved to convenient tones of the second chord; the upper voices can be moved in contrary motion to the bass voice, or the doubling in either or both chords may involve a tone other than the root. Study the given examples of voice leading. Note the ones which result in a change of position.

Root Movement of a Third Down or a Sixth Up, Major and Minor Modes

C: I   vi   c:i   VI   C:I   vi   c:i   VI   C:I   vi   c:i   VI   C:I   vi$_6$ c:i   VI$_6$

Root Movement of a Third Up or a Sixth Down, Major and Minor Modes

C: I   iii   c: i   III⁺c: i   III   C:I   iii   C:I   iii c: i   III   C:I   iii   c: i   III

The explanation which follows extends the principles of chord progression to include the use of the secondary triads with the primary triads in the major and minor modes. Since a number of the examples quoted illustrate more than one type of progression, the main group of illustrations is placed following the discussion.

A. Harmony based on the use of one or more of the one-common-tone chord progressions.

1. Chord progressions based on the root movement of a downward fifth (or the equivalent upward fourth).

The basic progression studied earlier was that from the major dominant to the major or minor tonic, and the principle was further applied in the root progression, tonic to subdominant. Both of these were practiced in the major and harmonic minor modes. The natural minor progression of a minor dominant to the minor tonic—quite acceptable to our ears—is found within phrases, but seldom is used as a final cadence.

In applying this principle to other degrees of the scale functioning as chord roots, one must spell each chord in accordance with the quality proper to the scale type being used. These relations of degree, mode, and chord quality were studied in Unit VIII.

The one-common-tone principle applies to triadic harmony based on the seven listed root movements of a downward fifth. The general function of this harmonic progression is that of *resolving* tension.

a. dominant to tonic—the basic progression. Remember to raise the leading tone when the major dominant of the harmonic minor mode is used.

b. supertonic to dominant—the contrary motion connection, which was studied as a free connection for I IV or V I in Unit VII, is used almost exclusively. The chord progres-

sion, II V I (in both major and minor modes), frequently
is used as a full cadence.

c. submediant to supertonic—use any form of the basic progression.

d. mediant to submediant—use any form of the basic progression.

e. leading tone to mediant—the principal use of the root
position leading tone chord is in sequential (see "sequence")
passages based on root progressions following a descending series of fifths.

f. subdominant to leading tone—occurs quite infrequently,
but when found is usually in sequential passages.

g. tonic to subdominant—familiar.

2. Harmony based on a *series of root movements* of a downward fifth.

It is quite logical that composers often used a series of
one-common-tone progressions, since the downward root
movement of a fifth seems so natural. In underlining the
logic of this progression, it is significant to note that, next
to the perfect octave, the most stable interval is the perfect
fifth.

Following the circle of fifths within the framework of the
key of C major gives the root movements C F B E A D G and
C. Translated into general terms any key's "circle of harmonies"
involves the succession based on the tonic, subdominant,
leading tone, mediant, submediant, supertonic, dominant,
and tonic roots. Note that in the major mode the intervals of
the major scale include a "built-in" adjustment of the size of
one fifth. This allows the circle of fifths to remain within the
original key. The subdominant thus moves an augmented
fourth up or a diminished fifth down to reach the leading
tone. *e.g.*:

Circle of Fifths Harmony in the Major Mode

C: I   IV   vii° iii   vi   ii   V   I

Note the use of two examples of contrary motion connection,
including that from ii to V, to keep the voices within a moderate range.

Circle of Fifths Harmony in the Minor Mode

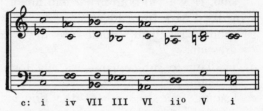

c: i   iv   VII   III   VI   ii°   V   i

Note the alternate use of contrary motion connections to form a descending sequence of harmonies. Note further the use of both the natural and the harmonic minor scales.

The use of a circle of harmonies in both the major and minor modes—occasionally an entire series, but more often a series of five or less chords—occurs frequently in traditional music. The ordinary one-common-tone connections—strict or free—are the basis for such harmony. It is obvious that constant use of this, or any other one technique tends to become monotonous, but it also is true that many of the very beautiful and effective passages of music are built on this harmonic basis.

This technique is an important characteristic of the music composed from the Baroque period up to the twentieth century. The explanation may be that the naturalness of the "circle of fifths" technique provided a most convenient, and occasionally a brilliant, way for extending the musical thought.

3. Chord progressions based on series of root movements of an upward fifth (or the equivalent downward fourth).

Two such root movements—IV I and I V—have been studied. Of these, the latter is the basis for the half cadence. Since this cadence lends a feeling of incompleteness, it is logical to expect that the effect of several such movements in succession would be cumulative. The use of progressions based on root movements of upward fifths is a means of *increasing* harmonic tension. *e.g.*:

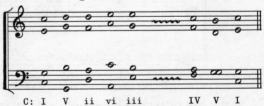

C: I   V   ii   vi   iii   IV   V   I

Note that the first five chords build up the tension; the IV V I cadence resolves it.

This rather direct manner of building tension from chord to chord is used occasionally, but more often the rise in tension occurs over a larger span of harmonies, and frequently is accompanied by momentary shifts of key to increase the effect. More will be said regarding this in dealing with tonality and modulation. Let us consider the easily understood example of tension which can be found in the inconclusive cadence on the dominant at the end of the first phrase of many a musical sentence. Such tension, created by using a half cadence in relation to the tonic key, often is resolved by using a conclusive cadence at the end of the following phrase, thus completing the sentence.

One device used for maintaining the level of harmonic tension is that of alternating a given chord with the chord whose root is a fifth higher, producing either a tonic-dominant-tonic effect or an effect akin to this, beginning on another degree. Or, the alternation may be with the chord whose root is a fifth lower, producing either the tonic-subdominant-tonic or the dominant-tonic-dominant effect.

B. Harmony based on the use of one or more of the no-common-tone chord progressions.

1. The chord progression based on the root movement of an ascending second.

   This progression is familiar as the subdominant-dominant contrary motion connection. Its principle is applicable to progressions based on the other functional degrees of the scale.

   a. tonic to supertonic—used quite often, in both modes.
   b. supertonic to mediant—used occasionally.
   c. mediant to subdominant—used often. When the raised leading tone is used in the minor mode, this degree most often should lead to the tonic degree.
   d. subdominant to dominant—the basic movement of this type.
   e. dominant to submediant—used frequently, either within a phrase or at its close as "the deceptive movement or cadence." The deceptive cadence*—V vi or V VI—is often used as the means for bringing about an inconclusive stop in a musical composition.
   f. submediant to leading tone—used only occasionally in major, but more often in natural minor (VI VII) where this progression sounds like the subdominant of the relative major moving to its dominant.
   g. leading tone to tonic—this occurs quite often, *especially* with the initial or both chords in the first inversion. This

use of the leading tone chord in major and harmonic minor is a part of its dominant function, since it actually acts like and sounds like a weaker, or occasionally more subtle, substitute for the dominant chord. In natural minor this progression is that of a deceptive cadence (V vi) in its relative major key.

Harmony Based On a Series of Root Movements of an Upward Second, Major and Minor Modes

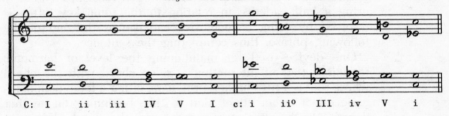

C: I   ii   iii   IV   V   I   c: i   ii°   III   iv   V   i

2. Chord progressions based on the root movement of a descending second.

     The downward root movement of a second is familiar as the progression of the dominant to the subdominant chord. Compared with the upward progression, the downward one is used less frequently, but is nevertheless important. The principle of this downward root movement applies also to other functional scale degrees.

     a. tonic to the leading tone—this occurs quite often, especially with the second or both chords in the first inversion, in the major or harmonic minor mode. The progression in the natural minor sounds like a submediant to the dominant of the relative major key.

     b. supertonic to tonic—occurs occasionally in both modes, again often with the use of the first inversion in the first or in both chords.

     c. mediant to supertonic—rarely used.

     d. subdominant to mediant—rarely used.

     e. dominant to subdominant—occurs at times, and sounds like a postponement of the dominant's resolution. The V IV I cadence (V iv i in harmonic minor) sounds like an authentic cadence which has undergone a plagal interruption—indeed, a pleasant sound!

     f. submediant to dominant—occurs quite often. The progression, vi V I (VI V i in harmonic minor) is one of the standard formulae for the full cadence.

g. leading tone to submediant—occurs often when the leading tone is lowered as in the natural minor scale, but only rarely when this tone is raised as in the other scale forms. In the natural minor this progression sounds like a dominant to the subdominant of the relative major.

Harmony Based On Descending Root Movements of a Second

C: vi   V   IV   iii   ii   I

Note: It is unusual to substitute a root movement of a seventh in the opposite direction for the basic root movement of a second. Such connections encourage complete parallelism in the upper voices, and this is contrary to the practice of tertian harmony. *e.g.*:

C: IV   V

C. Harmony based on the use of one or more of the two-common-tone chord progressions.

1. Chord progressions based on the root movement of a descending third (or ascending sixth).

The technique of the two-common-tone progression has been explained, but a word must be added about its application to each degree of the scale as a functioning chord root. The descending root movements of a third, especially those from the tonic and subdominant, occur more often than the ascending form. This may well be because the root of a chord a third down from a given chord root is a new tone, whereas the root of a chord a third up is the 3rd degree of the given chord.

a. tonic to sub-mediant—used very often. Note that in the major mode the submediant is the relative minor of the tonic.

b. supertonic to leading tone—rarely used. When this progression occurs in the natural minor the movement of the leading tone chord to the dominant chord of the relative major is suggested.

c. mediant to tonic—occurs at times, and often sounds like a weak form of the dominant moving to the tonic.

d. subdominant to supertonic—occurs often. Again, in the major mode the supertonic is the relative minor of the subdominant.

e. dominant to mediant—occurs at times. The mediant tends to sound like a weakened dominant because of the two common tones which are present.

f. submediant to subdominant—rarely used in major. When this progression occurs in the minor mode, a movement from the subdominant to the supertonic of the relative major is suggested.

g. leading tone to dominant—occurs occasionally where the raised leading tone is used, but in doing so the leading tone chord acts and sounds like a member of the dominant family. Rarely used when the leading tone is lowered in both chords.

Harmony Based On the Root Progressions of a Series of Downward Thirds

C: I   vi   IV   ii   vii⁰   V   I   c: i   VI   iv   ii⁰   VII   V   i

2. Chord progressions based on the root movement of an ascending third (or descending sixth).

This root movement tends to occur less often than the inverse progression just discussed.

a. tonic to mediant—quite common in major.

b. supertonic to subdominant—used at times.

c. mediant to dominant—used at times, but the mediant always sounds rather weak due to the common tones with the stronger dominant chord. In the natural minor this progression gives the effect of the relative major moving to its mediant, a much stronger progression.

   d. subdominant to submediant—used at times.

   e. dominant to leading tone—does not occur as often as the inverse progression, since the leading tone chord sounds much like a weaker member of the dominant family.

   f. submediant to tonic—used at times, but much less often than the inverse progression. In the natural minor this progression has the effect of its relative major's subdominant moving to submediant.

   g. leading tone to supertonic—rarely used.

Harmony Based On the Root Progression of a Series of Upward Thirds

C: vi   I   iii   V

D. Harmony based on the use of a combination of these techniques.

   The three principles of chord connection—those governed by one, two, or no common tones—can be used to explain the root progressions found in all music based on tertian harmony. There will be problems, however, since the complexity of the chordal structure usually goes beyond the level of simple triads. The use of primary and secondary harmony, the dominant seventh, ninth, and thirteenth chords, the inversions, the rhythmic duration of successive harmonies, and the use of non-harmonic tones will require our continued attention.

   In the examples note how, as well as how often, each principle of chord connection and root progression is employed. Note, also, the variety of progressions possible through a judicious selection from among the three basic techniques.

   The actual root movements of a fifth, second, or third take place only when the chords concerned are in root position. In dealing with inversions—either from the standpoint of writing or analysis—the sounded root present in one of the upper voices actually may not move at all. However, the progression should still be thought of in terms of its basic root position treatment.

This will clarify spellings and doublings, and will also suggest a logic of voice leading which can serve as a guide. It should be noted that the first inversion form of the mediant and the submediant are in general rarely used except in sequences of parallel sixth chords.

Note: The basic root movement is that of C to F, which implies one common tone with its consequent effect upon the voice leading.

In composing, variety and originality are the result of striving for new possibilities. The innate urge for the creative can be given a free, but disciplined, reign if experimentation is carried on from a solid foundation of understanding the several harmonic techniques.

SUGGESTIONS FOR STUDY

Several musical examples illustrating the basic types of harmonic progression are cited. A partial analysis has been made. Complete each one and work out the details suggested.

1. The mode. Whenever a minor key is involved, determine which minor scale types contribute to the particular "composite minor" used. Quite often music of the Baroque period will be found using the so-called modal signatures—including one less flat or one more sharp—rather than what we would call the proper minor signature. In such cases make the necessary adjustment so the example will more nearly conform with present day signatures.
2. The use of non-harmonic tones. The symbols R, R', S, S', P, and P' are familiar. A chord tone is indicated by the symbol "cht" whenever this fact needs mention. The presence of a non-harmonic tone which will be studied later is shown by the symbol "nh."
3. The name and chord progression involved in each cadence.
4. The use of the one-common, no-common, and two-common-tone progressions.
5. The use of each of the secondary triads of both the major and minor modes.

1. Hertzliebster Jesu, was hast du verbrochen   Bach

a: i⁸   V   vii°⁶   iv⁶   V

1. Note the alteration of tonic, dominant, and leading tone chords.
2. How is the voice leading of the two-common-tone progression handled?

2. Es stehn vor Gottes throne   Bach

g: i³ ———————   vii³   VI³ iv⁵ii° V³

1. The third soprano B♭ may be called an S′, but it is better to refer to it as a part of the dominant seventh chord. (This is to be studied in Unit XI).
2. Note the series of roots: g, C, f, B♭, E♭, a°, and D, following a circle of fifths within G natural minor. The chord qualities used are drawn from all three scales of the minor mode.

3. Wir Christenleut'   Bach

g: i⁶   v⁵   VI³

Observe that the second note in each of the four voices is called a non-harmonic tone. At the same time these four tones

form a vii°⁶ chord used between two tonic chord positions.
It is not necessary, or desirable, to show the eighth note harmonic rhythm the latter analysis would require, since the diminished chord is only a momentary embellishment. This is an
example of the use of non-harmonic tones having harmonic
implications, that is, a "selective use" of non-harmonic tones.
Also observe the deceptive cadence in the last two chords.

4.   Vater Unser   Bach

1. Note the use of first inversion chords.
2. Note the ambiguity of the third chord. It is a mediant sixth
   chord if the E♭ in the alto is considered as a chord tone,
   or, a dominant chord if the E♭ in the alto is considered to be
   a P′ replacing the D to which it moves. Either explanation
   may be considered correct.
3. Note that the first B in the alto of the last measure functions
   like the following C momentarily displaced. On the second
   eighth note of that measure the full 6/4 dissonance is present
   over the dominant bass— to be resolved during the second
   beat.
4. Note the five root circle of harmony as well as the no-common-
   tone progression found in this example.

5.   Helft mir Gott's güte preisen   Bach

The third chord is a "♭°⁶" for two reasons. First, the second
chord (F) has one common tone with the third chord, implying
that B could be the root of the third chord. Next, the third chord

leads to the C chord just as though it were a leading tone triad of that key. Thus the E in the bass must be considered to be a D momentarily out of place, hence, an P′.

Eins ist not!

1. Observe the use of change of chord position on the first two beats.
2. Observe how little effect the iii chord has on the V I cadence. In general: if a iii chord follows I it sounds like I, but if it follows V it sounds like a form of that chord.

7. Keinen hatt Gott verlassen

8. Freu' dich sehr, O meine seele

These two phrases—one basically in the minor mode and the other in the major mode—end with the characteristic inconclusive feeling of the Phrygian half cadence.* Take note of the approach to and the effect of each cadence.

ASSIGNMENT #29: Harmonic and non-harmonic analysis—primary chords, secondary chords, and non-harmonic tones.

This assignment, together with necessary instructions, is found on Work Sheet #34.

ASSIGNMENT #30: Part Writing—connecting primary and secondary triads in root position and first inversion in the major and the minor modes.

This assignment is found on Work Sheet #35.

FUNDAMENTALS

I. INTERVALS: The Augmented, up (Theory Skill #28);
The Diminished, up (Theory Skill #29)

The 12 simple interval sounds (m2, M2, m3, M3, P4, A4 or d5, P5, m6, M6, m7, M7, and P8) are now familiar. Each of the interval sounds must be interpreted, however, in relation to the context within which it is used. This suggests that the function of an interval determines its spelling as well as its name. In turn, this function often is modified by the voice leading appropriate to the mode used. Study the comparative functions of the augmented second and the minor third in the second measures of the illustrations in reference to the preceding explanation.

Consideration of the upward intervals will be completed with learning to spell the important augmented and diminished intervals. Remember that intervals are the components of melody and harmony, and that proficiency in spelling them is a necessary step towards familiarity with the tools of one's craft. Such proficiency is practical because it helps one to be literate in discussing the technicalities of music. Adeptness at hearing intervals makes one more keenly aware of what is happening in any given musical situation. Two principles for constructing augmented and diminished intervals are:

(1) Augmented intervals upward are formed by enlarging either a major or perfect interval one half step without changing the alphabetical letters.

e.g.: B F♯ is a perfect 5th, hence, B Fx is an augmented 5th (A5). Likewise, C A is a major 6th, hence, C A♯ is an augmented 6th (A6).

(2) Diminished intervals upward are formed by lowering the top tones of either minor or perfect intervals one half step in a similar fashion.

> *e.g.:* C♯ G♯ is a P5, hence, C♯ G is a diminished 5th (d5). Similarly, B D is a m3, hence, B D♭ is a d3.

Each of the 12 different intervals can be given at least two names, each one being proper under certain circumstances. For example, the interval "C D♯" is an augmented second, B♯ D♯ is a minor third, and C E♭ is also a minor third. Note that these interval sounds are identical and that the spellings are enharmonically equivalent. Study the table showing the various enharmonic possibilities—each of which gives rise to another name. To think in any given major scale, substitute that scale for the *Major Scale Numbers* shown. Note the interrelationships within as well as between the two tables—diagonally and vertically.

Type of Interval	The Relationship of the Interval Names												
Augmented		A1		A2		A3	A4		A5		A6		A7 A8
Major and Perfect		P1		M2		M3	P4		P5		M6		M7 P8
Minor and Diminished	d1		m2		m3	d4		d5		m6		m7	d8	
Diminished		d2		d3				d6		d7				
	Interval Relationships in Major Scale Numbers												
Augmented Numbers		1+		2+		3+	4+		5+		6+		7+ 8+
Major Scale Numbers		1		2		3	4		5		6		7 8
Diminished and Minor	1-		2-		3-	4-		5-		6-		7-	8-	
Diminished Numbers		2--		3--				6--		7--				
Lower Tone Number	1	1	1	1	1	1	1	1	1	1	1	1	1	1

These statements will simplify the interpretation of these tables.
(1) Raising any major or perfect interval a half step forms an augmented interval of the same number.
  e.g.: M3 becomes A3, and P5 becomes A5.
(2) Lowering any perfect interval a half step forms a diminished interval.
  e.g.: P4 becomes d4.
(3) A major interval lowered a half step becomes a minor interval.
  e.g.: M6 becomes m6.
(4) A minor interval lowered a half step becomes diminished.
  e.g.: m7 becomes d7.
(5) The major and perfect intervals and the major scale numbers are underscored to make them stand out. This is because *they are basic to an understanding of all the other intervals.*

(6) In considering intervals up, the bottom tone is always thought of as "1" for the purpose of measuring its distance.

    e.g.: B A♭ must be a d7, since B A♯ is a M7, and from this, B A is a m7; hence, B A♭ is a diminished 7th.

While a good understanding of the *formation* of the various augmented and diminished intervals is essential, proficiency in using only the more important ones will give a satisfactory background. The following assignment and proficiency tests therefore will be limited to the augmented second, fourth, fifth, and sixth, and to the diminished third, fourth, fifth, seventh, and octave.

SUGGESTIONS FOR STUDY

1. Practice reciting in letter names the foregoing augmented intervals listed, basing each one upon the tonic degree of each major scale.
2. Practice reciting the diminished intervals named, basing each one upon the tonic degree of each major scale.
3. Note that the diminished 7th up from C♭ requires a triple flat, which is impractical. Therefore, mark this interval "imp" whenever it occurs in an assignment or test.

ASSIGNMENT #31 (Part I): Augmented intervals, up.

    Write the A2, A4, A5, and A6 intervals up in four columns across the page following the 17 tones from D♯ through C♭. Alternate the use of treble, bass, alto, tenor, and soprano clefs on successive staffs and write in whole notes and accidentals. There are 68 intervals in this group, obtained by following through the 17 tone circle four times. Omitting the use of the other four tones of the 21 tone circle eliminates the impractical intervals. Use Work Sheet #36-1.

SATISFACTORY ATTAINMENT: the ability to spell correctly at least 20 augmented intervals up in five minutes. Write the test using whole notes and accidentals, and start on any of the 17 tones other than D♯, the beginning tone of the assignment.

ASSIGNMENT #31 (Part II): Diminished intervals, up.

    Write the d3, d4, d5, d7, and d8 intervals up in five columns across the page following the circle of 17 tones from E♯ through D♭. Alternate the clefs as in Part I, writing in whole notes and accidentals. There are 85 intervals in this group, of which 68 are practiced by following through the 17 tone circle four times. Omitting the use of the other four tones of the 21 tone circle eliminates the impractical intervals. Use Work Sheet #36-2.

SATISFACTORY ATTAINMENT: the ability to spell correctly at least 20 diminished intervals up in five minutes. Write the test using whole notes and accidentals, and start on any tone of the 17 tone major circle except E♯, the beginning tone of the assignment.

II. RHYTHM: Hemiola and cross-rhythm

It has been emphasized that the two basic rhythmic groupings are those of twos and threes and that illustrations of each type abound in music literature. It is also easy to find examples where the composer has achieved variety by disturbing the characteristic rhythmic groupings of the given meter. The rhythmic effect known as hemiola* always results from the conflict inherent in duple and triple organization.

There are three prevalent types of hemiola. *One* occurs when the prevailing organization of a triple meter is replaced by that of a meter whose measure is of the same size, but of the opposite organization. The pairs of meters which produce this type of hemiola are 3/4 and 6/8, 3/2 and 6/4, and 3/8 and 6/16. *e.g.*:

In the quoted excerpts from music literature, the conflicting rhythmic effect is that of replacing a group of three quarter note pulses from 3/4 meter by the two dotted quarter pulses of 6/8 meter.

The Brahms *Symphony No. 2 in D Major,* Opus 73, utilizes the hemiola effect a number of times, the excerpt following illustrating a clear example of the type just mentioned.

In Chopin *Waltz in Ab Major,* Opus 42, the hemiola is present throughout the first double period,* the right hand in effect playing in 6/8 meter, while the left hand accompanies in the basic 3/4 waltz rhythm. The upper melodic quarter notes (in reality dotted quarters) and their afterbeat accompanying figure are in 6/8 meter, while the left hand chords are in 3/4. Note that the effect of the upper two quarter notes against the three quarter notes of the accompaniment is that of a written out two against three. Chopin chose to express this combination of *quasi* 6/8 and 3/4 meters by changing the grouping of the six eighth note pulses, which are common to both meters.

Perhaps a composer of our day would have clarified the rhythmic intent by the use of a duplet bracket, or by dotting the melodic quarters as shown.

The *second* type of hemiola occurs when the prevailing organization of a triple meter is replaced by a similar organization in a measure twice as large. The rhythmic conflict is that shown. *e.g.*:

This hemiola often is used to give the effect of a notated ritardando,* and will occur as a *quasi* 3/2 bar replacing two 3/4 bars, a *quasi* 3/4 bar replacing two 3/8 bars, or a *quasi* 3/8 bars replacing two 3/16 bars. Study the following examples from Handel, Mozart, and Brahms. Composers from the Classic* and Romantic* periods seldom, if ever, actually notated the metric changes implied by the use of the hemiola effect. Rather, they expected the performers to notice and interpret the significance of the rhythmic conflicts used in achieving the varied effect they intended. Contemporary composers are more apt to notate the precise rhythmic effects intended by using each metric change needed.

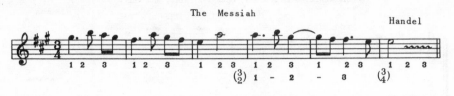

The Messiah

Handel

Symphony in G Minor, K. 550

Mozart

Symphony No. 2 in D Major, Opus 73

Brahms

To summarize the hemiola mentioned, the *first* type was caused by the use of the opposite organization in a measure of the same size. The *second* resulted from using the same organization in a measure twice the size. The *third* type of hemiola arises from the use of both duple and triple organizations within one bar, either vertically or horizontally. This type is already somewhat familiar since it is inherent in the use of duple and triple subdivisions. Its notation often can be written correctly in more than one way. Three illustrations of the *third* type of hemiola are given.

(1) the horizontal conflict between duple and triple subdivisions in 2/2 meter.

Symphony No. 3 in D Minor

Bruckner

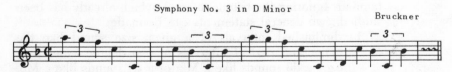

(2) the vertical conflict between duple and triple subdivisions in 4/4 meter.

Double Concerto in A Minor, Opus 102 (Vln., and vcl.)

Brahms

(3) the conflict between the three simple quarter note pulses of 3/4 meter and the duple group of half notes (sometimes notated as a duplet of quarter notes) which is their equivalent in time value.

Symphony No. 7 in E Major

Bruckner

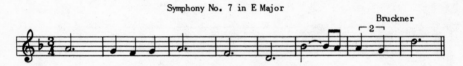

ASSIGNMENT #32: Hemiola

This assignment is found on Work Sheet #37.

MUSICIANSHIP

Pitch Ear Training

1. Review: practice singing, playing, recognizing, and hearing the major, minor, perfect, and tritone intervals up and down, as well as the four basic scales. Give attention also to the nine triad positions, in which the sound of the lower and upper tones must be recognized as that of the 3rd, 5th, or the 8th degrees.

2. The diminished and augmented intervals up.

   The problem in the recognition of the various diminished and augmented intervals is that of associating interval name and sound, since by now all of the sounds have become familiar. Ignoring the tritone interval, which already has been studied, two general statements can be made:

   1) diminished intervals of a given size sound like the major and perfect intervals of one degree lesser size.
      e.g.: a d3 sounds like a M2; or a d4 sounds like a M3.

2) augmented intervals of a given size sound like the minor and perfect intervals of one degree greater size. *e.g.*: an A2 sounds like a m3; or an A3 sounds like a P4.

In Theory Skills # 28 and #29 only certain diminished and augmented intervals were studied intensively, but this background should be adequate for spelling any desired diminished or augmented interval.

a. sing each pair of equivalent or enharmonic intervals as suggested.

la la, ma–jor 2–nd, la la, di–min–ished third,

b. practice the other pairs of enharmonic intervals in a similar manner.
1) P1 and d2
2) M3 and d4
3) P5 and d6
4) M6 and d7
5) M7 and d8

c. sing each enharmonic pair involving the augmented intervals as illustrated.

la la, min–or third, la la, aug–ment–ed sec – ond,

d. practice the other pairs of enharmonic intervals.
1) m2 and A1
2) P4 and A3
3) m6 and A5
4) m7 and A6
5) P8 and A7

e. practice recognizing each of the 13 sounds by the two names which are applicable. (Include the tritone).
1) P1 and d2
2) m2 and A1
3) M2 and d3
4) m3 and A2
5) M3 and d4

   6) P4 and A3
   7) A4 and d5
   8) P5 and d6
   9) m6 and A5
   10) M6 and d7
   11) m7 and A6
   12) M7 and d8
   13) P8 and A7

f. practice recognizing each of the 12 interval sounds (now omitting the P1 and d2 since no problem is involved) by whatever augmented or diminished name is applicable. In the case of the tritone, either the augmented or the diminished name may be used.

g. given the letter name of the lower tone, practice hearing the diminished and augmented intervals up. The response may be oral—naming the interval and spelling it, or written—recording the interval name and notating the pitches in the assigned clef. *e.g.*:

Rhythm Ear Training

1. In practicing the following rhythms it is suggested that each measure be counted according to the meter it momentarily suggests, since by now the regular characteristics of meter should be well understood. These rhythms, in various meters, include examples of hemiola.

(6) [musical notation in 6/8 meter]

(7) [musical notation in 6/8 meter]

(8) [musical notation in 6/16 meter]

2. Rhythm Skills for individual performance.
   Evaluate the performance of each rhythm skill in the usual manner.

   a. Hemiola: 3/4 and 6/8 meter, Flash Card Set #23, (*Rhythm Skill* #17)

   SATISFACTORY ATTAINMENT: the performance of these rhythms in any order and at any tempo up to 120 quarters per minute.

   b. Hemiola: 3/2 and 6/4 meters, Flash Card Set #24, (*Rhythm Skill* #18)

   SATISFACTORY ATTAINMENT: the performance of these rhythms in any order and at any tempo up to 144 quarter notes per minute.

Sight Singing: FORM EMPHASIS . . . Aria and Art Song

The aria* has found important use in opera* as a "lyric episode which relieves the dramatic tension of the action" (*Harvard Dictionary of Music*). Its place in the cantata* and oratorio* is quite comparable. One of its important forms was the da capo aria in which a first section led into a contrasting second section, and this was followed by a literal repetition, or "da capo" of the first section.

Another vocal form with considerable historical background, the German lied,* began mainly with the many artistic songs and song cycles of Schubert (1797-1826). Beethoven, Schuman, Brahms, and later, Wolf are also important lieder composers. Lieder and other art songs are often settings of vernacular poems of good literary quality. A tradition for the art songs also has developed in other countries including France, Spain, and Russia. Several of the following excerpts are drawn from this literature.

When possible it will be helpful to practice these and other art songs and arias from their original scores.

1. The Messiah

Handel

2. Es war ein Traum

Lassen

3. ''Er, den herrlichste von allen'' (Frauenliebe und Leben)

Schumann

*The symbol for the 'turn.' See terminology section.

4. "Haste Ye Shepherds" (Christmas Oratorio)

Bach

194

5. "Run, Run, Run Ye Souls" (St. John Passion)

Bach

6. Last Night

Kjerulf

7.   Du bist die Ruhe

Schubert

Keyboard Emphasis

Keyboard Skill #10—SATISFACTORY ATTAINMENT: performance of the illustrated (or similar) forms of the Phrygian half cadence in the minor and major modes at your highest level of competence as described:

"Minimum" Level—both types in each of two keys, major or minor as appropriate, using the given chord positions.

"Above-average" Level—both types in each of two keys, major or minor as appropriate. Alternate the use of the closed or the open positions of the 3rd, 5th, or the 8th in the first chord in successive keys.

"Superior" Level—both types in each of any two requested keys, major or minor as appropriate, using the closed or open positions of the 3rd, 5th, or the 8th in the first chord upon request.

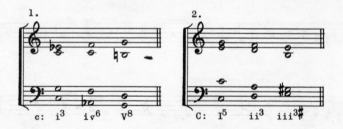

Dictation

1. Pitch.

   Pitch Skill #12—Hearing the Diminished and Augmented Intervals, Up.

   SATISFACTORY ATTAINMENT: demonstrated competence in hearing any of the diminished and augmented intervals up. Given the pitch and clef of the lower tone, respond by correctly recognizing and notating each of the ten intervals played.

e.g.:

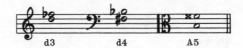

d3   d4   A5

Each interval and its analysis are considered to be one response. As with other pitch tests, compute the PROFICIENCY PERCENTAGE, note the pattern of error, and evaluate.

Pitch Achievement

These examples of pitch dictation consist of some sequence of the possible sounds from the minor second through the octave. Since all the sounds are known, and, since the major, minor, perfect, and tritone names in both directions, as well as the diminished and augmented names upward, are known, several correct answers can be devised for each exercise. With this in mind, it is suggested that the student response can be made in any of the following ways: 1) write the pitches as heard in terms of whatever notation comes to mind; 2) write the interval names, using only major, minor, perfect, and tritone intervals; 3) write the interval names using only the diminished and augmented forms, and 4) write the interval names, using the type which seems logically suggested by the context. Compute the PROFICIENCY PERCENTAGE by dividing the number of correct responses by the number attempted.

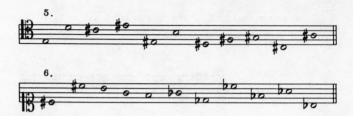

2. Rhythmic.

The rhythmic dictations offer practice in recognizing and hearing several of the possible hemiola patterns which may arise in simple and compound triple meters. Compute the PROFICIENCY PERCENTAGE by dividing the number of correct responses by the number attempted.

3. Melodic.

    a. write any well-known aria or art song in musical notation, without the aid of an instrument. Check your answers, if possible, with the actual score. The continued writing of familiar tunes and the composing of new ones afford valuable practice. Doing so becomes easier as the mind becomes accustomed to thinking of pitch and rhythm in terms of sound.

    b. notate only the bass voice of the following dictations. This will aid in developing the essential skill of selective listening. The musician often is attracted to or cognizant of the bass part of a composition because this voice serves as the foundation. Examples from Bach chorales are used because the individual voices are of a melodious character. The key, meter, tempo, and the pitch of the first bass note are given. The PROFICIENCY PERCENTAGE is obtained by dividing the number of correct responses by the number attempted. The proficiency can be determined for pitch alone, rhythm alone, and for both together in appraising competence in melodic dictation.

1.   Jesu, deine tiefe wunden (first phrase)

Bach

2. ——(second phrase)

3.——(fifth phrase)

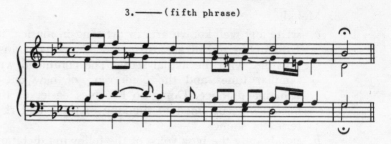

4.——(sixth phrase)

4. Harmonic.

The recognition of the harmonic function is continued in this unit with emphasis on selecting each supertonic, mediant, submediant, and leading tone chord that is heard used. No inverted chords are present.

a. recognize each of the root position primary chords on the first or second hearing, if possible identifying each by the proper Roman numeral and assigning the correct Arabic numeral for the soprano voice.

b. recognize each of the various secondary chords on successive hearings, using the same type of identification.

For purposes of evaluation each recognition attempted is one response. Compute the PROFICIENCY PERCENTAGE.

The recognition of cadences requires noting the harmonic function, since each cadence formula includes certain combinations of chord functions. Given the function of the first chord, name that of the chords following, and name the type of cadence. Note whether the voice leading is that of a perfect cadence. If necessary, again refer to the outline summary on "Cadences" found in the Appendix.

UNIT 10

1. SECONDARY CHORDS, INCLUDING THE SUPERTONIC SIX-FIVE CHORD

If the four basic scales, the four triad qualities, the various closed and open chord positions, the three principal triads and the four secondary triads of the major and the minor modes are well understood, then a functional use of many fundamentals of music has been achieved. If the three types of chord progression, as described in Unit IX, are understood as basic principles an important harmonic foundation has been laid, even though additional facility must be achieved.

In this unit, one assignment gives an opportunity to apply the three harmonic principles to part writing. In addition one new chord will be introduced, namely, the often used <u>first inversion of the supertonic seventh chord</u>, commonly known as the <u>supertonic six-five chord.</u>* Another assignment deals with analysis, putting emphasis upon the many possible forms of the six-four dissonance, principally those over the dominant root.

A. The Supertonic Chord.

1. Root position and first inversion.

The given examples show a familiar application of the principles governing the use of secondary harmonies.

Suite No. 1 in C Major (Orchestra)

Bach

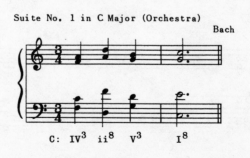

C: IV³   ii⁸   V³   I⁸

202

Note 1: The supertonic follows the subdominant chord using contrary motion rather than the two common tones.

Note 2: The supertonic leads to the dominant, but uses contrary motion in preference to the one-common-tone connection.

Sing Ye to the Lord (motet)

Bach

$B\flat$: V^6 I vi^3 ii^6 V^3 I^8

Note 1: Notice the four root circle of harmonies used in the full cadence.

Note 2: Notice the first inversion of the supertonic chord in the next to the last measure.

Note 3: Notice that the entire bass line shows that driving motion which the effective use of non-harmonic tones makes possible.

2. First inversion supertonic seventh—the supertonic six-five chord.

The use of the supertonic function preceding the dominant in cadences is common. However, the use of either the root position chord, or the first inversion supertonic chord, as in the two foregoing illustrations, is not as common as that of the supertonic chord with the added 7th degree above its root. In addition, the supertonic *seventh chord* is more often found in its first inversion form, called the supertonic six-five chord.

The first inversion of a supertonic (or any) seventh chord is called "six-five," written 6 over 5 ($\frac{6}{5}$). This is done because the root of a first inversion seventh chord is always (ignoring added octaves) a sixth above the bass tone, and the seventh of the same chord is similarly a fifth above the bass tone.

In the following illustrations observe how easily the 7th degree of the supertonic chord (always the 1st degree of the scale concerned) can be accounted for as a non-harmonic tone. In each of the following examples the seventh of the supertonic six-five chord appears as an accented suspension, in the first example, in the alto voice.

Note 1: The seventh of the supertonic chord is introduced like an accented suspension.

Note 2: Observe the interesting use of the first inversion of the subdominant and the dominant in the first full measure.

The next illustration shows the use of the seventh of the supertonic chord occurring as an accented suspension in the soprano voice.

The following excerpt from a Bach chorale shows an additional example of the supertonic six-five chord, the 7th occurring in the tenor voice.

Jesu, nun sei gepreiset

Bach

C: I⁶   V³   vi³ ii⁶₅ V⁵   I⁸

II. ALTERED CHORDS—the interchangeability of modes

Two instances showing the use of materials from one mode in the opposite mode have already been given. The first was that of the so-called Picardy third, and the second was the use of the minor subdominant chord in the major mode.

The root and inverted positions of other degrees of the minor scale also are effective when transferred or "translated" without change of function from the minor mode to the major mode. An illustration from Verdi shows a root position submediant chord of the minor mode used in A major in a chromatic passage. The analysis of the following chord built on B is not given. The Chopin excerpt shows the diminished first inversion supertonic chord from D minor used in the key of D major. In this latter illustration note how the two moving parts convey the effect of four part harmonic writing.

Requiem

Verdi

A: I⁶⁻⁵   3   8   iii³   VI³ vi°³〰〰〰 V

Prelude in D Major, Opus 28, No. 5

Chopin

D: I   ii°⁶   V   I

It is appropriate to mention that while single chords from the minor mode often are used without change of function to provide variety in the harmony of the major mode, upon occasion a composer will "translate" a complete musical thought to the opposite mode to achieve some desired musical effect. See how this has been done in the example quoted from Haydn.

Sonata in G Major

Haydn

III. NON-HARMONIC TONES

A. Horizontal combinations of Arabic numerals.

The meaning of the Arabic numbers such as 3, 5, 8, and 6 has become clear through use and study. In this unit the vertical combination, 6 over 5, is shown to indicate a seventh chord in its first inversion. Mention must also be made of several horizontal combinations which are often encountered such as 9-8, 7-8, 8-7, 7-6, 6-5, and 4-3. The figure 9-8, written horizontally, indicates that the 9th degree above a bass tone moves melodically to the 8th degree above the same bass tone. Similar reasoning can account for each of the other combinations. Note from the illustrations that the 9 in 9-8, the 7 in 7-8, the 7 in 8-7, the 7 in 7-6, either tone in 6-5, and the 4 in 4-3 can represent a non-harmonic tone. It is well to note, parenthetically, that non-harmonic tones are usually one step removed from a triad tone, that is, from a "1," a "3," a "5," or an "8." The implied harmony is shown for each illustration.

Study the two voiced illustrations and observe how each assigned horizontal Arabic combination achieves a non-harmonic effect. It is significant that one cannot name the non-harmonic effect (except as an appoggiatura, *q.v.*) until another approaching tone is added to the soprano voice, and that the type of non-harmonic combination can be altered by varying this added tone.

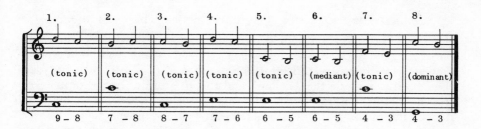

B. Passing six-four chord.

A common use of the second inversion chord is that of a passing function. The word "passing" suggests an embellishing effect. Previous illustrations have shown the dissonant 6/4 to be at best an unstable, though much used, sound. In its function as a passing six-four chord, this is again true. Study the illustrations, noting how the bass voice of the passing six-four chord occurs as the middle of three scale-wise tones, usually being between a root position and first inversion chord of the same function.

ASSIGNMENT #33: Part Writing—secondary chords; first inversion chords; supertonic 6/5; non-harmonic tones.

This assignment, together with necessary instructions, is on Work Sheet # 38.

ASSIGNMENT #34: Harmonic and non-harmonic analysis—primary and secondary harmony in root position and first inversion; cadences; forms of the dissonant sixth and fourth; other non-harmonic tones.

Review the use of the dissonant sixth and fourth over a dominant bass, and their identification as various combinations of non-harmonic tones over a dominant bass, as discussed in Units VII and VIII. This assignment is on Work Sheet #39.

FUNDAMENTALS

I. SCALES: The Four authentic church modes (Theory Skill #30)

Until the end of the Renaissance period, the music of the church was based largely upon the ecclesiastical modes.* There was, however, a tendency for theorists (reflecting the practice of composers) to broaden the modes to include the Aeolian* and Ionian* forms. These forms were similar to our natural minor and major scales. During the Baroque period, the major and minor scales became predominant, and, together with the concurrent development of tertian harmony, overshadowed the influence of the modes. Today, strangely enough, as composers seek new ways and means for creative expression, the appeal of the more quaint, austere, and mystical church modes is again apparent.

The church modes, as we know them, are the result of a partly erroneous adaptation of the Greek modes by the theorist, Boethius, who lived in the fifth century. The four basic modes are the Dorian,* Phrygian,* Lydian,* and Mixolydian,* known collectively as the authentic* modes. The so-called plagal* modes, whose individual names include the prefix "hypo-," are based upon the same tones as the mode whose name they share, but each has an octave gamut* sounding respectively a perfect fourth lower. The use of a hypo-mode* permits the selection of a range suitable for a lower voice while yet retaining some of the characteristics of the authentic form of the mode.

The ecclesiastical modes were not used in tonalities of more than one or two sharps or flats due to the difficulties of intonation. It must be remembered that the equal tempered scale* did not find acceptance on a broad basis until approximately 1800. Even though the modes were not freely transposed during the period of their common use, the present-day student who uses the tempered scale must be familiar with them beginning on any key tone, just as the major and minor scales are understood. Considered and learned in this way, the modes take their place as an additional resource for the discerning musician.

Our knowledge of the tetrachords can be applied to derive the modal scales.

(a) the Dorian mode consists of two minor tetrachords disjunct by a whole step.

(b) the Phrygian mode consists of two Phrygian tetrachords disjunct by a whole step.

(c) the Lydian mode consists of a Lydian tetrachord followed by a major tetrachord disjunct by a half step.

(d) the Mixolydian mode consists of a major tetrachord followed by a minor tetrachord disjunct by a whole step.

Understanding of the major and minor scales and their signatures can be applied to derive the signatures of the modal scales.

(a) the key signature of any Dorian scale is that of a major scale one whole step lower.
e.g.: the Dorian scale of 3 flats has the initial tone F.

(b) the key signature of any Phrygian scale is that of the major scale pitched a major third lower.
e.g.: the Phrygian scale of 2 flats has the initial tone D.

(c) the key signature of any Lydian scale is that of the major scale
pitched a perfect fourth lower.

   e.g.: the Lydian scale of 1 sharp has the initial tone C.

(d) the key signature of any Mixolydian scale is that of the major
scale pitched a perfect fifth lower.

   e.g.: the Mixolydian scale of 2 sharps has the initial tone A.

Each hypo-mode has a range which is a perfect fourth lower than
its authentic namesake. Thus the hypo-Dorian on "A" includes the same
tones as does the Dorian on "D," a perfect fourth higher, or the hypo-
Phrygian on "G" relates in the same way to the Phrygian built on "C."

Each modal type can be compared with its most similar major or
minor scale type.

(a) note that the Dorian mode is equivalent to a natural minor scale
with a raised 6th degree.

   Note: G minor has a two flat signature.

(b) note that the Phrygian mode is equivalent to a natural minor
scale whose 2nd degree is lowered a half step.

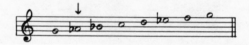

   Note: G minor has a two flat signature.

(c) note that the Lydian mode is equivalent to a major scale whose
4th degree has been raised a half step.

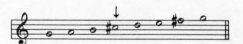

   Note: G major has a one sharp signature.

(d) note that the Mixolydian mode is equivalent to a major scale
whose 7th degree has been lowered a half step.

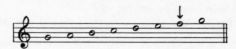

   Note: The G major scale has a one sharp signature.

SUGGESTIONS FOR STUDY

Adequate practice in spelling the modal scales can be obtained from each of the four modal types on the 13 tones which lie between D♯ and E♭ on the 21 tone circle (*e.g.*: D♯ G♯ C♯–B♭ E♭). Practice writing the four modal types using whole notes and accidentals, alternating the use of the five clefs studied. It is possible to spell 52 different scales. Work Sheet #40 is provided.

SATISFACTORY ATTAINMENT: the writing of at least eight modal scales in five minutes, alternating between scale types and clefs. Use the 13 tone circle from D♯ through E♭, beginning the test on any tone other than D♯.

II. INTERVALS

A. Review of basic principles of construction.

The intervals which have been studied are:

1. major and minor second, the whole and half step (M2, m2).
2. major and perfect intervals, up (M2 reviewed, M3, P4, P5, M6, M7, and P8).
3. minor and perfect intervals, down (m2 reviewed, m3, P4, P5, m6, m7, and P8).
4. minor, augmented fourth, and diminished fifth intervals, up (m3, A4, d5, m6, m7).
5. major, augmented fourth, and diminished fifth intervals, down (M3, A4, d5, M6, and M7).
6. selected augmented and diminished intervals, up.
   1) A2, A4 reviewed, A5, and A6.
   2) d3, d4, d5 reviewed, d7, and d8.

The basic principles governing intervals should now be clearly understood. Reconcile each of these statements with your knowledge of interval structure:

(1) A thorough knowledge of the major scales is a prerequisite to the study of intervals.

(2) Measured from the tonic degree upwards in scale tones, the major scale contains only perfect and major intervals.

(3) A minor interval is one-half step smaller than a major interval, but uses the same basic letter names. The differences are apparent from the combination of inflexion signs used.

(4) A major interval is one-half step larger than a minor interval, but uses the same basic letter names. The differences are apparent from the combination of inflexion signs used.

(5) The tritone spelled on any tone has two forms—that of the augmented fourth or of the diminished fifth.

(6) Augmented intervals are formed by enlarging either major or perfect intervals one-half step, using the same basic letter names.

(7) Diminished intervals are formed by reducing the size of either minor or perfect intervals one-half step, retaining the same letter names.

B. Eighteen Basic Intervals (Theory Skill #31)

The preceding discussion has reviewed 28 possible perfect, major, minor, diminished, and augmented intervals. Because of their melodic and harmonic importance 18 of these are selected for inclusion in a final test of proficiency in thinking simple intervals, up. The 18 intervals are—

M2	M3	P4	P5	M6	M7
m2	m3	A4	A5	m6	m7
A2	d3	d4	d5	A6	d7

For the purpose of the final proficiency test in spelling intervals, it will be sufficient to be thoroughly familiar with those based upon the 15 tones between D♯ and D♭ on the 21 tone circle of fifths.

SUGGESTIONS FOR STUDY

1. Practice the oral spelling of the above 18 intervals on each of the 15 tones specified.

2. Practice writing these 18 intervals following the 21 tone circle of fifths for the 15 tones between D♯ and D♭. For this purpose use Work Sheet #41.

ASSIGNMENT #35: The Study of melody through interval analysis. This assignment is found on Work Sheet #42.

III. RHYTHM: Other cross-rhythms

In the previous unit hemiola was explained as being that type of cross-rhythm in which the rhythmic variety is achieved by substituting or superimposing duple organization for or upon triple organization, or vice versa. Hemiola produces an interesting rhythmic conflict, but there is a sense of regularity in the disturbance since the effect involved is that of two pulses balanced against three. There is something to be learned from studying other cross-rhythms, which might well be called irregular to distinguish them from the more regular hemiola cross-rhythms.

Any rhythmic effect which disturbs or reorganizes the indicated or implied metric pulse is a cross-rhythm. *One* general type is that caused by an ostinato* like repetition of a rhythmic pattern. Cursory notice was taken of such patterns in the study of irregular meters, such as those with 5 and 7 as numerators. *e.g.*:

1. the repetition of a non-characteristic pattern in some regular meter, such as 4/4.

2. the repetition of any possible rhythm pattern in some irregular meter, such as 7/8.

A *second* general type of cross-rhythm is that resulting from the non-repetitive use of rhythm patterns, in either a regular or an irregular meter. *e.g.*:

1. the non-repetitive use of non-characteristic rhythm patterns in a regular meter, such as 4/4.

2. the non-repetitive use of possible rhythm patterns in some irregular meter, such as 5/4. Such rhythmic combinations—irregular by their grouping and organization—are normal in the irregular meters.

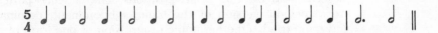

A *third* general type occurs when there are rapid changes of meter. Quite often, for example, in modern choral compositions where the rhythm of the words is an important factor, musical phrases and sentences can be made up of measures of several different lengths. There is usually a note value common to each pair of adjacent meters. This note value may, or may not, be a denominator value in the two meters, and may, or may not, be organized in similar fashion in the adjacent meters. Many interesting conflicts are found among the possibilities suggested by the description.

The Hundredth Psalm

Vaughan Williams

Serve the Lord   with glad-ness, and come be-fore His pres-ence   wi th   a   song.

(Printed by permission of the copyright owners: Galaxy Music Corporation, New York.)

Note: 1) for common denominator pulses occurring in contrasting organization see ms. 2 and 3; 3 and 4; and 4 and 5.

2) see ms. 1 and 2 for a common value which is one-half of the
denominator in the first meter, and the denominator value in
the second.

A number of rhythmic possibilities—examples of cross-rhythms—
were shown to be possible when considering the use of 1, 5, and 7 as
numerators in dealing with irregular meters in Unit IV. Numerators
such as 6 and 8, whose size permit the juxtaposition of various combinations of 1, 2, 3, and 4 pulses can be used to create rhythmic effects which
can be quite disturbing in their cross-rhythmic pulsing. The essence of
cross-rhythm thus is rhythmic conflict.

   ASSIGNMENT #36: The Study of melody through rhythm.
   This assignment is found on Work Sheet #43.

MUSICIANSHIP

Pitch Ear Training

1. Review: practice singing, playing, recognizing, and hearing
the major, minor, and tritone intervals down, the four cadence
patterns, and the nine triad positions. The cadence patterns
are a melodic version of the tonic, subdominant, dominant,
and tonic triads (the harmonic progression of one form of the
full cadence) in each of the four basic scales. The nine triad
positions include each triad degree—root, 3rd, and 5th—in
either or both the lower or upper voices.

2. All intervals, up.

   In listening to the 13 interval sounds (including the unison)
one is most likely to recognize them as the basic major, minor,
perfect, and tritone sounds unless some special circumstance
dictates otherwise.

   a. sing each interval sound, using its name as a word for
vocalization.

b. which basic intervals can be heard as representing augmented intervals? Practice each sound using in turn the basic name and the augmented name.

c. which basic intervals can be interpreted as representing diminished intervals? Similarly practice these using both possible names.

d. practice in turn each interval from the half step through the octave, using both names.

e. practice recognizing each interval by its basic name and also by the applicable augmented or diminished name.

f. practice hearing and analyzing the upward intervals, recording the quality and notating each in the assigned clef, given the letter name of the 1st degree.

e.g.:

M2	A4	d8	M6	d7
(d3)	(d5)	(M7)	(d7)	(M6)

3. The four modal scales.

Knowledge of the spelling and sound of the major, minor, Phrygian, and Lydian tetrachords and their combinations is the basis for recognizing the four modal scales.

a. sing two minor tetrachords, the one beginning a whole step above the upper tone of the first. Compare and contrast this Dorian scale form with that of the four basic major and minor scales.

b. sing two Phrygian tetrachords which are similarly disjunct by a whole step. Compare and contrast this Phrygian scale form and sound with that of the five types of scales now known.

c. sing a Lydian and a major tetrachord disjunct by a half step. Compare and contrast this Lydian scale form and sound with the six scale types learned.

d. sing a major and a minor tetrachord disjunct by a whole step. Compare and contrast this Mixolydian scale form with the seven preceding scale types.

e. practice singing, playing, and recognizing the four modal scales to gain proficiency.

f. practice hearing and analyzing the four types of modal scales, recording the quality and notating each in the

assigned clef, given the letter name of the 1st degree.
e.g.:

Rhythm Ear Training

Each cross-rhythm can best be understood and counted in terms of the particular meter it momentarily suggests. Unity is obtained through relating successive rhythmic units by a common rhythmic value.

1. Practice each of the examples of cross-rhythm previously given in this unit. Then practice the following exercises which include various types of cross-rhythm other than ordinary hemiola.

2. Rhythm Skills for individual performance.
   Evaluate performance as previously suggested.

   a. Other Cross-rhythms: 4/4 meter, Flash Card Set #25.
      (*Rhythm Skill* #19)
      SATISFACTORY ATTAINMENT: the performance of these
      rhythms in any order and at any tempo up to 120 quarter notes
      per minute.

   b. Other Cross-rhythms: 7/8 meter, Flash Card Set #26.
      (*Rhythm Skill* # 20)
      SATISFACTORY ATTAINMENT: the performance of these
      rhythms in any order and at any tempo up to 192 eighth notes
      per minute.

Sight Singing: FORM EMPHASIS—plainsong or plainchant

Plainsong* is the basic type of music found in the rite of the
Roman Catholic Church. It is especially important in the Mass.*
The uniquely melodic character, organized in a freely rhythmic
style derived from origins spanning many centuries, and the
ethereal aloofness derived from its basis in the church modes,
make the chant an ideal vehicle for worship in the ritualistic
churches. Further, the anonymity of authorship of the plainsong,
and also the circumstances of its usage, encourage humble performance. Many composers, but notably Palestrina (ca. 1525-
1595), wrote contrapuntal music steeped in the tradition of the
plainsong. Many settings of the unchanging musical sections of
the Mass (the Kyrie, Gloria, Credo, Sanctus, and Agnus Dei), as
well as many motets* for use in conjunction with the Catholic
rites, were composed during the Ars Nova and Renaissance
periods. Some of the same quality that permeates plainsong is
found in the works of composers of these periods, reaching a
climax in the choral works of Palestrina. This same influence
also permeates the tunes of such Protestant hymns as *Veni
Immanuel,* quoted in the examples for sight singing. Those examples of the character of plainsong should be sung in a steadily
moving but not rigid unit of pulse. The end of each phrase
should be broadened.

Liber Usualis, 'Pueri Hebrorum,' page 583

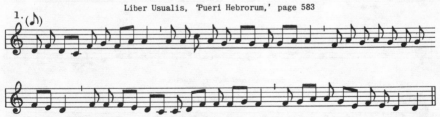

(The first three musical examples are transcribed from the LIBER USUALIS
with the permission of the publishers, DESCLEE CO., Tournai (Belgium), New York.)

2. ♪   Liber Usualis, 'Kyrie fons bonitatis,' page 19

Ky–ri–e – – – – – – – – – – – – e–le – i–son.

3. (♪)   Liber Usualis, 'Alleluia,' page 97

Al – le – – – – – – – lu – ia.

Hymn Tune, 'Jam Lucis'

Plainsong Melody

4. (♩)

Hymn Tune, 'Veni Creator Spiritus'

Ancient Plainsong

5. (♩)

Hymn Tune, 'Veni Immanuel'

Ancient Plainsong

6. (♩)

Sonata in C Major, Opus 1

Brahms

7. (♩.)

ff   *rit. e dim.*   *Presto*   *f*

218

Scherzo in B♭ Minor, Opus 31

Chopin

sotto voce

Symphony No. 3 in E♭, Opus 55

Beethoven

KEYBOARD EMPHASIS

Keyboard Skill #11—SATISFACTORY ATTAINMENT: the ability to play the full cadence using the supertonic six-five chord in both the major and harmonic minor modes at the highest level of competence you can attain.

"Minimum" Level—in any two major and any two harmonic minor keys.

"Above-average" Level—in any four major and any four harmonic minor keys.

"Superior" Level—in any four requested major and any four requested harmonic minor keys.

Dictation

1. Pitch.

For each type of pitch dictation compute the PROFICIENCY PERCENTAGE, analyze the pattern of error, and evaluate the level of achievement.

Pitch Skill # 13—Hearing All Intervals, Up.

SATISFACTORY ATTAINMENT: demonstrated competence in hearing each of the upward simple intervals from the half step through the octave. Given the pitch and clef of the lower tone, respond by correctly recognizing and consistently notating each of ten intervals played. Remember that minor and perfect sounds can be recognized and notated as augmented intervals and major and perfect sounds as diminished intervals—with the exception of the tritone which is either an augmented fourth or a diminished fifth. *e.g.*:

Pitch Achievement

The dictations are based upon the four church modes. Since their whole and half step structure differs from that of the major and minor scales, there seems to be a certain strangeness in their sound. The fact that the basic patterns are not the same as those found in the four basic scales causes one to be more aware of differences in sound. This awareness is one of the goals of ear training.

2. Rhythmic.

These exercises give further practice in recognizing and hearing various cross-rhythms. For purposes of evaluation consider the numbers below each exercise to represent or indicate a response. Compute the PROFICIENCY PERCENTAGE by dividing the number of correct responses by the total number attempted.

3. Melodic.

The following chorale excerpts give practice in isolating either the soprano or the tenor voice from the four-voiced texture. At one time record in proper pitch and rhythm notation the soprano voice, given the key, meter, tempo, and pitch of the first note. Separately, record the tenor voice similarly. As before, determine your proficiency in the pitch aspect alone, the rhythm aspect alone, and both together as an index to proficiency in melodic dictation. The PROFICIENCY PERCENTAGE equals the number of correct responses over the number attempted.

b. practice ordinary melodic dictation by listening to examples such as those suggested. The key, meter, tempo, and pitch of the first note is given. Determine your PROFICIENCY PERCENTAGE in the usual manner.

4. Harmonic.

Proficiency in recognizing and hearing harmonic progressions depends on 1) the ability to recognize the shape of two melodic lines—the soprano and the bass, and 2) the ability to recognize vertical harmonic concepts. Since melodic dictation is the basis for point one, and the recognition of chord qualities is the basis for point two, both are of importance as background for harmonic dictation.

The following examples of harmonic dictation include root position primary and secondary chords in both the major and minor mode. Given the pitch of the first bass tone, the response may take any of three forms, in each instance noting which, if any, of the standard cadences is used.

a. record only the sequence of Roman and Arabic numerals. For evaluation count each separate numeral as a response.

 b. notate the soprano and bass voice together with the Roman and Arabic numerals. For evaluation count each notated pitch as a response and add the Roman/Arabic responses.

 c. notate all four voices together with the Roman/Arabic numerals. For evaluation, count each notated pitch as a separate response and add the Roman/Arabic numerals.

Compute the PROFICIENCY PERCENTAGE, dividing the number of correct responses by the number attempted, and evaluate.

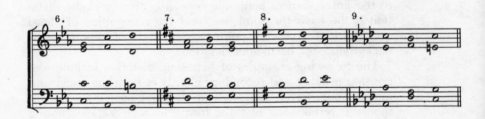

UNIT 11

HARMONY

I. THE DOMINANT FAMILY—the dominant seventh chord, the leading tone chord.

In beginning special study of the dominant family* we are dealing with a most dynamic harmonic factor. The dominant seventh chord,* more than any other, has given life and spirit to the music of the past two hundred years. The music student of today can experience some of the same satisfaction his Baroque ancestors must have enjoyed as they enriched their harmonic vocabulary while exploring the dominant seventh chord's many uses. Especially important is its use in cadences. Doubtless the dominant seventh's tritone and its tendencies, activated by the circle of fifths tension inherent in the dominant-tonic bass movement, together with the many ramifications of the dominant family, are responsible for the musical prestige of the dominant hierarchy. Several aspects of the dominant seventh and leading tone chords will be discussed and illustrated, including complete and incomplete seventh forms and their resolutions, the melodic use of the dominant seventh chord, irregular (or free) resolutions of this chord, as well as the first inversion leading tone chord as a dominant function. These aspects will be considered after proficiency in spelling the dominant seventh chord is attained.

    A. The Dominant Seventh Chord.

       1. Spelling (*Theory Skill* #32)

          An essential step in attaining proficiency in dominant seventh chords is learning to spell them in root position and in the first, second, and third inversions. For this purpose the simplest form of each position is used, and the four chord tones are written on only one clef. *e.g.*:

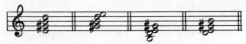

      Note: the E dominant seventh chord functions equally well as the dominant seventh of either the key of A major or of A minor.

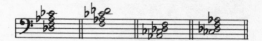

Note: the Db dominant seventh shown is the dominant of
Gb major. It would serve the minor key of Gb equally
well, but this key is rarely used since it requires a signature of 9 flats. Rather, the respective enharmonic
chord—the C♯ dominant seventh—is used with the
equivalent key of F♯ minor, whose signature is three
sharps.

SUGGESTIONS FOR STUDY
Practice spelling the dominant seventh chord in two ways.
1. Given the key, mode, and inversion of the desired dominant
seventh chord, recite the answer.
2. Write the dominant seventh chord forms according to the
plan suggested on Work Sheet #44.

SATISFACTORY ATTAINMENT: correctly notate at least 12
dominant seventh chord positions in a period of five minutes.
Follow a plan of alternating keys, clefs, positions, signatures, and
accidentals such as that used on Work Sheet #44. Write each
chord in whole notes.

2. Root positions of the dominant seventh chord.
   As was the case with the sixth chord, the positions of the
dominant seventh (hereafter also written V7) chord will be
closed, open, or mixed, the choice depending upon the desired effect. Note how the illustrated chords fall within the
already familiar voicings of closed and open positions. *e.g.*:

C: V⁷ (complete)   C: V⁷ (incomplete; without 5ᵗʰ)

3. Resolutions of the root position dominant seventh chord.
   a. *complete* V7 to *incomplete* I.
      —move the root of the first chord to the root of the tonic
      chord.
      —move the 3rd of the V7 (hereafter also called the leading
      tone) a half step up to the tonic degree.
      —move the 7th of the V7 chord down one step to the 3rd
      degree of the tonic chord.

—move the 5th degree of the V7 chord one step down to the tonic degree.

This procedure applies no matter which chord position is used, and will always result in an incomplete tonic chord, that is, one with three roots and a 3rd, without a 5th. Hence, the COMPLETE V7 resolves to an INCOMPLETE I. There are two differences between the resolution in the major and the harmonic minor mode: 1) the leading tone of the harmonic minor scale must be raised a half step accidentally to make available a true leading tone, and 2) the 3rd degree of the minor tonic chord is, of course, a half step lower than that of the major tonic chord.

Note: Bracketing the tritone serves as a reminder of its special function in the dominant seventh chord. "tr" designates a tripled root in the chord described.

b. incomplete V7 to complete I.

Two points must be remembered in resolving the incomplete V7 to a complete I, namely, 1) double the root of the V7 chord, and 2) omit the 5th degree of the V7 chord. This leaves the incomplete V7 chord with a doubled *root* and a *tritone*, the *essential* dominant elements. As for the resolution to the tonic, the additional root is held over as a common tone, thus assuring that the INCOMPLETE V7 resolves to a COMPLETE I.

c. other V7 chord resolutions.

    1) using the melodic 7th degree

        The 7th degree of the dominant seventh chord can occur within melodic patterns whose shapes are similar to those arising from the use of non-harmonic tones. Such voice leading, including a degree of contrapuntal independence, is encouraged. From the standpoint of analysis and writing, both the contrapuntal and harmonic aspects are important.

    Note: Each numbered item refers to the corresponding numbered example.

        (1) Note the passing 7th degree of the dominant chord.

        (2) Note how the resolution of the 7th degree of the dominant chord is interrupted by the escape tone* figure.

        (3) Note how the 7th degree of the dominant chord is introduced by a cambiata* movement in the alto voice.

        (4) Note how the 7th degree of the dominant chord is introduced by a change of chord position, again resulting in a cambiata figure.

    2) complete V7 to complete I.

        There are times when it is desirable to change the voice leading, the root movement, or even the constituency of the dominant seventh chord. These situations are the more free, or irregular treatment of the V7 chord. Where a COMPLETE tonic is desired following a COMPLETE V7, take note of this suggestion: when the leading tone is in the alto or tenor voice, it may resolve by leap of a third down to the 5th degree of the tonic chord, thus forming a complete tonic chord.

This disruption of the melodic tendency of the leading tone is a harmonic, rather than a contrapuntal
consideration. Its most effective use, therefore, is in
final cadences, where a complete tonic chord is often
desirable.

It is much less usual for this leap to occur in the
soprano voice, but an occasional illustration can be
found in the Bach chorales.

3) V7 to I6

The first inversion of the tonic triad may follow the
V7 chord. This is an effective movement where the
sense of finality is not as important as the sense of
forward motion, as, for instance, within a phrase.
Whenever the 7th of the dominant chord cannot lead
to the 3rd of the tonic, since the bass voice has already
done so (V7 I6), it resolves upward one degree to the
5th of the tonic.

4) V7 to I with a doubled 3rd degree.

The 5th of the V7 chord can also move upward one
degree to the 3rd of the tonic. This results in a tonic

chord with a doubled third since the 7th degree of the
V7 chord naturally resolves to the tonic 3rd degree.

5) V7 to IV or to IV6

The basic movement of triadic harmony is that of the
dominant to its tonic. Gradually, however, as the logic
of harmony becomes functional and meaningful, a feeling of and desire for originality will suggest many irregular movements to other than the tonic. For illustration the movement of the dominant seventh to the
subdominant chord will be shown.

Since such deceptive cadence movements cannot satisfy
the demand for resolution, there is in them a feeling
of postponement of resolution. For this reason, these
progressions are helpful as a means of extending the
thought of the musical phrase, or sentence. The V7
chord moves very effectively to IV6, possibly because
of the similarity of IV6 to vi. The next example illus-

trates the resolution, V7 to vi, the most usual form of
the deceptive cadence.

4. The Leading Tone Triad—the V7 without its root.

If the root of the dominant seventh chord is omitted, the
diminished triad found on the leading tone remains. Inasmuch
as this triad sounds and functions like a member of the dominant family more often than not, it will usually be considered
to be a dominant seventh chord without its root. Although
the triad on the leading tone is seldom used in root position,
an exception was shown in certain sequential progressions
under the discussion of secondary triad harmony. It is *often*
found in its first inversion—acting like a member of the dominant family.

Note: In each example observe how the motion of the voices
       which share the tones of the tritone, F—B, compares
       with that used in the dominant seventh resolutions.

SUGGESTIONS FOR STUDY

These exercises give practice in resolving the root position dominant
seventh chord in different ways and keys. Each progression consists
of two chords—a dominant form and its resolution to some form of the
tonic or other chord. Write these exercises in either signature or
accidentals, using basically whole notes.

Dominant form	Key	Position	Remarks
—complete V7	C♯	3rd	—(position of the 3rd in the soprano voice). Resolve to an incomplete tonic.
—incomplete V7	e	7th	—resolve to a complete tonic.
—V	F♯	3rd	—introduce the passing 7th in half notes, then resolve to an incomplete tonic.
—V	d	5th	—introduce the 7th with the cambiata figure, then resolve to a complete tonic.
—V	b	8th	—introduce the 7th by a position change in the upper three voices, then resolve to a complete tonic.
—complete V7	B	5th	—resolve to a complete tonic.
—V7	f	7th	—resolve to I6.
—complete V7	E	5th	—resolve to an incomplete tonic with a doubled 3rd.
—complete V7	c♯	7th	—resolve to a complete tonic with a doubled 3rd.
—incomplete V7	E♭	8th	—move to IV.
—complete V7	a	5th	—move to iv6.

B. Inversions of the Dominant Seventh Chord.

    1. Descriptive Arabic symbols or numerals.

        a. when the root is the bass tone ....$\begin{smallmatrix}7\\5\\3\end{smallmatrix}$

        b. when the 3rd degree is the bass tone ....$\begin{smallmatrix}6\\5\\3\end{smallmatrix}$

        c. when the 5th degree is the bass tone ......$\begin{smallmatrix}6\\4\\3\end{smallmatrix}$

        d. when the 7th degree is the bass tone...........$\begin{smallmatrix}6\\4\\2\end{smallmatrix}$

The complete Arabic descriptions normally are given only when made necessary by the use of alteration, as, for instance, the use of the leading tone of the harmonic minor scale as illustrated.

$$c: \quad V_3^7 \natural \qquad V_4^6 \natural \qquad V_2^4 \natural$$
$$3$$

For ordinary usage the following abbreviations are adequate:

(1) the fundamental position 7

(2) the first inversion .... $\begin{matrix} 6 \\ 5 \end{matrix}$

(3) the second inversion .... $\begin{matrix} 4 \\ 3 \end{matrix}$

(4) the third inversion .... 2, or, $\begin{matrix} 4 \\ 2 \end{matrix}$

Two associations between the numbers used and what they signify are important and should be noted:

  (1) any Arabic numerals included with a figured bass designate the intervals of distance desired above a given bass tone for a particular chord. The particular octave desired is not indicated, however, thus leaving this a matter of choice.

  (2) by learned association these same Arabic numerals connote certain harmonic situations, as, for example, the numeral "6" connotes the first inversion of a chord.

2. Regular resolutions.

Considered from the standpoint of voice leading, there is much similarity between the resolution of a root position V7 chord and that of each of its inversions. The *one* difference is that the root which appears in an upper voice of the inversions of the dominant seventh chord usually is held over as a common tone. It follows, therefore, that a *complete* inverted dominant seventh chord resolves to a *complete* tonic chord.

It can be said that each tone of the dominant seventh chord has a characteristic movement which is not affected by spacing or by the distribution of the voices. Note how each illustration is described by the following statements:

  (1) the root of the inverted seventh chord remains as a common tone in the next chord.

  (2) the leading tone moves up a half step, *as before.*

(3) the seventh moves down one step, *as before*.
(4) the 5th degree moves down one step, *as before*.
(5) consequently, the V6/5 and V4/3 chords regularly resolve to a I chord, and V2 resolves regularly to a I6.

3. Other resolutions.

   a. Incomplete inverted V7.

   In the first and third inversions the 5th of the dominant seventh chord may be omitted, and the root doubled in its place. The doubled root may either remain as a common tone, or it may move freely.

   b. V6/5 to I6.

   The V6/5 occasionally may resolve to I6 when a weak resolution is wanted. *Note*: move the 7th degree of the dominant seventh chord to the 5th degree of the tonic chord.

c. V4/3 to I6.

The second inversion of the dominant seventh chord may lead to the I6 chord when a weak resolution is desired. Note that the 7th of the dominant chord moves up one step to the 5th of the tonic chord in this case. The harmonic movement, I V4/3 I6, is called that of the passing dominant four-three, since the two "d's" in the five note bass pattern are passing tones in the melodic sense. This chord is similar to that of the passing six-four discussed in Unit X.

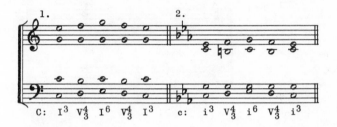

C: I³ V⁴₃ I⁶ V⁴₃ I³   c: i³ V⁴₃ i⁶ V⁴₃ i³

d. V2 to I.

Only occasionally does the V2 resolve directly to the root position I chord. In this movement the harmonic color of the V2 chord is evident, but the resolution of the bass is strongly subdominant in character (IV I).

C: V²   I⁵   c: V²   i³

e. V7 and V7 inversions to IV and IV6.

Just as was the case with the V7 chord, the inversions of the V7 can move to IV, and with especial ease to IV6.

C: V⁶₅ IV⁶ I³   c: V² iv³ i⁵

4. Dominant prolongation.

Those resolutions of the dominant seventh chord in which the voices do not move characteristically are irregular. Any dominant form of chord can be followed by any other dominant form with which connection by good voice leading is possible. The last of such dominant forms is then resolved properly to complete the progression. This changing around among the available positions and chords of the dominant family is referred to as dominant prolongation.*

C: V^7 2 $\frac{4}{3}$ 7 $\frac{6}{5}$ I^8

SUGGESTIONS FOR STUDY

The following exercises will provide practice in resolving inversions of the dominant seventh chord in several keys in both the major and minor modes.

1. Progressions involving two chords using whole notes and accidentals.

Dominant chord	Starting position	Key	Remarks
—complete V6/5	root in the S	B♭	regular resolution
—incomplete V6/5	root in the S	b	regular resolution
—complete V4/3	LT in the S	d♯	regular resolution
—incomplete V2	LT in the S	a♭	regular resolution
—complete V6/5	fifth in the S	c♯	resolve to i6
—V6/5	fifth in the S	G	move to IV6, doubling the 3rd of IV if necessary

2. Progressions involving dominant prolongation.
   —V V6 V2 V4/3, beginning with the leading tone in the S voice of the first chord, resolving the last dominant position to the tonic in any suitable manner, in the key of E♭ major.
   —V7 V2 V6/5 V4/3 V2 V6/5, beginning with the fifth in the S voice of the first chord, resolving the last dominant position to the tonic in any suitable manner, in the key of d minor.

A number of illustrations from music literature including the dominant seventh and leading tone chords have been used previously for other reasons. Ten of these are suggested for further study of their use of the dominant function.

1. Page 98, example #3 (Lyons, adapted from Johann Haydn).
2. Page 98, example #4 (Dundee).
3. Page 144, Bach chorale, Vater unser.
4. Page 145, Gottes sohn ist kommen.
5. Page 147, Bach chorale, O wir armen sünder.
6. Page 147, Bach chorale, Ich dank dir.
7. Page 181, Bach chorale, Hertzliebster Jesu.
8. Page 181, Wir christenleut!
9. Page 183, Bach chorale, Eins ist not!
10. Page 183, Bach chorale, Keinen hatt Gott verlassen.

II. NON-HARMONIC TONES

A. The Anticipation.

This non-harmonic tone is a great favorite in traditional harmony. It became prominent during, and, in certain forms is characteristic of the musical style of, the Baroque period. Stated harmonically, the anticipation* results from introducing one or more notes of a chord before the harmonic rhythm has changed to that chord. The chord affected is very often the final cadence chord of a section, but it can occur anywhere. Contrapuntally, the anticipation is introduced by either a step or a leap, and is left by repetition. Its nature is such that it occurs most often in a non-accented metrical position, but its sound is such that it gives the effect of a subtle accent. The illustrations show several types of anticipation.

1. in one voice.

   a. embellishing the soprano as a cadence decoration.

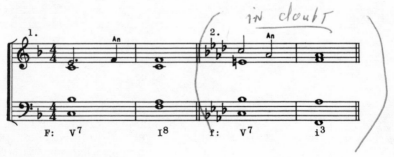

   b. the "Corelli clash"*

In the special instance that the anticipated tone is the tonic degree, and this tone is sounded against the leading

tone, the resulting dissonance is called the "Corelli clash"
in honor of the earlier contemporary of Bach in whose
music this figure abounds.

2. in two voices.

Note the parallel fifths in the first example. Such fifths are
common in music literature, and are acceptable when they
result either from the combination of a chord tone and a
non-harmonic tone, or from the use of two different types of
non-harmonic tones. The final guide must be the reaction
of the ear to the sound, but experience is needed to make the
ear a reliable judge.

3. in more than two voices.

Occasionally the anticipation is found in all four voices.
It would appear that this apparent syncopation* of the harmonic rhythm would be quite disrupting, but, peculiarly
enough, provided that the foregoing harmony is stylistically
compatible, the real change in harmonic rhythm does not
seem to occur until the primary accent on the following first
beat is reached. This feeling persists in spite of the fact that
the entire tonic chord is sounded too early. Thus the appro-
priateness of the name "anticipation" is again made evident.

4. as a melodic characteristic.

An anticipatory style of melodic movement often is encountered, and this lends a certain restlessness, which is frequently of good effect. In such instances, the anticipation
becomes a characteristic part of the musical texture.

B. The escape tone.*

1. the traditional form.

This non-harmonic tone, whose name is very appropriate
to its movement and character, is approached by step and
left by a leap. In its traditional form a voice which moves
by step between chords is momentarily deflected by a step
movement in the opposite direction (the escape tone), and this
is followed by a leap of a third back to the original destination. The examples illustrate.

2. a broader interpretation of the "escape" movement.

If neither the direction of the step nor the length of the leap is curtailed, the designation "escape tone" can be used to cover additional non-harmonic situations which are similar in nature and effect to the traditional form. The study of these combinations is worthwhile, since they exemplify one of the freedoms of contemporary music, namely, a more liberal use of non-harmonic tones.

[handwritten margin note: Trying to apply old laws to new age — can't do it]

3. as a decoration of another non-harmonic tone.

The escape tone can serve as the decoration of any other non-harmonic tone based upon a step movement, such as the returning tone, the suspension, and the passing tone.

ASSIGNMENT #37: Harmonic and non-harmonic analysis; including excerpts from the piano sonatas of Haydn and Beethoven.

This assignment, together with necessary instructions, is found on Work Sheet #45.

ASSIGNMENT #38: Part Writing using the dominant seventh chord, secondary chords and non-harmonic tones.

This assignment, together with necessary instructions, is found on Work Sheet #46.

FUNDAMENTALS

I. SCALES. The Eight Basic Scales (Theory Skill #33)

In the previous units the *four* basic scales (the major, and the natural, harmonic, and melodic minor), and the four church modes have become familiar and meaningful. Since these eight scale types are, collectively, the basis of much secular and sacred music, it is essential that the musician be able to write, sing, play, recognize, and hear any and all of these *eight basic scale* types with a high degree of accuracy.

SUGGESTIONS FOR STUDY

Practice writing the eight basic scale types in succession, using whole notes and accidentals, and following the 13 tone circle from D♯ through E♭. Use the five clefs in succession—two scales per clef—repeating the sequence of clefs after ten scales. A total of 104 scales can be written before a repetition will occur. Work Sheet #47 serves as an example of the format and procedure.

SATISFACTORY ATTAINMENT: writing at least eight scales in a five minute period, following the general format practiced in the suggestions for study. Choose any beginning tone except the ones used to begin drills.

This group of eight basic scale types does not exhaust the possible number of eight tone scale types to be found within our 12 tone octave. To supplement this list it is suggested that the student consult any standard musical dictionary regarding such other scales as the pentatonic, the Hungarian minor, and the whole tone. A number of "synthetic scales" constructed from the five tetrachords already familiar will be dealt with in the "Musicianship" section of a later unit.

II. RHYTHM: Syncopation

The subject of cross-rhythm has been discussed in previous units. In this discussion very little attention was given to syncopation. Cross-rhythm may produce syncopated effects, and syncopation often can be interpreted as cross-rhythm. There are, however, at least two additional rhythmic effects which have not yet been mentioned. These can more logically be referred to as syncopation rather than as cross-rhythm. These rhythmic effects can be accomplished by:

(1) shifting the principal pulse from the first to some other beat within the measure, without otherwise tampering with the meter, and,

(2) the use of rests on strong beats of the measure.

Shifting the principal pulse from the first beat of the measure can be done by:

(1) the use of a tie across a barline, or within a measure. *e.g.*:

Symphony No. 2 in D Major, Opus 73

Brahms

(2) the use of accents* on other than the first beat of a measure. *e.g.*:

Symphony No. 2 in D Major, Opus 73

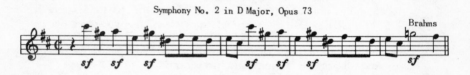

Brahms

The use of rests on strong beats leaves no alternative but that the weaker beats will receive a greater degree of emphasis. *e.g.*:

Symphony No. 2 in D Major, Opus 73

Brahms

In homophonic music (see homophony*) the syncopated effect is often confined to one voice, and particularly to the one which carries the melody. Nevertheless, this need not always apply. Careful thought will suggest other possibilities. As Walter Piston (*Counterpoint*) has pointed out: 1) the melodic rhythm* may or may not agree with the metrical rhythm,* 2) the harmonic rhythm may or may not agree with the metrical rhythm, and 3) the actual metrical rhythm may or may not agree with the meter. These varying rhythmic factors, organized with a degree of flexibility and originality, react with each other in what may be called a "counterpoint of rhythms." This is one of the characteristics of contrapuntal music (see counterpoint*). Many of these cross accents—melodic versus harmonic and metric, harmonic versus melodic and metric, or metric versus melodic and harmonic—are subtle examples of syncopation used to achieve variety and interest in the music they affect. The effects may occur melodically, harmonically, metrically, or in a combined form in any one or more voices.

ASSIGNMENT #39: The influence of syncopation upon rhythmic effect.

This assignment is found on Work Sheet #48.

MUSICIANSHIP

Pitch Ear Training

1. Review: practice singing, playing, recognizing, and hearing all simple intervals, up and down—major, minor, perfect, and tritone. Continue the practice of the nine major triad positions, and add the nine corresponding positions based on the minor triad.

2. The eight basic scales.

The ability to spell, sing, and recognize the eight basic scales depends on 1) understanding their step arrangement, and 2) being familiar with the sound patterns involved. Step one was drilled in minor, and the modal scales separately (Pitch Skill #8 in Unit VII and Pitch Achievement in Unit X).

   a. Sing the following tetrachord combinations and name the scale type formed.

   1. M plus m (a whole step apart)
   2. m plus m (a whole step apart)
   3. m plus hm (a whole step apart)
   4. Lyd plus M (a half step apart)
   5. m plus ph (a whole step apart)
   6. M plus M (a whole step apart)
   7. m plus M (a whole step apart)
   8. ph plus ph (a whole step apart)

   b. practice singing and playing each scale type from a common tonic, or 1st degree.

   c. practice recognizing and spelling each scale type, given the pitch of the 1st degree.

3. The dominant seventh chord.

The pleasant sound of the dominant seventh chord, a major chord with an added minor seventh interval, results from a composite of interval qualities. Notice that 12 different intervals can be found in the simplest forms of the root and inverted seventh chord positions. Of these, two are the tritone in two spellings, two are minor thirds and two are major sixths. The interblending of this composite of qualities creates a problem in recognition, but the many interval sounds included also are the means by which one can mentally orientate the total sound.

C: V^7 M3 P5 m7 m3 d5 m3   C: V$^6_5$ m3 d5 m6 m3 P4 M2

C: V$^4_3$ m3 P4 M6 M2 A4 M3   C: V^2 M2 A4 M6 M3 P5 m3

  a. practice singing and playing the many seventh chords in root position and in each of the three inversions, using a variety of bass tones and roots.

F^7 C$^6_5$ A$^4_3$ D^2

  b. practice singing and playing each of the possible dominant seventh chord positions from one tone to give orientation in successive keys and position types.

C: V^7 A♭: V$^6_5$ F: V$^4_3$ D: V^2
(or) G^7 E♭$^6_5$ c$^4_3$ A^2

  c. practice hearing and analyzing the four basic dominant seventh chord positions. Record the analysis and notate each one in the assigned clef, given the letter name of the lowest tone of each chord. *e.g.*:

Rhythm Ear Training

1. Drill the given examples of syncopation. Note the means by which the syncopation is achieved.

   a. syncopation arising from *shifting* the pulse from the first to some other beat within the measure.

(music notation examples 1–4)

   b. syncopation arising from *omitting* the first beat of a measure and thus throwing the emphasis on some other part of the measure.

(music notation examples 1–4)

2. Rhythm Skills for individual performance.

Evaluate the performance of these skills in the usual manner.

a. Syncopation: 4/4 meter, Flash Card Set #27.
(*Rhythm Skill* #21)

SATISFACTORY ATTAINMENT: the performance of these
rhythms in any order and at any tempo up to 132 quarter
notes per minute.

b. Syncopation: 2/4 meter, Flash Card Set #28.
(*Rhythm Skill* #22)

SATISFACTORY ATTAINMENT: the performance of these
rhythms in any order and at any tempo up to 132 quarter notes
per minute.

Sight Singing: FORM EMPHASIS—two part open form, the
invention, and contrapuntal imitation.

Johann Sebastian Bach's *15 Two Part Inventions* and *15 Three
Part Symphonies* (referred to as inventions*) are excellent examples of two and three part contrapuntal writing based upon
a clearly organized harmonic foundation. As far as their form is
concerned, many of them can be divided into two easily discernible sections or paragraphs. In some inventions the hint of a three
part form is obvious in the closing section, relating both the
key and the subject matter to the beginning. In the usual invention the first paragraph begins in the tonic, maneuvers into
a related area, and cadences there; then the second paragraph
begins in the related area, works its way back to the tonic area,
and cadences at home. Often the last measures of each paragraph
are similar except for key, illustrating what is known as "cadence
rime."* This formal scheme, very common in the music of the
Baroque period, is known as "two part open form."*

Generally, the related area is the dominant in the major mode,
and the relative major in the minor mode. Since every invention is contrapuntal, each abounds in imitation.* This technique
can be used either to build up a voice or passage through sequences or to carry forward the composition through the inter-
play of motives among the voices.

Occasionally, the device of contrapuntal interchange,* or invertible counterpoint,* is found in the Inventions. Examples of
this can be found in "Two Part Inventions" number 6 and 8 and
"Three Part Invention" number 9. It is suggested that the word
"interchangeable" be used to designate the contrapuntal technique through which two or more voices can serve as basses for
each other. This would still leave the word "invert" (and "in-

version") at least two duties, namely, that of describing the contrapuntal technique of turning a theme or an interval upside down, and of describing a chord whose root is not in the bass voice.

As you practice these sight singing examples (four of which are taken from the Inventions) observe their contrapuntal aspects.

1. Two Part Invention in C Major

Bach

2. Two Part Invention in D Major

Bach

3. Two Part Invention in E Major

Bach

4. Two Part Invention in D Minor

Bach

5. Two Part Invention in A Minor

Bach

6. Prelude and Fugue in F# Major (WTC I)

Bach

7. Scenes from Childhood, Opus 15

Schumann

Keyboard Emphasis
Keyboard Skill #12

This keyboard skill includes the dominant seventh chord in root position and in each inversion, *the* deceptive cadence, and a full cadence using one form of the cadential six-four dissonance.

SATISFACTORY ATTAINMENT: the ability to play this keyboard skill at your highest level of competence:

"Minimum" Level—in any four major and any four minor keys.

"Above-average" Level—in any eight major and any eight minor keys.

"Superior" Level—in any four requested major and minor keys.

Dictation

Evaluate the level of achievement in each type of dictation skill done.

1. Pitch.

   Pitch Skill #14—Hearing the Dominant Seventh Chord.

   SATISFACTORY ATTAINMENT: demonstrated competence in hearing the dominant seventh chord in root position and in each of the three inversions. Given the pitch and clef of the lowest tone, respond by recognizing and correctly notating each of the ten dominant seventh chord positions played. For evaluation the Arabic symbol and the spelling count as one response. *e.g.*:

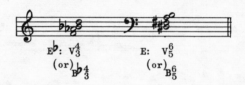

$$\text{E}^{\flat}: \text{V}^{4}_{3} \qquad \text{E}: \text{V}^{6}_{5}$$
$$(\text{or})_{\text{B}^{\flat}}{}^{4}_{3} \qquad (\text{or})_{\text{B}}{}^{6}_{5}$$

Pitch Achievement

Review recognizing the sound of the five qualities of tetra-chords—

1) listen to one of the given tetrachords played. After recognizing its quality, spell each of the scales from the eight basic types that include this tetrachord. To illustrate, the major tetrachord—C D E F—is the first tetrachord of the C major and the C Mixolydian scales, and the second tetrachord of the F major and the F melodic minor scales. *e.g.*:

Tetrachords

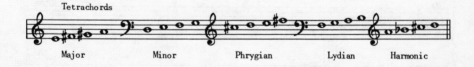

Major   Minor   Phrygian   Lydian   Harmonic

2) continue this type of practice with the four remaining tetrachords, or with each of the various types of tetra-chords spelled on still other degrees.

2. Rhythmic.

   These three measure rhythm dictations afford practice in recognizing and notating syncopation and cross-rhythm in several meters. Compute the PROFICIENCY PERCENTAGE by dividing the number of correct responses by the total number attempted. For convenience in doing this each response is numbered.

3. Melodic.

    a. practice notating the given excerpts from hearing them played. Each one illustrates some form of the contrapuntal technique of imitation, as applied in a melodic line.

1. Three Part Invention in D Major   Bach

2. Piano Sonata in F Major   Haydn

3. Two Part Invention in A Minor   Bach

4. Three Part Invention in C Minor   Bach

5. Intermezzo in A Minor, Op. 119, No. 3

Brahms

b. continue the development of selective listening by notating only the alto voice of the next phrases. The key, meter, tempo, and pitch distribution or voicing of the first chord are given. The PROFICIENCY PERCENTAGE is obtained by dividing the number of correct responses by the number attempted.

Chorale: "O Thou the True and Only Light," St. Paul

Mendelssohn

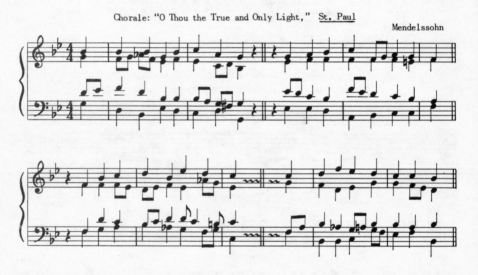

4. Harmonic.

This dictation practice includes the primary and secondary triads and the resolution of the root position and inverted dominant seventh chords. The key and the pitch of the tonic degree are given. The response may be in Roman/Arabic numerals— one of each for each chord. Always note the type of cadence and its state of perfection or imperfection. Consider each Roman and each Arabic numeral used for each chord a separate response in computing the PROFICIENCY PERCENTAGE obtained by dividing the number of correct responses by the total number attempted.

UNIT 12

HARMONY

I. DIATONIC MODULATION—by direct pivot chord, by two common tones pivot, by one common tone pivot.

The three principal chords in any key are the foundation of traditional harmony. Their continued, unrelieved use in one key soon becomes monotonous, however, since the ear knows in advance what to anticipate. Because of such limitations, composers developed the technique of modulation* to add variety and interest to their musical compositions. In perusing music literature to observe the use of modulation, one finds that in very many instances the composer was content with only small changes in key. Many classical sonatas contain a modulation into the dominant or into the relative key for the subordinate theme group.* These same modulations were also quite standard in the various dances of the suite of the Baroque period. Analysis shows that certain modulations have been used frequently and these should be thoroughly familiar. They include:

(1) modulation from the major tonic to the major dominant key (a signature difference of one sharp or flat).

(2) modulation from the minor tonic to the minor dominant (the same difference in key signature).

(3) modulation from a major key to its relative minor (no difference in key signature).

(4) modulation from a minor key to its relative major (also with no difference in key signature).

Thorough acquaintance with these and other modulations, and with the various techniques for achieving modulation, can serve as a means of increasing one's understanding of musical form.* This is true particularly in the analytical study of the development section of the sonata form.*

For the study of modulation certain already familiar knowledge is prerequisite. To summarize—

(1) major and minor keys and signatures.

256

(2) the proper spelling of the primary and secondary chords, their first inversions, and the various dominant seventh chord forms. These should be understood in both the major and minor modes, remembering the three minor scale types, each of which contributes to the total meaning of the minor mode.

(3) the various cadences.

Modulation can be accomplished in several ways. A common way is merely that of starting in a new key without bridging the tonal gap from the initial key to the key of destination. This type of modulation depends for its effect upon the juxtaposition of two independent tonalities. Their contrasting sound produces an effective result which should be noted. Observe how Beethoven used such a modulation in the beginning of Opus 53.

Sonata in C, Opus 53, " 1st"

Beethoven

Another means of modulation is that of striking the dominant chord (or a chord of the dominant family) of a new key. Again the effectiveness will depend upon the kind of contrast achieved between the two tonalities concerned.

Sonata in E♭ Major, Opus 7, " 1st"

Beethoven

A. Diatonic Modulation.

The modulations just presented are somewhat impromptu in style. Another very important, but much less impromptu, type of modulation is achieved, however, by the use of a pivot—common to both keys—which may consist of: 1) one or more chords of any quality, 2) two chord tones, or 3) even a single chord tone. This type is known as diatonic modulation.* It requires three procedural steps. These are:

—establish the initial key through the use of a cadence or a logical succession of chords belonging to the initial key.

—select an appropriate pivot which indicates a clear relationship to both the initial key and the key of destination.

—establish the key of destination through the use of the desired cadence.

We see, then, that modulation between two keys is partly a matter of writing convincing cadences before and after a pivot. To the composer it also means writing music which sounds convincing in its context. As suggested there are various techniques of diatonic modulation by which certain effective changes of key can be made. Let us examine them.

1. Modulation by direct pivot chord—the possibilities.

Direct pivot chord* modulations are possible whenever the initial key and the key of destination have one or more chords in common. This situation occurs when two keys which are relative to each other are concerned. For example, a major key and its relative minor key have all chords in common when the *natural* relative minor is considered. A major key and its *harmonic* relative minor key have only four common chords, however, and a major key and its relative *melodic* minor key have only one chord in common.

Chart of Chords Available in a Major Key and the Three Relative Scales

It is obvious from the chart that the natural minor scale provides the greatest number of pivot chords in this instance, but it is also obvious that the harmonic and melodic scale forms provide added pivot possibilities with scales other than the relative major. In planning a modulation involving a minor key, the possibilities within all the minor scale types therefore must be considered before selecting the pivot to use. Regardless of how the pivoting can best be accomplished, it is quite certain that a convincing cadence in the new key will require the raised leading tone of the harmonic minor scale. Modulation by a direct pivot chord is also possible when two keys (major or minor) have signatures differing by either one or two flats or sharps. A signature difference of one flat or one sharp permits *four* direct pivot chords, whereas a signature difference of two flats or sharps allows only *two* pivot chords to remain, that is, considering only the natural minor scale which is entirely controlled by its signature. If the signatures of two keys differ by more than two flats or sharps, modulation must be accomplished in some way other than by the use of the direct pivot chord. For clarification let us examine certain modulations using the direct pivot chord.

a. Major and minor keys that are relative, having the same signature.

1) a modulation from G major to E minor.

a) the available chords of G major are: (the tonic
chord is underlined)

G a b C D e f♯°

b) the available chords of E (natural) minor are:
(for ease of comparison, chords on the same basic
letter name are written one below the other)

G a b C D e f♯°

c) since all the chords of the first key are found in
the next key, it is obvious that the modulation can
be effected only by showing in some manner that
the function of one or more chords has changed.
Study the illustration.

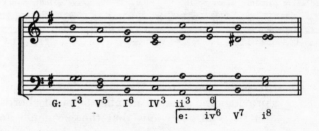

Note that the first five chords belong to the key of
G major, but that the function of the first inversion
A minor chord is clearly the subdominant of E minor
rather than the supertonic of G major, hence it has
performed the function of a direct pivot between the
two keys.

2) a modulation from E minor back to its relative, G
major.

Note in the illustrated modulation that the A minor
chord again functions as the pivot, this time changing
from a subdominant in the key of origin to a supertonic
in the key of destination.

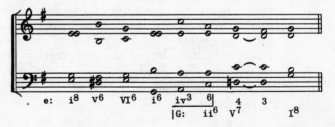

b. Major keys differing by one flat or one sharp.

For an example let us consider the modulation from A major to the key of its dominant, E major.

1) the available chords of A major are:

A b c♯ D E f♯ g♯°

2) the available chords in E major are:

A b c♯ d♯° E f♯ g♯

3) the four common chords, called possible *direct pivot chords*, are:

A c♯ E f♯

4) a possible modulation using the first common chord, that of A major, is shown, and an example of its use in the music of Mozart gives a further illustration.

Sonata in A Minor, K. 310

Mozart

SUGGESTIONS FOR STUDY

Write simple modulations similar to those which have been shown after completing the necessary steps to determine the available pivot chords.

(1) use the subdominant chord of F major as a direct pivot chord to D minor.

(2) use the diminished supertonic chord of A minor as a direct pivot chord to C major.

(3) use the mediant chord of B♭ major as a direct pivot chord to F major.

(4) use the dominant chord of D major as a direct pivot chord to A major.

(5) use the submediant chord of E major as a direct pivot chord to A major.

c. Major and minor keys differing by one flat or one sharp.

There are four pivots between a major key and the natural form of a minor key differing by one flat or one sharp in its signature. Before determining the pivot to use, it is well to note what effect the harmonic and melodic minor scale forms have on the pivot chords available. After surveying the possibilities, one can arrange the modulation which seems most effective under the given circumstances. To illustrate, let us consider a modulation from D major to F♯ minor.

1) the possible chords in D major are:

$$D \quad e \quad f\sharp \quad G \quad A \quad b \quad c\sharp°$$

2) the possible chords in F♯ minor (the natural scale) are:

$$D \quad E \quad f\sharp \quad g\sharp° \quad A \quad b \quad c\sharp$$

3) the four pivot chords are:

$$D \quad f\sharp \quad A \quad b$$

4) the harmonic minor scale adds these chords:

$$A^+ \quad C\sharp \quad e\sharp°$$

It should be noted that since these chords are not common to both keys they are of no direct assistance in modulating from D major to F♯ minor.

5) the melodic minor scale adds the following chords:

$$g\sharp \quad B \quad d\sharp°$$

Again note that these three chords will be of no direct assistance in modulating from D major to F♯ minor. It is therefore logical to use one of the four pivots mentioned under previous item 3. The one selected for this example is the submediant chord of D major. It is used as a direct pivot by becoming the subdominant of F♯ minor. An example from the music of Bach shows how he handled this same type of modulation. Complete the analysis of each example.

French Suite No. 3 in B Minor

Bach

SUGGESTIONS FOR STUDY

(1) write three other modulations from the key of D major to F♯ minor, using, in turn, the D major, F♯ minor, and A major chords as the direct pivot.

(2) analyze harmonically the given example assuming that the B diminished chord is the pivot in the modulation from C major to D minor.

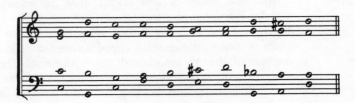

d. Major and minor keys differing by two flats or two sharps.

Although not frequently used, a direct pivot modulation between two major and minor keys whose signatures differ by two flats or two sharps is readily understood. Such a modulation (as from C major to G minor) is cited as a final pivot chord illustration.

1) the available chords in C major are:

C   d   e   F   G   a   b°

2) the available chords in G (composite) minor are:

c   d   E♭   F   g   a°   B♭
C   D   e°   f♯°   a   B♭+

3) the possible direct pivots are:

C   d   F   a

Two of these pivot chords (d and F) are the expected pivots from the G natural minor scale and the other two (c and a) are derived from the G melodic minor scale.

4) a suggested illustration of this modulation using the D minor pivot chord is given. In this instance, the minor quality chord from the natural minor scale is used for pivoting to G minor, but the D major chord from the harmonic minor scale is used for effecting a strong dominant feeling, which is further strengthened by the final plagal cadence. Complete the analysis.

2. Modulation by the two common tones pivot.

Any two tones of one chord may be common to other chords. For example, the tones C and E♭, the root and 3rd degrees of the C minor chord, may be the root and 3rd degrees of the C diminished chord as well as the 3rd and 5th degrees of the A♭ major and the A diminished chords. Consideration of the various seventh chords—of which the supertonic, dominant, and leading tone are known—would reveal further possible associations for the two tones in question. These two tones, thus serve as a direct pivot in effecting modulations between those tonalities or keys which share the chords to which the given pair of tones are common. Alternate forms of modulations learned earlier, as well as new modulations, may be devised by means of this two common tone technique.

Study the following modulation from Haydn which illustrates an interesting means of moving from E major to its dominant minor, B.

Quartet in D Major, Op. 76, No. 5

Haydn

E: I

b:ii°⁶₅

SUGGESTIONS FOR STUDY

(1) using the two notes E and B, determine the number of three-tone and four-tone chords to which these are common.

(2) using this information, determine several modulations which are made possible by the E and B—two common tones—pivot. Express these as root progressions using Roman numerals.

3. Modulation by the one common tone pivot.

It is immediately apparent that a single chord tone is not as limited in function as are two chord tones. In dealing with triads, any given tone may be present in a chord as either the root, 3rd, or 5th degree, or, also, as the 7th degree when dealing with seventh chords. For example, E can be the root of either a major, minor, diminished, or augmented chord; the 3rd degree of the C major, the C augmented, the C♯ minor, and C♯ diminished chords. Further, considering E as any one of the possible tones of a seventh chord suggests several more possible chords.

Note that in the given modulation the C major triad is not
found in the A major scale, and conversely, the A major triad
is not a part of the C major scale. The E, the 3rd degree in
the C major chord of the initial key, thus serves as a direct
pivot by becoming the 5th degree of the A major chord, the
tonic of the key of destination.

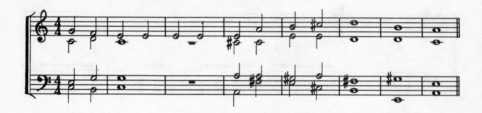

Analysis of the foregoing suggests that the one common
tone pivot technique can make possible modulation between
quite distant keys. In the C major scale the tone B is the
most distant degree in terms of its potential major key signature. Note further that this tone can be the 3rd degree of
the dominant chord of C major. The example shows a simple
modulation bridging the tonal gap from C major to B major.
Make a harmonic analysis.

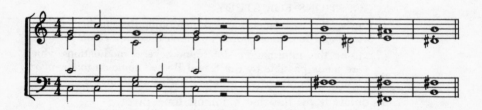

Perhaps the greatest use of the one common tone pivot is
that of providing alternate ways of making the simpler and
more usual modulations. The last illustration shows how
Beethoven uses the one common tone technique as an alternative solution to modulation which ordinarily would involve
two common tones, or, stated otherwise, which implies the
presence of two common tones.

Sonata in C Minor, Op. 10, No. 1

Beethoven

SUGGESTIONS FOR STUDY

Study of the material on modulation by direct pivot should provide answers to questions such as the following:

(1) What are the harmonic functions (tonic chord, etc.) that a major chord can assume in the major and minor modes?

(2) What modulations can be accomplished using a D major pivot chord as a I in the initial key and allowing its function to vary in the key of destination?

(3) What are the harmonic functions that a minor chord can assume in the major and minor modes?

(4) What modulations can be accomplished using an E minor pivot chord as a iv in the initial key and allowing its function to vary in the key of destination?

(5) What are the harmonic functions that a diminished chord can assume in the major and minor modes?

(6) What modulations can be accomplished using a G diminished chord as a vii° in the initial key and allowing its function to vary in the key of destination?

(7) Why is the augmented chord not useful for modulations such as the foregoing?

ASSIGNMENT #40: Harmonic and non-harmonic analysis including direct pivot modulation.

This assignment, together with necessary instructions, is found on Work Sheet #49.

ASSIGNMENT #41 (Part I): Melodic harmonization including the use of the direct pivot chord.

(Part II); Writing modulations.

This assignment, together with necessary instructions, is found on Work Sheet #50-1 and 50-2.

II. SECONDARY DOMINANT CHORDS—INTRODUCTION

The music of approximately two centuries preceding 1900 was enriched by the use of the secondary dominant* chords, that is, chords that are dominant in function to other degrees than the tonic. Previous study has shown that 1) the tonic chord of each major or minor key is enhanced by a major dominant chord—the primary dominant—whose root lies a perfect fifth above the tonic; 2) each tonic chord is major or minor in quality according to the mode of the key; and 3) either major or minor chords can be found on all but the 7th degree of the major mode and on each degree of some scale of the minor mode. It follows logically, therefore, that whenever a major or minor chord is found within a mode, that chord can be enhanced by the major chord which is dominant to it in function.

The chords which serve this purpose—other than the primary dominant—are known as secondary dominant chords. Thus the dominant of a degree other than the tonic is called a secondary dominant, speaking generally, and the dominant of the supertonic, or the dominant of the submediant, etc., speaking specifically. The use of secondary dominant chords will of necessity introduce alterations into the scale tones of the basic tonality. The presence of such alterations can alert one to detect the use of secondary dominant functions, a fact which the perceptive ear will confirm. Extensive use of secondary dominant harmony is one of the characteristics of chromaticism,* which in turn is one of the characteristics found in music of especially the last half of the nineteenth century.

The knowledge of the primary dominant, the three principal triads, and the four secondary triads can be utilized to give understanding and proficiency in the thinking of secondary dominants. Also, remembering the 21 tone circle of fifths can be of help. It is now meaningful to re-emphasize that each tone of the 21 tone circle is the dominant of the next tone in the sequence, or that the dominant degree of any tone on the circle (except the first) is the tone that precedes it. This is, of course, equivalent to thinking in downward perfect fifth or upward perfect fourth intervals.

e.g.: Part of the 21 tone circle of fifths is shown:

C♯	F♯	B	E	A	D	G	C	F	B♭	E♭
B: V	I	IV					B♭: V	I		IV
E: V	I	IV								

Thinking in the key of G major, the tonic chord is G major and the primary dominant is D major; the supertonic chord is A minor and its dominant is thus E major; the mediant chord is B minor and its dominant is thus F♯ major. In the key of C minor, the tonic chord is C minor and the primary dominant is G major. The supertonic diminished of the harmonic minor cannot support a dominant chord, and possibly for this reason a secondary dominant relationship to the supertonic is rarely established, even though the melodic form of minor scale gives the supertonic degree a minor quality. Similarly the augmented mediant chord of the C harmonic minor scale cannot support a dominant chord, but the major mediant of the C natural minor scale does have a dominant chord of B♭ major. In each instance, the basic scale tones are altered, as needed, to spell the desired secondary dominant properly.

The secondary dominants include root position chords, seventh, ninth, and thirteenth chords, as well as the related leading tone triads and leading tone seventh chords and their inversions. Since the dominant seventh chord is the *basic* form, our main emphasis will be placed upon understanding this type of secondary dominant.

If each resolution is thought of as a dominant function resolving to its temporary tonic, and this temporary tonic is recognized as having some other-than-tonic function within the main key and tonality, an adequate understanding of secondary dominants readily can be achieved. The given example illustrates a use of the five secondary dominant chords which are possible in the major mode. Note that since the leading tone chord of the major mode is diminished in quality it cannot support a secondary dominant function.

The following secondary dominants are possible in the minor mode in its composite form.

(1) V/ii, based upon the melodic minor scale.

(2) V/III, based upon the natural minor scale.

(3) V/iv, based upon the natural and harmonic minor scales.
    Also, V/IV, based upon the melodic minor scale.

(4) V/V, based upon the harmonic and melodic minor scales.
Also, V/v, based upon the natural minor scale.

(5) V/VI, based upon the natural and harmonic minor scales.

(6) V/VII, based upon the natural minor scale.

SUGGESTIONS FOR STUDY

1. Spelling the Secondary Dominant Seventh Chord (*Theory Skill* #34)

Practice spelling the secondary dominant seventh chord related to all other-than-tonic degrees except the leading tone of each major scale, and to all the other-than-tonic degrees of each minor scale. Work Sheet #51 provides a convenient format for organizing this information.

2. To become familiar with the use of the secondary dominant chords—

   a. write and resolve the first inversion of the dominant seventh chord of the mediant for each odd numbered minor flat key (thinking degree roots in the natural minor scale).

   b. play and resolve on the keyboard the root position dominant seventh chord of the subdominant of C major and each of the even numbered flat keys.

   c. write and resolve the second inversion of the dominant seventh chord of the lowered leading tone of A minor, and of each even numbered flat key (thinking, as suggested before, in the natural minor scale).

   d. play and resolve the third inversion of the dominant seventh chord of the submediant of C major and each even numbered major sharp key.

3. Several examples of the secondary dominant function are available in this unit. Study each illustration cited in relation to the analysis suggested. Carefully note each resolution.

   a. page 274, *Intermezzo,* Op. 10, No. 3, Brahms.

      1) a leading tone seventh chord in bar one (b: vii°⁷).

      2) a leading tone seventh chord of the subdominant in bar four (b: vii°⁷/iv).

      3) a leading tone seventh chord of the dominant in bar five (b: vii° 7/V).

   b. page 284, Bach chorale, *Sei lob und ehr'.*

      1) bar 3, 4th quarter note—a V²/V in G major.

      2) bar 5, 4th quarter note—a V²/vi in D major.

      3) bar 8, 2nd eighth note—a V⁶/⁵/ii in G Major.

      4) bar 10, 1st quarter note—V⁶/V in G major. The 7th is not used in this instance.

FUNDAMENTALS

I. RHYTHM—A SUMMARY

The study of rhythm is based upon a number of principles which have been discussed in the previous 11 units. A brief summary of these principles and their application follows.

A. Meter signature and size.

The various simple notes and rests can be combined in numerous ways within the limitations prescribed by the size of each meter signature. This size is the same as the value of the largest possible note in a meter, and both are indicated by the value of the meter signature. A numerator of 4 or smaller indicates a simple meter, whereas one of 5 or larger shows a compound meter. *e.g.:*

(1)   (2)   (3)

B. Numerator influence and denominator function.

The denominator of the meter signature designates the size of the note value which is influenced by the numerator of the signature.

e.g.:—in 3/4 meter it is the quarter note.

—in 2/2 meter it is the half note.

—in 6/8 meter it is the eighth note.

A numerator of 2, 4, or possibly 8 signifies that the denominator value is grouped in twos, or in duple fashion.

e.g.:—in 4/4 one thinks in twos; in 2/2 also in twos, the main difference being the size of the denominator value which is influenced.

When the numerator is 3, 6, 9, or 12, the organization of the denominator value is in threes, or triple.

e.g.:(1) in 3/8 meter there is one group of triple denominator pulses per bar.

(2) in 6/8 meter there are two groups of triple denominator pulses per bar.

(3) in 9/16 meter there are three groups of triple demoninator pulses per bar.

(4) in 12/16 meter there are four groups of triple denominator pulses per bar.

Whenever the numerator is 5, 7, 8, or larger, the organization may be some additive combination of ones, twos, threes, and fours, which is best illustrated through the use of music notation. *e.g.*:

C. Characteristic rhythms.

Rhythms are characteristic of a meter when note values of the size of the denominator or larger are grouped in agreement with the organization implied by the numerator. Varied rhythms, still characteristic of the meter, can be obtained by using either or both duple or triple subdivisions of the denominator value. In the examples, note the clarity of the pulse despite the subdivisions.
e.g.:

Further variety is available by using any desired subdivision of any possible simple notes in either duple or triple meters. *e.g.*:

D. Uncharacteristic rhythms.

1. Hemiola and other cross-rhythms.

Any desired subdivisions also can be applied in triple meters to the larger dotted notes which consist of one or more triple denominator pulse groups. Whenever the grouping of such subdivisions conflicts with the characteristic organization of the meter, a cross-rhythmic effect is produced.

When this effect suggests a two against three conflict, or vice versa, the resulting cross-rhythm is known as hemiola. *e.g.*:

More drastic cross-rhythms result from juxtaposing dissimilar note groups or measures with or without similar denominators. These cross-rhythms result also from the ostinato-like repetition of especially non-characteristic or irregular pulse or note groupings. *e.g.*:

(1)

(2)

(3)

2. Syncopation.

Rhythmic disruptions, known better as syncopations, derive their effect by shifting the point of accent within the bar or by omitting the main accents through replacing them by rests. These syncopations may concern only the melody, the entire texture, or, more subtly, the harmonic rhythm of a composition. Three musical excerpts give partial illustration to these types of syncopation.

Scenes from Childhood

Schumann

i   V   i
(Tonic Pedal)

Intermezzo, Op. 10, No. 3

Brahms

Sonata in E♭, Op. No. 7

Beethoven

f: i   V♯♮   i   V♯♮

There is a rhythmic plan in all music. It can be discerned by becoming aware of the characteristics of a meter, by observing the variety achieved through subdivisions and groupings of its denominator, and by noting the conflicts and disruptions arising from the use of hemiola, cross-rhythm, and syncopation.

ASSIGNMENT #42: Rhythmic facts and principles.

This assignment is found on Work Sheet #52.

MUSICIANSHIP

Pitch Ear Training

1. Review: practice recognizing and hearing the eight basic scales in three ways—1) recognize the constituent tetrachords

and thereby deduce the type of scale, 2) recognize the quality of each scale as a unit, and 3) recognize and notate each scale given its initial pitch. Further, practice recognizing and hearing the root and inverted position dominant seventh chords in three ways—1) recognize the lower and upper chord degrees and deduce the chord position used, 2) recognize the chord as being in root position, 1st, 2nd, or 3rd inversion, and 3) recognize and notate each chord given the pitch of its lowest tone.

2. All intervals down: think each downward interval in relation to the upper tonic (or 8th) degree of a major scale.

   a. using the basic names—major, minor, perfect, and tritone (called either tritone, augmented fourth, or diminished fifth, as desired)—as descriptive words for vocalization, sing alternately the 8th scale degree of any major scale and each successive semitone lower.

   e.g.:

   b. similarly, sing each successively larger interval, interpolating each augmented interval in its proper place. The augmented intervals sound like the nearest larger minor or perfect interval.

   e.g.:

c. sing each successively larger interval, interpolating each diminished interval in its proper place. The diminished intervals sound like the nearest smaller major or perfect interval.

e.g.:

d. sing each successive interval, first vocalizing the interval's basic name then its enharmonic name. (See enharmonic intervals.*)

e.g.:

e. practice hearing and analyzing the downward intervals, recording the quality and notating each in the assigned clef, given the letter name of the upper tone. In parentheses beneath each analysis write the name of the enharmonic interval.

e.g.:

Rhythm Ear Training

Check through the "Musicianship" section of each of the preceding 11 units and review any of the rhythm exercises and num-

bered Rhythm Skills which still present problems in performance. The knowledge and experience now available—together
with additional needed practice—should be sufficient to solve any
remaining difficulties.

Sight Singing: FORM EMPHASIS—two part open form in the Bach Suites.

The French* and English Suites* of Bach are a part of this
composer's very important contributions to the suite form, a
form which became almost extinct after his death in 1750. More
recently, interest in the suite form has revived, but the modern
examples tend to include a succession of free movements of differing character rather than a sequence of idealized dances,
as was the custom of the Baroque period. The acrostic, A C S O
G*, is useful in remembering the group of dances usually found
in the Bach suites. Those included are the allemande,* courante,*
sarabande,* the "optional group,"* and the gigue.* The larger
number of suite movements are two part open forms, but occasionally a three part form can be found, usually in the optional
dance group. In these two part open forms, a modulation to,
and the establishment of, a related key occur in or by the end
of the first section. The second section of the form begins in
the related key, using the same thematic material transposed,
modulates to the tonic area and convincingly establishes that
key center, often using an extensive cadence rhyme. In the
major mode the related key usually is either the dominant or the
relative minor; in the minor mode it is either the dominant
(major or minor) or the relative major.

Each of these sight singing examples represents a theme or
melody from some movement of the many instrumental suites
written by Johann Sebastian Bach.

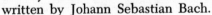

1. French Suite No. 1 in d " Sarabande"   Bach

2. French Suite No. 1 in d "Courante"

Bach

3. Orchestral Suite No. 2 in b "Minuet" *

Bach

4. English Suite No. 6 in d "Gavotte" *

Bach

5. English Suite No. 5 in e " Passepied I " *

Bach

6. Partita * No. 1 in b " Bourree "

Bach

279

7. French Suite No. 6 in E "Bourrée" *

Bach

8. Suite #1 in G "Gigue" *

Bach

Keyboard Emphasis

Keyboard Skill #13

SATISFACTORY ATTAINMENT: play the following exercise illustrating the secondary dominant seventh chords found in the major and minor modes at the highest level of competence you can attain.

"Minimum" Level—in any two major and any two minor keys.

"Above-average" Level—in any four major and any four minor keys.

"Superior" Level—in any four requested major and any four requested minor keys.

(1)

(2)

Dictation

Evaluate the level of achievement attained in each type of dictation.

1. Pitch.

Pitch Skill #15—Hearing All Intervals, Down

SATISFACTORY ATTAINMENT: competence in hearing each of the downward simple intervals from the half step through the octave. Given the pitch and clef of the upper tone, respond by correctly recognizing and consistently notating each of ten intervals played. In parentheses beneath the analysis of each interval write the name of the corresponding enharmonic interval. Each spelling and its complete analysis is one response.

Pitch Achievement

The positions of the half steps in a scale determine its type. Listen to the following (or similar) scales played and recognize each scale type by indicating the positions of the half steps. *e.g.*: the natural minor scale type heard would be diagrammed as follows:

The suggested dictations are based on various positions of the dominant seventh chord in the major and minor modes. Given the pitch and clef of the first tone, respond by correctly notating each example. For ease of evaluation each example contains ten intervals.

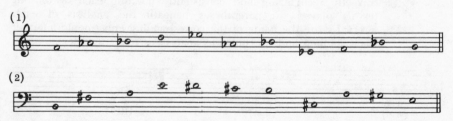

2. Rhythmic.

The examples of rhythmic dictation illustrate the categories of rhythm which have been studied. For each dictation the tempo should be designated as "moderate," "fast," or "very slow." The meter may be announced, or it can be suggested by announcing the denominator value and indicating the numerator by the appropriate conducting pattern. In a more subtle manner the meter can be implied by announcing the size of the pulse unit and showing the appropriate accompanying conductor's beat.

3. Melodic.

  a. record phrase by phrase in proper pitch and rhythmic
  notation the alto from two phrases and the tenor from the
  other three phrases of this example to gain further experience in selective listening for a single voice line of a four
  part texture. The key, meter, tempo, and the pitch of the
  first tone will be given. Compute the PROFICIENCY
  PERCENTAGE in the usual manner.

Sei lob und ehr' dem hochsten Gut

Bach

b. practice one voice melodic dictation. The examples are selected from the Bach Suites and Inventions. The pitch of the first note and the key, meter, and tempo should be given. Compute the PROFICIENCY PERCENTAGE.

1. French Suite No. 4 in E♭ Major "gigue"

Bach

2. French Suite No. 5 in G Major "gavotte"

Bach

3. French Suite No. 6 in E Major "gigue"

Bach

4. Suite in E♭ Major "menuet ✱2"

Bach

4. Harmonic.

These examples of harmonic dictation reduce modulation by a common or pivot chord to the barest essentials, namely, a tonic chord, a pivot chord, and a cadence into the key of destination. The response may be in Roman and Arabic symbols—each counted independently—or it may be in music notation together with the Roman/Arabic symbols. In the

latter instance, evaluate the recorded notation by comparing
it note for note with the examples played. Compute the
PROFICIENCY PERCENTAGE.

UNIT 13

HARMONY

I. CHORDS OF THE DOMINANT FAMILY—dominant ninth, leading tone seventh, dominant thirteenth, dominant eleventh.

The composers of the Baroque, Classic, and Romantic periods (approximately 1700 to 1900) explored many of the harmonic uses of the dominant family. The use of the dominant seventh, ninth, eleventh, and thirteenth chords is a notable characteristic of the music written during this time. Bach used the dominant seventh chord extensively, Mozart and Haydn gave the dominant ninth chord some prominence and its use became an important facet of the harmonic style of Beethoven. The harmonic resources of the dominant, as well as the secondary dominant, families were skillfully used by such composers as Brahms, Mahler, Bruckner, Franck, and Strauss. With Debussy, a contemporary of Strauss, a gradual change into the music of the modern period began. Representative composers such as Bartok, Schoenberg and his school, and Stravinsky and his following, complete the transition to the "Modern Period."* A study of their music reveals strong roots in the traditions of the past, even though their harmonic paths diverge sharply from the chromatic harmony of their immediate predecessors.

The study of certain harmonic and contrapuntal techniques will give an understanding of the ninth, eleventh, and thirteenth chords of the dominant family. The root progression, V I, together with its extended form, V⁷ I, provides the foundation for understanding the more advanced chords of this group. Whenever the 9th, 11th, or 13th degree is used above the dominant root, each is a dissonant tone which must be resolved by some motion to a tone of the tonic chord. When the dissonance is resolved by a stepwise motion there is much similarity to the usual resolution of certain non-harmonic tones. This similarity will be pointed out as each added member of the dominant family is discussed. The fact that these motions take place under specific harmonic tensions and are analyzable as harmonic movements does not detract from their effectiveness as contrapuntal dissonances.

287

A. The Dominant ninth chord.

  1. Root in bass voice (root position).

      a. positions (including the minor dominant ninth chord in the major mode as an "Altered Chord").

         In four part writing the dominant ninth chord usually consists of the root and the tritone already studied under the dominant seventh chord, and the ninth above the root, thus, of necessity, omitting the fifth of the dominant chord. As illustrated, many positions are possible, the main consideration being that the root and the ninth are not *usually* placed on adjacent degrees. The ninth usually is placed in the soprano voice but may, however, be placed in any of the upper voices. In the major mode, the 6th degree of the scale gives the dissonant ninth of the ninth chord a major quality, whereas correspondingly, in the minor mode the quality of the ninth is minor. As another extension of the principle of interchangeability of modes, the dominant minor ninth of the harmonic minor mode also often is used in the major mode. The opposite modal interchange is, however, seldom encountered.

Note: the last example is best interpreted as a non-harmonic "A" in the tenor voice (an upward accented suspension) replacing the leading tone momentarily.

      b. resolution.

         The dominant seventh part of the ninth chord—the root and the tritone—are resolved as previously learned. Both strict and free resolutions will be found useful. The basic root and tritone resolution is shown.

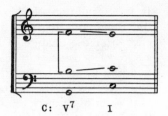

c: V^7 I

The resolution of the dominant ninth chord admits of varied treatment, including two basic "harmonic" as well as several "non-harmonic" resolutions. The problem is that of handling the dissonant 9th degree in relation to the three voiced dominant seventh resolution whose well-known habits have just been mentioned.

1) harmonic

Study the two resolutions.

c: V^9 I V^9 I

The ninth resolves a step downard in the first example and by a leap in the second but, significantly, at the same moment as when the change of harmonic rhythm occurs. This latter fact is the reason for labelling such resolutions as "harmonic" in character.

2) non-harmonic

Study the three resolutions.

c: V^9 I V^9 I V^9 2 I^6

If the resolution of the ninth downward one step to the dominant degree (the traditional resolution) occurs *after* the change of harmony, the effect is that of a 6-5 suspension, either unaccented or accented, depending upon whether the dissonant tone is tied over or reiterated at the moment of harmonic change. The first example illustrates the unaccented suspension of the dissonant 9th degree. If the ninth comes down one step before the change in harmonic rhythm takes place (as in the second example), the *effect* of an anticipation (An) is evident, even though the anticipated tone is not dissonant to the first chord. In the third instance the ninth is replaced by the substitution of another member of the dominant family of chords in one of the many possible applications of the familiar technique of dominant prolongation.

c. voicing.

The dissonant ninth may occur in any of the three upper voices in both the fundamental position and the inversions. It is important to remember that each type of voicing is not equally effective in every instance, especially when the ninth is placed in the inner voices, where its freedom of movement is more restricted. Experiment with possible chord positions and their respective resolutions in order to achieve the most musical results.

Note from the following illustrations that the interval of a ninth between the ninth and the root can occur in any pair of voices. This is an accepted corollary to the rule learned earlier regarding fundamental voicing of triad chords in which the distance between adjacent voices was limited to an octave. *e.g.*:

(1)   (2)   (3)

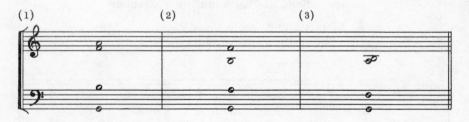

SUGGESTIONS FOR STUDY: The Dominant ninth chord, and its resolutions.

—practice spelling the dominant ninth chord of the major and harmonic minor keys.

e.g.: 1) the dominant ninth of F major is "C E B♭ D."

2) the dominant ninth of D minor is "A C♯ G B♭."

—compare the dominant ninth chord of both modes with the dominant seventh chord of both modes in parallel major/minor keys.

—practice resolving the V9 to I in B♭ major in several ways. Remember that the dominant chord can be close-knit or wide-spread in voicing; the 9th degree may occur in any of the upper three voices; and, the 9th degree can be resolved in at least five ways.

—practice resolving V9 to i in F♯ minor giving consideration to the factors enumerated under the item immediately preceding.

—note the use of the dominant ninth chord in the given illustration.

1. Today There is Ringing

F. Melius Christiansen

(St. Olaf Choir Series #63, Copyright 1956 Augsburg Publishing House, Minneapolis, Minnesota. Used by permission.)

2. Prelude, Chorale, and Fugue

Franck

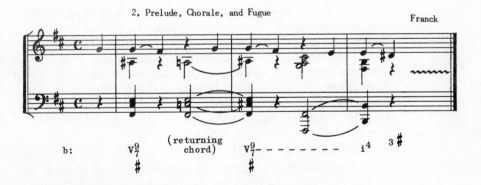

3. Prelude in A Major, Op. 28, No. 7

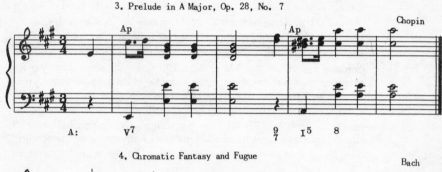

4. Chromatic Fantasy and Fugue

5. Scherzo in B♭ Minor, Opus 31

2. In first and third inversions.

Study of the inversions of the dominant ninth chord poses few new problems. The root will occur in one of the three upper voices, and, as in resolving the inversions of the dominant seventh chord, it will most frequently be held as a common tone, thus giving a complete chord of resolution. The tritone is resolved as before, and, of course, the 5th degree of the dominant chord is not used, being replaced by the dissonant 9th degree. Hence, the second inversion is not of use in four part writing.

a. positions, and numerals for identification.

Positions of the ninth chord with the leading tone, or the 7th degree in the bass are named as shown following.

Arabic numerals specify interval distances above a given bass tone. After a given set of figures is learned, it connotes a specific harmonic concept. The accidental sign used with Arabic numerals indicates the raised leading tone of the harmonic minor. Its particular form varies with the sharpness or flatness of the key concerned.

1) V7 ....first inversion of the   see examples 1-3,
   6   dominant ninth chord   above.
   5   in the major mode.

2) V7♭ ....first inversion of the   interpret examples
   6   dominant ninth chord   1-3 in harmonic
   5   in the harmonic minor minor.
                mode, assuming the
                presence of the raised
                leading tone of the
                harmonic minor in the
                bass voice.

3) V10 ....third inversion of the   see examples 4-7,
   4   dominant ninth chord   above.
   2   of the major mode.

4) V10♭ ....third inversion of the   Interpret examples
   4   dominant ninth chord   4-7 in C harmonic
   2   in the harmonic minor minor.
                mode.

  b. resolutions.

Applying the information learned under root position resolutions, determine which of the illustrated resolutions are harmonic, that is, the dissonant ninth resolves at the moment of chord change; also, which are non-harmonic, that is, the dissonant ninth resolves at other than the moment of harmonic change. Note that the root and tritone are an inverted dominant seventh chord, and that the ninth acts in each of the five ways outlined under the root position resolutions.

SUGGESTIONS FOR STUDY: The Inverted Dominant Ninth Chord, and its Resolutions.

—practice spelling the first inversion of the dominant ninth chord in the major and harmonic minor keys.

—practice resolving the V 7/6/5 chord to I in A major and to i in A harmonic minor in several ways. Remember the variety of possible voicings, the possible placement of either the root or the ninth in any of the three upper voices, and the several ways of treating the dissonant 9th degree. Evaluate the most effective resolutions; determine why they are effective.

—practice spelling the third inversion of the dominant ninth chord of each of several major and minor keys.

—practice resolving the V 10/4/2 chord to I in E♭ major and to i in E♭ minor in several ways, considering the factors which were suggested under "resolutions."

B. The Leading Tone Seventh Chord (diminished seventh chord).

The seventh chord based on the leading tone of the major and harmonic minor scales can function in several ways. One of these is to act like a member of the dominant family, that is, subservient to the influence of the dominant root, whether or not the dominant root is literally present. This reasoning is the same as that used to describe the resolution of the leading tone triad chord to the tonic chord. In this resolution the vii° either resolves to I or i, or becomes absorbed by the V chord which normally resolves to the tonic chord.

1. Spelling.

a. the diminished/minor seventh chord (*Theory Skill* #35)

The leading tone seventh chord* based on a major scale consists of a diminished triad plus the interval of a minor seventh above the leading tone. There are 15 major keys, and therefore, 15 diminished/minor leading tone seventh chords. Practice spelling these chords on Work Sheet #53.

D: vii°⁷   G: vii°⁷   C: vii°⁷   F: vii°⁷

SATISFACTORY ATTAINMENT: the correct notation of 12 diminished/minor seventh chords in a period of five minutes, given either the key signature or the key. Use whole notes and accidentals.

b. the diminished/diminished seventh chord (*Theory Skill* #36)

The leading tone seventh chord based on the harmonic minor scale is the "true" diminished seventh chord,* consisting of a diminished triad plus the interval of a diminished seventh above the leading tone. Although this diminished seventh chord originates in the harmonic minor scale, it is useful in *both* the major and minor modes. Because of the difference in parallel signatures, the diminished seventh interval is written in the major mode by lowering the 6th degree of the major scale.

e.g.: in C major the diminished/diminished seventh chord is spelled B D F A♭. Note that A♭ is the 6th degree of the C major scale, lowered a half step to form the required diminished 7th interval from B up to A♭.

In studying the diminished seventh chord, note that the keys, A♯, D♯, and G♯ are only minor, the keys C♯ F♯ B E A D G C F B♭ E♭ and A♭ are either major or minor, and that the keys D♭, G♭, and C♭ are only major. Hence, there are 18 diminished seventh chords associated with either or both the 15 major keys and the 15 minor keys.

Use Work Sheet #54.

g♯: vii°⁷   c♯: vii°⁷   f♯: vii°⁷   a♭: vii°⁷

SATISFACTORY ATTAINMENT: the correct notation of at least 12 diminished/diminished leading tone seventh chords in a period of five minutes, when given either the key and the mode, or the key signature and the mode. Alternate treble and bass clef and use whole notes and accidentals.

2. Resolutions.

    a. in the major mode.

        Study the following illustrations showing resolutions of the leading tone seventh chord to the tonic chord of the major mode. Note that the voice leading—particularly that of the tritone—is guided by the dominant root, which however, is not present. In this resolution it is usual to double the 3rd degree of the tonic chord. The two examples of the third inversion of the leading tone seventh chord are shown resolving to the second inversion of the tonic chord. No difficulty is encountered if it is remembered that the second inversion of the tonic chord usually functions like a dominant root beneath dissonant 6th and 4th degrees. The Arabic numerals used are, of course, those for seventh chords, namely, 7, 6/5, 4/3, and 2, or 4/2.

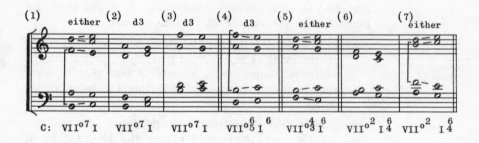

    b. in the minor mode; "Altered Chord" in major mode,

        Study the next examples showing the resolution of the diminished/diminished seventh chord to either a major or to a minor tonic chord. Note that the 1st and 5th degrees of the diminished seventh chord are the *tritone* of the dominant seventh chord and must be resolved in the same manner, that is, as a diminished fifth contracting to a major or minor third. If these two tones are inverted they become an augmented fourth and resolve by spreading out into a minor or major sixth. The 3rd and 7th degrees form *another tritone* which is resolved in a similar manner. This treatment usually results in a doubled third in the tonic chord.

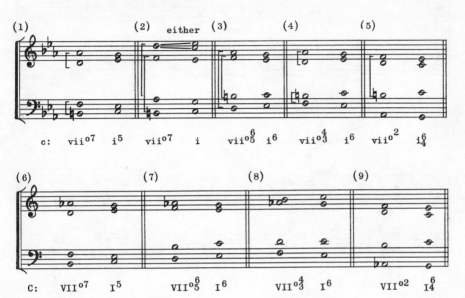

SUGGESTIONS FOR STUDY: The Leading Tone Seventh Chord and its Resolutions.

—resolve the following forms of the leading tone seventh chord of the major mode in several major keys:

—the diminished/minor seventh chord in fundamental or root position.

—the same type of chord in its first inversion.

—the same type of chord in its second inversion.

—the same type of chord in its third inversion.

—resolve the following forms of the leading tone seventh chord of the minor mode in several major and several minor keys:

—the diminished/diminished seventh chord in fundamental position to either a major or to a minor tonic chord.

—the first inversion of this chord in either mode.

—the second inversion of this chord in either mode.

—the third inversion of this chord in either mode.

—examine the illustrations from music literature which include the leading tone seventh chord of both modes. Two are secondary diminished seventh chords, that is, they belong to other than the basic key, for example, the diminished seventh of the subdominant function in the second illustration.

C. The Dominant Thirteenth Chord.

1. Positions and numerals for identification.

The Arabic numerals for the positions of the dominant thirteenth chord* are outlined. Remember that the Arabic numerals indicate interval distances above given bass tones and denote the bass tone's relation to the function indicated by the Roman numeral. By associating the Arabic combinations with the position name, one knows what to call any particular inversion of the dominant thirteenth chord.

a. V13, or V13—root position, major 7 mode

b. V13♭, or V13♭—root position,
   7   (harmonic) minor
   3   mode

interpret the illus-
tration above in C
harmonic minor.

c. V 11—first inversion, major mode
   6
   5

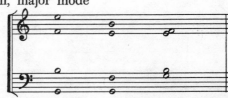

c. V 11—first inversion, major mode
   6   (harmonic) minor mode
   5

interpret the illus-
tration above in C
harmonic minor.

e. V 7—third inversion, major mode
   4
   2

f. V 7♭—third inversion,
   4♮ (harmonic) minor mode
   2

interpret the illus-
tration above in C
harmonic minor.

2. Resolutions.

   a. in root position.

   The resolutions of the dominant ninth chord differed
from those of the dominant seventh chord in one essential
way, namely, the treatment of the dissonant 9th degree.
Similarly, the only new problem in resolving the dominant
thirteenth chord is that of handling the dissonant 13th
degree. The resolutions can be grouped into harmonic
and non-harmonic categories.

1) harmonic.

 The three examples show the harmonic use of the dominant thirteenth chord. The dissonant 13th degree can resolve respectively by a leap to the 1st degree of the tonic chord, by common tone to the 3rd degree of the tonic chord, or by a leap to the 5th degree of the tonic chord. In each instance the movement coincides with the change in harmonic rhythm. The root and tritone are, of course, handled as they were under the dominant seventh and dominant ninth chord resolutions.

2) non-harmonic.

 Study the two examples. In the first the 13th degree is resolved by a downward step movement to the 5th degree of the dominant seventh chord, that is, it acts like the 5th degree one step out of place. The type of non-harmonic movement involved is designated by the symbols, R', P', S, S', or Ap', depending upon the note preceding the dissonant 13th degree. The second example uses the technique of dominant prolongation, that is, another member of this chord family replaces the thirteenth chord without changing the dominant harmony.

SUGGESTIONS FOR STUDY: The Root position dominant thirteenth chord and its resolutions.

—practice spelling the dominant thirteenth chords of the major and minor keys.

    e.g.: 1) the dominant thirteenth of F major is "C E B♭ and A."
           2) the dominant thirteenth of D minor is "A C♯ G and F."

—compare the form of the dominant seventh, ninth, and thirteenth chords of a major key with the corresponding dominant chords of a parallel minor key.

—practice resolving the V 13 to I in D major and to i in D minor in different ways, remembering the possible variety in the positions, the placement of the 13th degree in any of the three upper voices, and the possible ways of handling the dissonant 13th degree.

—examine the following excerpts which give illustration of the use of the dominant thirteenth chord in music literature.

b. the first and third inversions.

The inversions of the dominant thirteenth chord are as simple to handle as were the inversions of the dominant seventh and the dominant ninth chords. The resolutions of the dominant root and tritone are unchanged, and again, the second inversion is not available in four part writing. Further, the harmonic and non-harmonic ways of resolving the dissonant 13th degree again apply but the student should be selective and experimental in order to achieve the best musical effect in the various resolutions. Study the following examples.

1) the first inversion—V 11/6/5 to 1 or to i.

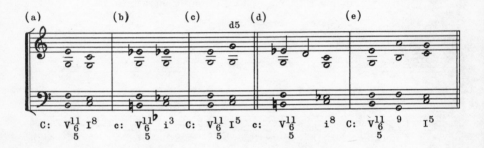

2) the third inversion—V/7/4/2 to I or to i.

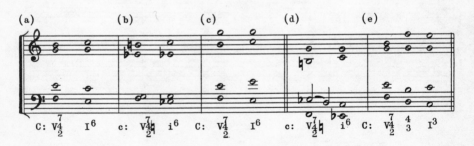

SUGGESTIONS FOR STUDY: The Inverted Dominant Thirteenth Chord and Resolutions.

—practice spelling the first inversion of the dominant thirteenth chords in the major and minor keys.

—practice resolving the V 11/6/5 to I in G major and to i in G minor in several ways remembering varied voicing, placement of the root or thirteenth in any of the three upper voices, and the several possible harmonic or non-harmonic resolutions of the dissonant 13th degree.

—practice spelling the third inversion of the dominant thirteenth chords in the major and minor keys.

—practice resolving the V 7/4/2 to I in E major and to i in E minor in several ways considering the factors suggested under the foregoing second item.

—examine the illustration from literature which shows the first inversion dominant thirteenth chord.

Sonata in C Minor, Op. 10, No. 1

Beethoven

D. The Dominant Eleventh Chord.

The dominant eleventh chord* is peculiar in nature. The 11th degree above the dominant root is the tonic note of any major or minor scale. This immediately poses a problem because the leading tone and its resolution (the tonic degree) sound simultaneously, if the root, tritone, and the "dissonant" 11th degree are accepted as the normal structure of this chord.

Actually there are a number of combinations of tones which may satisfactorily represent the dominant eleventh chord. The selection of tones in the six given forms of the dominant eleventh chord are, except for the last one, logically explained as non-harmnoic movements based upon dominant chords other than the eleventh.

(1)   (2)   (3)   (4)   (5)   (6)

Let us show how example 1 can be explained non-harmonically. In this example the C in the soprano can be called a B (or the leading tone) momentarily out of place. This suggests that the dissonant 11th degree can be approached in several different ways, each with a different non-harmonic name. Study the four illustrations of these possibilities as shown next.

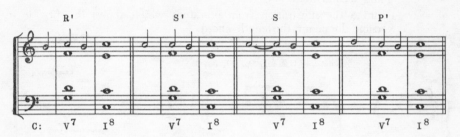

Similar and equally effective explanations based on a knowledge of non-harmonic tones may apply to the foregoing examples "2" through "5." The last example, 6, which should, by the standards used for the dominant ninth and thirteenth chords, be a satisfactory dominant eleventh chord, is least well explained by the non-harmonic technique. Attempting to explain this dissonant 11th degree as an anticipation of the tonic degree is not logical, since its duration is the same as that of the dominant root and tritone with which it is associated. This situation is not usual in traditional harmony, and is quite different from the "Corelli clash" of the Baroque period (q.v.). This harmonic form of the dominant eleventh chord is found, however, in the work of such a contemporary composer as Kodaly, whose music has a distinctly traditional orientation. The harmonic dominant eleventh chord—including root, tritone, and dissonant 11th degree—is a true harmonic form, since the 11th degree does not act non-harmonically, but rather, functions as a dissonant chord tone guided in its resolution by the dominant chord root, as illustrated. Note in particular the interesting sound of the harmonic eleventh chord on the dominant root.

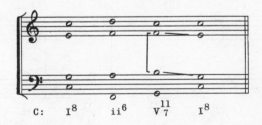

II. NON-HARMONIC TONES: the appoggiatura; the non-harmonic
diminished chord.

A. The *appoggiatura** is a non-harmonic tone which is either approached by leap and left by step or is an unprepared dissonance,
that is, sounded without a prior preparatory tone. It most
frequently and effectively occurs in its accented form, usually,
but not necessarily, in the uppermost voice. The unaccented
form of the appoggiatura is sometimes called the cambiata.
Like other non-harmonic tones it can be used in more than one
voice simultaneously, as well as in combination with other non-
harmonic tones, *e.g.*:

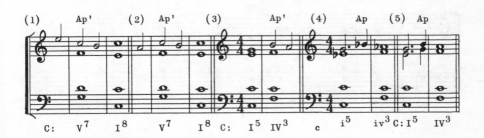

B. The *Non-harmonic* (non-dominant) *diminished chord* is a form
of diminished seventh chord which performs an embellishing
rather than a harmonic function. This chord usually can be
recognized by the common tone held between it and the following chord of resolution, always a major chord in the major
mode, and usually the tonic or the dominant. In each instance
the common tone is the 7th degree of the diminished and the
root of the principal chord acting as the chord of resolution.
Since the embellishing chord is subservient in nature, it can well
be accounted for as a group of simultaneous non-harmonic tones.
It also can be analyzed as an altered chord. The diminished
seventh chord embellishing the tonic is an altered supertonic
seventh, and that embellishing the dominant is an altered submediant seventh chord. Study the three examples, noting both
the non-harmonic as well as the more positive Roman/Arabic
analysis. It is of interest that the second chord from the end of
the Christmas hymn is *almost* an embellishing diminished seventh
chord of the tonic based on the altered supertonic (note the
effect of changing the tenor B♭ to C).

ASSIGNMENT #43: Part writing involving the use of the dominant ninth, thirteenth, and leading tone seventh chords, as well as non-harmonic tones.

This assignment is found on Work Sheet #55.

ASSIGNMENT #44: Harmonic and Non-harmonic analysis including the use of the dominant seventh, ninth, and thirteenth chords, and non-harmonic tones including the six-four dissonance.

This assignment is found on Work Sheet #56.

MUSICIANSHIP

Pitch Ear Training

1. Review: practice singing, recognizing, and hearing all the basic downward intervals (major, minor, perfect, and tritone), and various forms of the root and inverted positions of the dominant seventh chord. Use the procedures outlined in the corresponding section of Unit XII.

2. Twenty-Five Scales—common and synthetic.

    Five tetrachords representing as many common scalar sound patterns have been studied. The combination of certain pairs of these tetrachords into the eight basic scales is now familiar knowledge.

In this section the five types of tetrachords are combined
with each other in all possible pairs. All previous scales are
thus reviewed, the whole tone scale* is brought out, and 15
synthetic scales,* many of which provide interesting aural
and vocal practice, are formed. Study the chart showing these
25 scales. Practice singing, playing, and recognizing each one
by naming its constituent tetrachords.

First tetrachord	Second tetrachord	Interval separating tetrachords	Name of Scale	Remarks
M	M	whole step	—major	—basic scale.
M	m	whole step	—Mixoly-dian	—basic modal scale.
M	ph	whole step	....	—sounds like a melodic minor scale starting on its 5th degree; a synthetic scale.
M	L	half step	....	—synthetic scale.
M	hm	whole step	....	—synthetic scale.
m	M	whole step	—melodic minor, ascending	—basic scale.
m	m	whole step	—Dorian	—basic modal scale.
m	ph	whole step	—natural minor	—also known as Aeolian; a basic scale.
m	L	half step	....	—synthetic scale.
m	hm	whole step	—harmonic minor	—basic scale.
ph	M	whole step	....	—synthetic scale.
ph	m	whole step	....	—synthetic scale.
ph	ph	whole step	—Phrygian	—basic modal scale.
ph	L	half step	—Locrian	—another modal scale, not included in the four basic modal scales.
ph	hm	whole step	....	—synthetic scale.
L	M	half step	—Lydian	—basic modal scale.
L	m	half step	....	—sounds like an ascending melodic minor starting on its 4th degree; a synthetic scale.
L	ph	half step	....	—synthetic scale.
L	L	none; the two overlap	—whole	—the scale familiar as being an important factor in the style of Debussy.
L	hm	half step	....	—synthetic scale.
hm	M	whole step	....	—synthetic scale.
hm	m	whole step	....	—synthetic scale.
hm	ph	whole step	....	—sounds like a harmonic minor scale starting on its 5th degree; a synthetic scale.
hm	L	half step	....	—synthetic scale.
hm	hm	whole step	....	—synthetic scale.

3. The dominant ninth chord—major and minor modes.

In Unit XI we observed that the dominant seventh chord combines a complex of intervals based upon superimposed major and minor triads. The addition of one more major or minor third forms the dominant ninth chord of the corresponding mode.

It will be remembered that the root position ninth chord includes a root, a leading tone, a seventh, and either a major or a minor 9th degree, all intervals measured upward from the root. Or this chord can be said to consist of an incomplete dominant seventh chord (that is, without its 5th), plus a major or a minor third above its 7th degree. Or finally, the dominant ninth can be thought of as a chord pattern built upward in thirds, a major third, a minor third, another minor third, together with either a final major or minor third.

    a. practice singing and playing these and other positions of major and minor mode dominant ninth chords. Sing each chord as an upward arpeggio. Note the inversions used.

    b. practice singing and playing many pairs of major and minor ninth chords from one tone to give orientation in successive keys, to compare major and minor modes, and to contrast the several position types. Some pairs are suggested.

c. practice hearing and analyzing the various major and minor dominant 9th positions when played. Given the pitch of the bass tone, record the analysis—either in Roman/Arabic symbols or in letter-name/Arabic symbols—and notate each chord on one or two staffs as needed. Note that the Roman/Arabic symbols show chord function as well as position, whereas the letter-name/Arabic symbols show quality, but require that the user deduce the function.

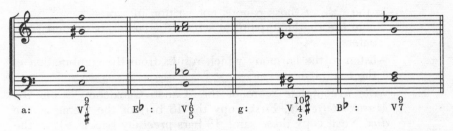

Rhythm Ear Training

In Unit XII it was suggested that the student should review and re-study any rhythmic problems from the first 12 units still requiring further understanding and performance proficiency. The satisfactory completion of this final project concludes the consideration of rhythm as a separate concept. The proficiency acquired should be of material assistance in promoting achievement in sight singing and in melodic dictation, with consequent growth in over-all musicianship.

Sight Singing: FORM EMPHASIS—canon

The simple canons* called rounds* and catches* are well known. The phrase or subject heard in the first voice, dux,* is answered at the appropriate rhythmic interval by the second voice, comes,* sounding the phrase either at the same pitch (or octave) or transposed to some other degree. Once started, the canon continues according to its "rule." If the imitation in the second voice sounds identically-sized intervals in reply, the canon is said to be "real" (see real imitation*), but if the imitation is relative rather than identical it is called "tonal" (see tonal imitation*). The pitch interval at which the second voice imitates the first voice is most often the octave, but it may be at any interval from the unison through the twelfth. Illustrations of the use of canons in serious music can be found in Bach, *Musical Offering*, and in Franck, *Symphony in D Minor*.

During the Renaissance and the Baroque periods the composition of riddle canons* was, for musicians, a favorite intellectual pastime. These canons were not written out in full. Only their theme and their "rule," the latter written in enigmatic form, were given. For this reason the solution of these canons is often difficult, and this is especially true in the case of the crab canon,* or canon canzicrans.

Study the given canons as suggested:

—in the case of those canons not written in score—

—note the rhythmic point at which the *comes,* or second voice enters.

—listen to the harmony which results from the combination of the two or more voices.

—write a complete score of the "Canon Canzicrans" from the *Musical Offering.* First, copy the 18 bars of the theme as the *dux.* Next, copy these same 18 bars precisely backwards as the *comes,* beginning, therefore, with the last note. These two voices begin at the same moment. Analyze the resulting harmonic background in the usual manner.

4. Sonata in the Form of Thirty Variations "Variation 3" Wendell Otey

a little ritard ....

(used by permission granted by the composer.)

5. The Musical Offering "Canon Canzicrans" Bach

6. Canon (with entries at successive fifths) Bach

311

7. Infinite Canon in Three Parts

Palestrina

8. Quintet for Wind Instruments, K. 516b

Mozart

Keyboard Emphasis

Evaluate these keyboard skills according to the "SUGGESTED STANDARDS" found in the Appendix.

Keyboard Skill #14—SATISFACTORY ATTAINMENT: performance of the two harmonic progressions, the first illustrating a modulating sequence of dominant ninth chords in the major mode, and the second,

a similar sequence in the harmonic form of the minor mode. Since
both are modulating sequences,* each covers all the keys in a given
mode.

Dictation

1. Pitch.

Pitch Skill #16—Hearing the Dominant Ninth Chord.

SATISFACTORY ATTAINMENT: competence in hearing the
various positions and distributions of the dominant ninth chord
in the major and minor modes. Given the pitch and the clef of the
bass voice, respond by correctly notating each of five chords
played in an arpeggiated manner. The analysis may be either the
key, mode, and Roman/Arabic numerals, or the key, mode, and

letter-name/Arabic numerals. For evaluating count each total response as a single item. Compute the PROFICIENCY PERCENTAGE.

e.g.:

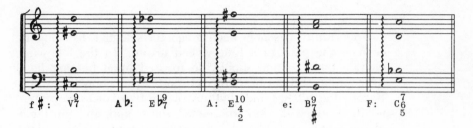

Pitch Achievement

Since the 25 scale forms studied in this unit include a number of patterns not frequently heard, listening to several of these scales can be a broadening ear training experience. In each instance note especially the pair of tetrachords used to form the given scale. The response may take either of two forms—

1) write the numbers from one through eight and diagram the location of the half steps.

   e.g.:

   <u>1 2</u> 3 <u>4 5</u> 6 7 8 (this would be the correct answer if a scale consisting of the Phrygian and Lydian tetrachords were played.)

   (or)

2) record the particular pair of tetrachords heard, without recording the half step locations. *e.g.:*

   Ph tet plus Lyd tet (the response for recognizing the foregoing scale given.)

2. Melodic.

Opportunity has now been given for selective listening to each of the parts of a four voiced texture. In the following chorale the attention should be focused upon hearing *both* the soprano and the bass voices from the polyphonic* texture. Record the pitches and rhythms of the two voices in proper notation, given the key, the meter, the tempo, and the pitch of the first tone of the two voices being copied. For evaluation count each note as either right or wrong—considering the pitch and rhythm of each note as totaling one response—and on this basis compute the PROFICIENCY PERCENTAGE by dividing the number of correct responses by the number attempted.

Christ, der du bist der helle tag

Bach

Canons, or themes used canonically in the compositions from which they are taken, provide examples for the usual type of melodic dictation.

1. Sonata in D Major, K 576 — Mozart

2. Goldberg Variations — Bach

3. Art of the Fugue "Canon No. 1" — Bach

4. Sonata in A Major (violin and piano) — Franck

5. Panis Angelicus — Franck

6. Symphony in D Minor   Franck

3. Harmonic.

   The examples of harmonic dictation include typical forms of the dominant ninth and thirteenth chords in the major and minor modes. Each progression has the characteristics of some kind of cadence, either authentic or half, perfect or imperfect, hence, conclusive or inconclusive. The response may be in Roman/Arabic numerals—each evaluated independently—or it may be in music notation together with both analytical symbols. In the latter instance evaluate the recorded notation note for note. Compute the PROFICIENCY PERCENTAGE.

UNIT 14

1. CHROMATIC MODULATION—by alteration of chords, by indirect pivot chord.

Diatonic modulation by the use of a direct pivot consisting of one or more common chords, two common tones, or one common tone was introduced in Unit XII. Let us review the concepts. The use of a *direct pivot chord* between major keys is limited to those keys whose combined signature differences do not exceed two flats or sharps. Because of the variant 6th and 7th degrees of the harmonic and melodic minor scales, the signatures of a major and a minor key, or of two minor keys, may differ by any combination of as many as five flats or sharps. *e.g.*:

G: IV   f: V♮

A pivot consisting of two tones is somewhat more flexible. An interval of a major third can be common to two keys differing by any combination of five flats or sharps (Ex. a), and a minor third to two keys differing by any combination of six flats or sharps (Ex. b)—considering both intervals in relation to all forms of the minor scale. Under similar circumstances, the single tone pivot can be related to scales as divergent as the B major (5 sharps) and the C harmonic minor (3 flats), a combined signature difference of eight flats and sharps (Ex. c).

a.   *b.*   *c.*

G: IV   f: V♮   D: ii   f: vii°   B: I   c: vii°
e: VI

Diatonic modulations provide a basic means of achieving many of the needed key changes in music. Keeping the concepts of diatonic modulation in mind, let us proceed to the consideration of a technique of modulation by means of chords which include tones foreign to one or both of the keys concerned. This technique, known as chromatic modulation,* makes it possible to bridge some key relationships other than those previously considered. It also provides numerous alternative means for writing the various diatonic modulations.

A. Chromatic Modulation.

   1. by the alteration of chords.

      Changing the interval size and relationship of any chord will give an entirely new perspective of that chord's function. A major chord becomes diminished if its root is raised a half step, minor if its 3rd degree is lowered a half step, and augmented if its 5th degree is raised a half step. This alteration may concern more than one chord tone, and may be applied to chords of any quality as well as to other chords more complex than triads. By alteration, a chord which cannot serve as a *direct* pivot between two keys can be made to take on characteristics which make it suitable for modulation. Study the following example.

Sonata in A Major, Op. 2, No. 2, "1st"

Beethoven

By the fifth measure of this excerpt from the Beethoven sonata it is clear that the key of E major—the dominant of the original key—has been reached. The development section* is about to begin. In the tenth bar Beethoven chromatically lowers G♯ to G, thus changing the quality of the E major chord to E minor. Even with the 5th degree of the chord omitted, one still hears E minor, but also easily senses the propriety of what follows, namely, the C major chord which begins the development section. Note that E and G, which were the first and third degrees of the E minor chord, act as a two common tone pivot and become the 3rd and 5th degrees of the C major chord in completing the modulation. Beethoven has effectively combined two techniques of modulation, that of chromatic alteration, and the two common tone pivot, to achieve this change from E major to C major, a signature difference of four less sharps.

In the next example from the same sonata movement, Beethoven alters one tone of a diminished seventh chord, thus changing its function as well as its allegiance.

Sonata in A Major, Op. 2, No. 2, "1st"

Beethoven

The first three bars clearly indicate the tonality of E minor. In the fourth bar D♯ is lowered to D. This causes the D♯ diminished seventh chord—strongly dominant to E minor—to become a D 6/5 chord which is equally dominant to the key of G major. Complete the analysis by giving attention to the non-harmonic tones found in the example.

The dominant seventh chord is versatile in that it can function equally well as the dominant of parallel major and minor keys. Within the context of music written in four sharps, the B dominant seventh chord should resolve to the E major tonic chord, but in the example which follows, it resolves instead to an E minor tonic chord which begins the next section of the movement. This differs from the technique of modal interchange*—often encountered—in which material already heard in one mode is immediately presented in the parallel mode. Rather, in the present instance, the contrast of the new section with the preceding one gives the impression that a modulation to the parallel minor mode has taken place. In essence, the effect is that of a major tonality's having been chromatically altered to a minor tonality.

Sonata in C Major, Op. 2, No. 3, "Adagio"

Beethoven

The chromatic alteration of two tones of the tonic chord to make it connect more smoothly with the G major chord of the next bar is illustrated in Beethoven's *Sonata in F Minor*. In this instance—as frequently happens—the chromatically altered chord takes on a dominant function. More extensive examination of the entire section from which this excerpt is taken would show that the G major chord is not a tonic chord, however, but is itself, rather, the dominant of C minor. The explanation of indirect pivot chord which follows the example concerns the use of the primary and secondary dominant seventh chords in modulation.

Sonata in F Minor, Op. 2, No. 1, "last"

Beethoven

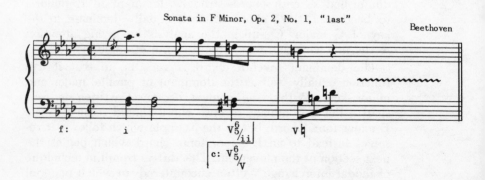

2. by the indirect pivot chord.

Major keys whose signatures differ by a total combination of three to five flats or sharps share no common chord which can be a direct pivot. There are in such instances, however, one to three common scale degrees, each of which may serve as the root of a major chord in one key, and as the root of a minor chord in the other key. Since parallel major and minor chords have a common dominant seventh chord, this dominant chord—primary or secondary as the case may be— can serve as an indirect pivot chord* for purposes of modulation. For example, the primary dominant in the key of origin could be resolved as the secondary dominant seventh chord of the subdominant in the key of destination.

Such an indirect pivot chord could be the dominant of any one of several degrees in the key of origin, and resolve as the dominant of any one of several degrees in the key of destination. Perhaps the most important use of the secondary dominant seventh chord in effecting indirect pivot modulations is that of adding the richness of their sound to modulations which technically could be done without their assistance.

a. major and minor keys whose signatures differ by three flats or sharps or some equivalent combination.

Consider, for example, the keys of A♭ major and F major:
1) the available chords of A♭ major are:

A♭ b♭ c D♭ E♭ f g°

2) the available chords of F major are:

a B♭ C d e° F g

3) there are no common chords, but there are three common scale degrees which are the roots of parallel major and minor chords. These are, B♭/b♭, C/c, and F/f. Three dominant seventh chords—F7, G7, and C7—belong to these parallel major/minor scale degrees, and each one can serve as an indirect pivot chord between the two keys, A♭ major and F major.

4) note how in the following example Beethoven applies the indirect pivot principle to accomplish a modulation from G major to B♭ major. The G7 chord in bar five is the secondary dominant of the subdominant in the key of origin, and the secondary dominant of the supertonic in the key of destination, B♭ major.

Quartet in Bb Major, Op. 18, No. 6

Beethoven

5) apply the principle illustrated in the foregoing example to make an harmonic analysis of the one which follows.

6) the modulation from C major to A major (just analyzed) could also be accomplished by using secondary
dominant seventh chords from either the B⁷ or the A⁷
families as indirect pivots. The B⁷ family is related as
the secondary dominant of E minor (the mediant or
iii in C major) and the secondary dominant of E
major (the dominant or V in A major). Similarly, the
A⁷ family is related as the secondary dominant of D
minor (the supertonic of C major) and the secondary
dominant of D major (the subdominant of A major).
The basic harmonic concept of the secondary dominant
function can be reviewed on pages 268-270.

The indirect pivotal function of each of the foregoing pivots described could be detailed in symbols as
shown.

a) in C major: B⁷ is V⁷/iii; in A major: B⁷ is V⁷/V.

b) in C major: A⁷ is V⁷/ii; in A major: A⁷ is V⁷/IV.

SUGGESTIONS FOR STUDY
—Write a modulation from the key of D major to the key
of B major, using the indirect pivotal relationship of V⁷/iii
becoming V⁷/V.
—Write a modulation from the key of F major to A♭ major,
using the indirect pivotal relationship of V⁷/IV becoming
V⁷/ii.

b. major and minor keys whose signatures differ by a total
combination of four flats or sharps.

Comparing the chord qualities found on parallel degrees of the C major and the E major scales reveals two
degrees, E and A, each of which is the root of a minor
quality chord in C major, and a major quality chord in E
major. The two dominants, B⁷ (V⁷ of E, M/m) and E⁷
(V⁷ of A, M/m), therefore are the possible indirect pivots
for bridging the four-sharp gap between these two keys.

c. major and minor keys whose signatures differ by a total
combination of five flats or sharps.

The difference of a total combination of three flats or
sharps gives rise to three indirect pivot chords, and the
difference of four yields two such possible pivots. Logically, then, a signature difference of a total combination of
five flats or sharps will permit only one indirect pivot, and
a larger key difference will allow *no* pivot chord. Given
the key of C major and one as remote as D♭ major with
five flats, the one parallel major/minor scale degree is F/f,

whose secondary dominant seventh chord (C⁷) can function as an indirect pivot between the keys.

In each of the cases discussed under item "2," the number of indirect pivot chords associated with total signature differences of three flats and sharps, four flats and sharps, or five flats and sharps would also pertain to modulations between major and minor keys, and between minor keys. The indirect pivots mentioned in this unit are based upon the natural minor scale. By experimenting, determine what further pivots are made possible through the use of the harmonic and melodic minor scales. In general it can be stated: base the pivot area upon all the resources of the minor mode when at least one minor key is involved, but base the final cadence upon the harmonic minor scale.

Study and analyze the following examples which illustrate the use of the dominant seventh chord—primary and secondary—as an indirect pivot.

(4)

e: g:

SUGGESTIONS FOR STUDY

—Make a chart showing the indirect pivot chords which have been studied in this unit. In each case reduce the pivotal function to keys and Roman numerals, which then can be compared.

—Work out in keys and Roman numerals the indirect pivot function of the G7 chord in five different modulations. The C major chord can be a tonic, mediant, subdominant, dominant, submediant, or leading tone chord in some key of the major and minor mode. Likewise the C minor chord can function in every capacity except that of the leading tone chord in some key of the major and minor modes.

—Compare the parallel chord qualities of the E major and the A natural minor scale. Note what happens when the comparison includes the chords found in the A melodic minor scale. What indirect pivots between the two distant keys are technically possible? Write a short modulation using one of these pivots.

ASSIGNMENT #45: Harmonic and Non-harmonic Analysis— including Chromatic Modulation, Diatonic Modulation, Secondary Seventh Chords, and non-harmonic tones.

This assignment, together with the necessary explanations, is found on Work Sheet #57.

II. HARMONIC CONTRAPUNTAL WRITING.

Writing simple successions of chordal harmony involves three essential steps. These are:

(1) devise a logical series of root progressions and their harmonic rhythm.

(2) make the appropriate chord connections suggested by each successive pair of roots.

(3) create interest in the horizontal melodic lines, within the limitations of the various types of chord connection.

Much of the interest in any musical composition centers about its individual voice lines, both as to how they are unified as well as to how they contrast with each other. When chords are connected strictly there is almost no latitude possible in the movement of the individual voices.

This results in what can be called "block harmony," the kind found in many folk songs and in simple hymn tune harmonizations.

Such chordal harmony—also often called note against note harmony, or simple vertical harmony—is limited both in interest and effect. However, it is logical to review certain of the concepts presented previously which serve in giving some freedom when considering particular harmonic or non-harmonic situations. These concepts are useful in the quest for more free and melodic voice lines which also will show organization in terms of unity and contrast. Restated they are:

(1) use one or more changes of chord position over a held bass tone or chord root.

  This allows for the use of a rather angular type of melodic line based on the tones of a given chord. Bugle calls are a readily understandable, though certainly not a unique, example of this technique.

(2) use one or more changes of chord position or harmony under a held melodic tone.

  This technique permits a variety of rhythmic and harmonic change to occur in the other three voices.

(3) use each type of non-harmonic tone, singly, or in combination with itself or other non-harmonic tones.

  The motion introduced by non-harmonic tones does much to impart rhythmic and melodic freedom to the voice lines. This is especially true if specific rhythm patterns are allowed to become apparent through the use of the various non-harmonic tones. The use of such rhythmic and melodic patterns, derived from the use of non-harmonic tones, leads directly into a conscious application of certain contrapuntal techniques. For instance, imitation easily can result from the use of rhythmic non-harmonic motives in a single voice, or in any part of the voice texture.

(4) use differing rhythmic non-harmonic patterns as contrasting motives. This type of contrast can arise naturally, since each non-harmonic tone tends to lend itself to somewhat different melodic patterns which can be identified as differing motives.

A step-by-step application of these principles of harmonic-contrapuntal writing is given. Since a reorientation of thinking, rather than the use of entirely new concepts is involved, it is essential to study the effect produced by each successive step.

Step 1: Select a root progression.

  The root progression, I IV V I, is selected since it is basic, solid, and effective. A harmonic rhythm of one chord change per measure of 3/4 meter is used.

Step 2: Connect these chord roots in simple chordal harmony.

This can be accomplished in closed position, open position, a combination of both, or in free, irregular connections still using only the dotted half note in each voice part. The first three illustrations are in open position, in closed to open position, and in positions resulting from using consecutive contrary motion connections. The last illustration employs a more free connection between IV and V.

Step 3: Combine change of chord position over a held harmony with the use of the first inversion chord.

Quite a noticeable degree of melodic freedom—especially in the bass line—is apparent from the application of this technique to the basic harmony progression given in step one.

Step 4: The incidental use of non-harmonic tones.

Non-harmonic tones can be used in a variety of ways. A certain non-harmonic tone can be introduced into one or more voices at those points where its incorporation is logical; or more than one non-harmonic tone can be used, singly or together, as is desired. Once a degree of competence is achieved, the

natural result is to attempt to be original. This is certainly to
be encouraged.

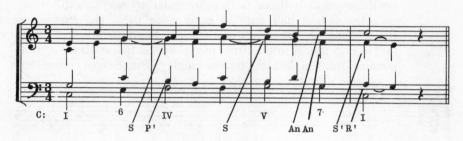

C: I   6   IV   V   7.   I
          S P'   S   An An   S'R'

Step 5: The use of motives formed by combining non-harmonic tones
with specific rhythm patterns.

By subdividing the denominator into two eighth notes, or by
the use of dotted subdivisions of the quarter note, motives with
some rhythmic vitality are developed. The number of motives
used in a short composition should be few. Often a composer
is able to develop a composition of some length from a very
small amount of musical material. As an illustration, see "Fugue
#16 in G Minor" (*Well Tempered Clavier*, Book I), in which
almost the entire composition is traceable to the motives found
in its subject. Another illustration of this economical use of
material is found in Bach's "Invention #9 in F Minor," in which
three rhythmic non-harmonic motives serve as the thematic
material.

In the following example, motive "a" (♩. ♪) is used six times,
twice without non-harmonic tones. Motive "b" (♪♪) occurs 13
times, each time in conjunction with non-harmonic tones. The
non-harmonic tones used include a number of returning tones,
suspensions, passing tones, escape tones, and one anticipation
tone. Each appears in one or the other of the two motives. Some
attempt has been made to impart a degree of interest to each
voice line. Each motive lends its own unity, and the use of the
two provides some contrast. There is a suggestion of the technique of imitation, and of course, the whole is based upon the
simple given pattern of chords, I IV V I.

This type of writing exemplifies a form of free counterpoint
developed from a harmonic background. By means of further
study this example could be refined, the use of non-harmonic
tones be made selective rather than prolific, and the imitative
process developed more thoroughly to increase the contrapuntal
interest and effect. *e.g.*:

C: I^3 8   5 IV^3 6 V^5 7   3 I^8

SUGGESTIONS FOR STUDY

Under "Sight Singing" in Unit XI, mention was made of the Bach "Two Part Inventions." In connection with them such terms as two part form, cadence rime, contrapuntal interchange or invertible counterpoint, sequence, motive, and imitation were used. Read a discussion of these terms and such others as arise in a standard musical dictionary. Then complete the following assignment.

ASSIGNMENT #46: Contrapuntal Study—the Bach Two Part Inventions and original work.

This assignment is found on Work Sheet #58.

III. SPELLING SECONDARY SEVENTH CHORDS OF THE MAJOR AND MINOR MODES.

An important characteristic of the secondary *dominant* chord is its ability to enhance any of the secondary major or minor chords found within the two modes. For example, the dominant of the mediant, preceding and resolving to the mediant chord, tends to emphasize that chord's position in any harmonic texture.

However, this emphasis is precisely what is lacking in the sound of the secondary seventh chords.* Since they are not dominant in form, their 3rd and 7th degrees—though contributing to their generally dissonant effect—are not as limited in movement as are the tritone notes of the dominant family chords. Secondary seventh chords can be built on each degree, except the dominant, of any major or minor scale, and include only the tones available in the scale used. The quality of each triad and 7th degree thus is governed by the structure of the scale type used.

The following illustrations show the exact quality of the triad and of the interval of the seventh which combine to form each of the seventh chords found on the degrees of the four scale types. Note that seven different combinations are identified.

Major Mode—the C major scale.

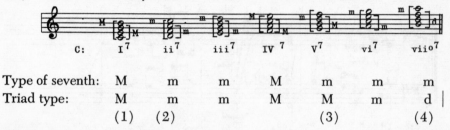

Type of seventh:	M	m	m	M	m	m	m
Triad type:	M	m	m	M	M	m	d
	(1)	(2)			(3)		(4)

Minor Mode—the C natural minor scale.

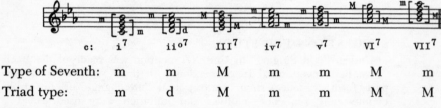

Type of Seventh:	m	m	M	m	m	M	m
Triad type:	m	d	M	m	m	M	M

Minor Mode—the C harmonic minor scale.

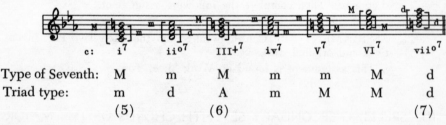

Type of Seventh:	M	m	M	m	m	M	d
Triad type:	m	d	A	m	M	M	d
	(5)		(6)				(7)

Minor Mode—the C melodic minor scale.

Type of Seventh:	M	m	M	m	m	m	m
Triad type:	m	m	A	M	M	d	d

Each of the combinations forming seventh chords has its own distinctive sound and function in a musical setting. A brief description of each type is given—(all are secondary seventh chords unless noted differently).

1) $\frac{M}{M}$—a bright, dissonant sound with the stable background of a major triad.

2) $\frac{m}{m}$—a rather dull, bland, yet pleasant sound with the stable background of a dark minor triad.

3) $\dfrac{m}{M}$ –the characteristic dominant seventh sound which can tend to over-lushness, especially with the use of many secondary dominant seventh chords. When this chord occurs as a dominant function, that is, a primary dominant (V), or a secondary dominant (V/various degrees), it is *not* a secondary seventh. When this chord occurs on the subdominant of melodic minor it is a *secondary seventh in function.*

4) $\dfrac{m}{d}$ –the tame dissonance of the minor seventh interval combined with the instability of the diminished triad. The result: a chord which can act *either* as a member of the dominant family or as a secondary seventh chord (when it is a supertonic function).

5) $\dfrac{M}{m}$ –the biting dissonance of the major seventh interval combined with the dark stability of the minor triad to form a chord color of considerable interest.

6) $\dfrac{M}{A}$ –the dissonance of the major seventh interval combined with the bright instability of the augmented triad to form a rather brilliant chord color.

7) $\dfrac{d}{d}$ –the soothing sound of the diminished seventh interval combined with the indecisiveness of the diminished triad to form a chord which functions equally well in many keys and in both modes. Its usual role is that of a member of the dominant family, either as a primary dominant or as a secondary dominant chord. Its role as a secondary seventh chord is of less importance.

SUGGESTIONS FOR STUDY

Spelling the various possible secondary seventh chords is accomplished by visualizing the degree pattern—1 3 5 7—on each degree within any scale type. Thus an understanding and knowledge of the four basic scales, the four triad qualities, and the major, minor, and diminished seventh intervals are essential.

Using each of several key tones, always including the four parallel major-minor scales:

(1) Practice spelling the secondary seventh chord found on the tonic degree.

(2) Review spelling the secondary seventh chord found on the supertonic degree. This chord was first introduced in Unit X, with emphasis upon its first inversion form.

(3) Practice spelling the secondary seventh chord found on the mediant degree.

(4) Practice spelling the secondary seventh chord found on the subdominant degree.

(5) Review spelling the m/m dominant seventh chord of the natural minor scale. Note how this chord differs both in spelling and effect from the usual dominant seventh form of chord.

(6) Practice spelling the secondary seventh chord found on the submediant degree.

(7) Review the varied forms of the leading tone seventh chord. The form of this chord found in the major scale—the m/d form, and the d/d seventh chord of the harmonic minor scale are now familiar. Note that the m/d form of the major mode is also that found in the melodic minor scale. Further note that the seventh chord found on the lowered leading tone of the natural minor scale is the m/M form found in the ordinary dominant seventh chord.

(8) Practice writing the secondary seventh chords related to the four basic scales following the format shown on Work Sheet #59.

SATISFACTORY ATTAINMENT: Spelling Secondary Seventh Chords (*Theory Skill* #37).

The ability to spell a minimum of 12 secondary seventh chords related to the four basic scale types of the major and minor modes in a five minute period, using whole notes and accidentals.

MUSICIANSHIP

Pitch Ear Training

1. Review: practice singing, recognizing, and hearing—
    a. all the downward intervals in both their basic and enharmonic forms.
    b. the 25 scales made possible by combining pairs of the five tetrachords.
    c. the various forms of the root and inverted positions of the dominant ninth chord, utilizing the procedure outlined in the corresponding section of Unit XIII.

2. The dominant thirteenth chord in the major and harmonic minor modes.

The interval structure of the dominant seventh and ninth chords is familiar. The dominant thirteenth chord adds more complexity, namely, the dissonance created by the presence of the 3rd degree of the scale (functioning as the 13th) in combination with the dominant seventh chord. Listen to and isolate the root, the leading tone, and the 7th degree of the dominant seventh chord. Then note that the presence of the 13th degree (the 3rd of the scale) adds the tension of a major 7th interval above and in relation to, the 7th degree of the dominant seventh chord in the major mode. Correspondingly, this interval becomes that of a minor seventh in the harmonic form of the minor mode.

Notice further that the minor 7th dissonance becomes an interval of the 2nd when the dissonant 13th degree occurs below the 7th degree of the dominant chord.

a. practice singing and playing the indicated (and other) positions of the dominant thirteenth chord of the major and minor modes. Note the use of inversions, and compare the sound of the major and minor mode.

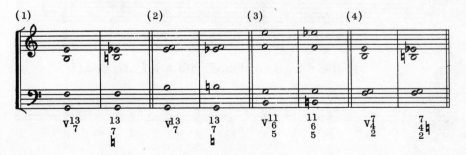

b. practice hearing and analyzing the various major and minor dominant thirteenth chord positions. Given the pitch of the bass tone, record the analysis—either Roman/Arabic symbols or in letter-name/Arabic symbols—and notate each chord on one or two staffs as needed.

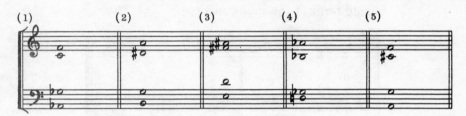

3. Secondary Seventh Chord sounds—Major and Minor Modes.
   The characteristic sound of each of the possible secondary seventh chords found in the major and minor modes should become familiar to the ear. To achieve this, each of the four triad qualities should be associated with the forms of the 7th interval as discussed earlier in this unit in connection with spelling these chords.

a. practice singing, playing, and recognizing—

   1) the M triad combined with either a m7, or a M7.

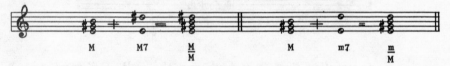

   2) the m triad combined with either a m7, or a M7.

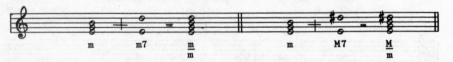

   3) the d triad combined with a m7, d7, or M7.

4) the A triad combined with either a M7, or a m7.

b. practice recognizing the nine types of root position secondary seventh chords. The response should be that of noting
the quality of the seventh in relation to that of the triad.

$$e.g.: \quad \frac{M}{M} \text{ means a } \frac{\text{major 7th}}{\text{major triad}}; \quad \frac{d}{d} \text{ means a } \frac{\text{dim'd 7th}}{\text{dim'd triad}}$$

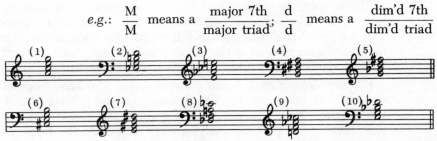

c. practice associating the sound of the secondary seventh
chords with their locations in the major and minor scales.
This association of type and location of the seventh chords
was discussed in the harmony section of this unit.

d. practice hearing, that is, properly recognizing and spelling
the nine root position secondary seventh chords, given
the pitch and clef of the lowest tone. It will be sufficient
to become proficient in hearing the closed position chords,
such as those shown under item "b."

Sight Singing: FORM EMPHASIS—Fugue

The use of fugue* as a compositional device is so widespread
and the structure of fugue so varied that it is customary to refer
to the entire fugal technique as a procedure rather than as a
specific musical form. This is true even though many fugues
exist as separate movements, usually preceded by a prelude.*

The acknowledged master of fugue is Johann Sebastian Bach.
The 48 preludes and fugues in the *Well Tempered Clavier,* the
19 canons and fugues in the *Art of the Fugue,* the many organ
fugues, and the choral fugues in the church cantatas constitute
an eloquent testimonial to his ingenious and masterly utilization
of fugal procedure.

All fugues are based on a theme called the subject,* which appears successively in three or four (less often, two or five) voices. If the same counterpoint is presented in conjunction with most entrances of the subject and answer* it is known as a countersubject.* The succession of entrances of the subject and its answer form the first exposition.* Many fugues consist of three or more expositions separated from each other by episodes* in which motives from the subject or countersubject often are given contrapuntal treatment. Such treatment includes the use of imitation, sequence, motives derived from the thematic material of the fugue, and interchange of the voices. Often the middle expositions (there may be more than one) will include inversion of the subject, its diminution,* its augmentation,* and its combination in the technique of stretto.* The fugue often closes with a coda* based on a tonic pedal point.* An example which is quite easily understood is the "Fugue in C Minor" from the first book of the *Well Tempered Clavier* (often abbreviated *WTC I*).

Practice singing each fugue example using your knowledge of rhythm, intervals, and triads to determine the correct sound. Where two, three, or four voiced texture are given, learn to sing each voice part correctly—always without help from an instrument.

1. Requiem   Verdi

2. B Minor Mass   Bach

3. "Fugue in A Minor" (WTC I)   Bach

4. Fugue in F Major

Buxtehude

2. Subject, with answer and countersubject.

"Fugue in D Minor" (WTC I)

Bach

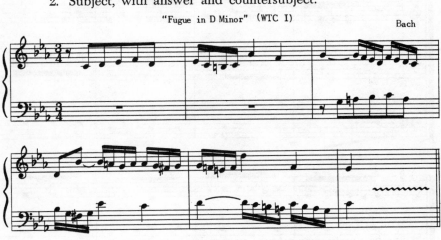

3. First exposition, four voiced vocal fugue.

3. "All Breathing Life" (Sing Ye to the Lord)

Bach

4. Subject in stretto.

(1) "Fugue in C Major" (WTC I)   Bach

(2) "Fugue in C Major" (WTC I)   Bach

5. Middle exposition of a fugue showing subject, subject inverted, stretto, and episode.

"Fugue in D Minor" (WTC I)

Bach

Keyboard Emphasis

Keyboard Skill #15—SATISFACTORY ATTAINMENT: play the following exercise illustrating the secondary seventh chords in the major and minor modes at the highest level of competence you can attain.

"Minimum" level—in any two major and any two minor keys.

"Above-average" level—in any four major and any four minor keys.

"Superior" level—in any four requested major and four requested minor keys.

(1)

(2)

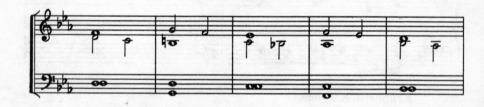

Dictation

1. Pitch.

   Pitch Skill #17—Hearing the Dominant Thirteenth Chord.

   SATISFACTORY ATTAINMENT: competence in hearing the various positions and voice distributions of the dominant thirteenth chord in the major and minor modes. Given the pitch and the clef of the bass voice, respond by correctly notating each of the five chords played in an arpeggiated manner. The analysis may be either the key, mode, and Roman/Arabic numerals or the key, mode, and the letter-name/Arabic numerals. For evaluation each

total response counts as one item. Determine the PROFICIENCY
PERCENTAGE. *e.g.*:

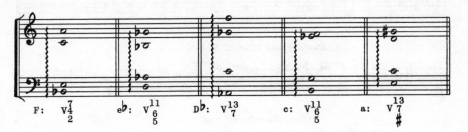

$$\text{F:}\quad \text{V}^{7}_{4\,2} \qquad \text{e}\flat\text{:}\quad \text{V}^{11}_{6\,5} \qquad \text{D}\flat\text{:}\quad \text{V}^{13}_{7} \qquad \text{c:}\quad \text{V}^{11}_{6\,5} \qquad \text{a:}\quad \text{V}^{13}_{7\,\#}$$

Pitch Achievement

Review the Pitch Skills and Pitch Achievements studied in
Units I through VI.

2. Melodic.

Each of the examples of a single melodic line dictation is
the subject of a fugue. As before, evaluate your proficiency.

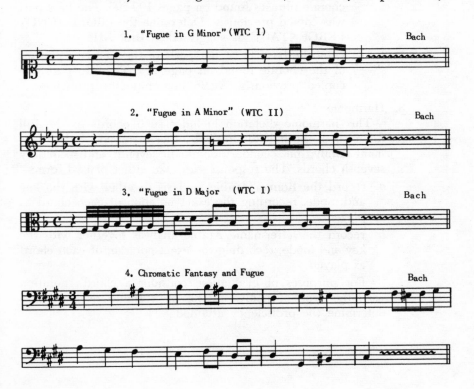

1. "Fugue in G Minor" (WTC I)   Bach

2. "Fugue in A Minor" (WTC II)   Bach

3. "Fugue in D Major (WTC I)   Bach

4. Chromatic Fantasy and Fugue   Bach

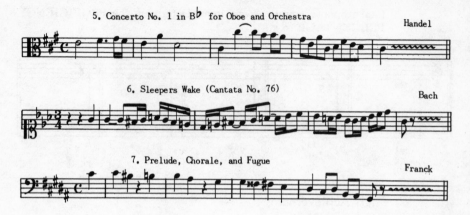

5. Concerto No. 1 in B♭ for Oboe and Orchestra

Handel

6. Sleepers Wake (Cantata No. 76)

Bach

7. Prelude, Chorale, and Fugue

Franck

To continue the practice of selective listening, copy two of the four sounding parts of a Bach chorale as suggested:

1) copy the soprano and alto parts of the first two chorale phrases found on pages 199-200. The bass part was copied previously. Determine the PROFICIENCY PERCENTAGE as suggested in Unit XIII.

2) copy the bass and tenor parts of the first two phrases of the chorale found on page 254. The alto part was copied previously. Again determine the proficiency.

3. Harmonic.

This harmonic dictation includes such chords as the full diminished, the half diminished, other members of the dominant family, the secondary dominant seventh, and secondary seventh chords. The response can take either of two forms—

a. record the Roman/Arabic analysis together with the key and mode, recording the exact notation of each chord as played.

b. record the letter-name/Arabic analysis together with the key and mode, recording the exact notation of each chord as played.

For purposes of evaluation, consider a chord's notation with the type of analysis done as a single response and determine the proficiency attained.

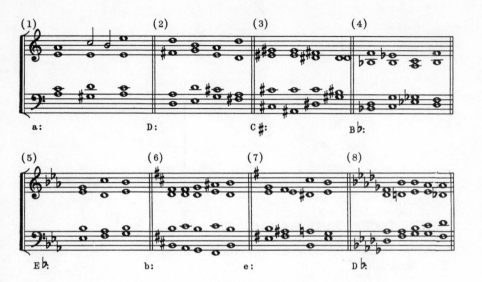

UNIT 15

HARMONY

I. SECONDARY SEVENTH CHORDS.

A. Secondary Seventh Chords—their harmonic and non-harmonic function.

Since its earliest usage in the late Renaissance and early Baroque period, the secondary seventh chord, some aspects of which have been introduced in certain earlier units, has been an important element of harmonic structure. In fact, its varied, non-dominant, yet distinctive sound continues to be found in the music of our contemporary composers.

Some uses of secondary seventh chord harmony already are familiar. The use of the supertonic seventh chord was discussed and illustrated (Unit X). Particular attention was given to its first inversion form, whose use is a stylistic characteristic in much music of the late Baroque period. The use of the leading tone seventh chord as a member of the dominant family, in both the major and minor modes, was studied (Unit XIII). In numerous instances the seventh intervals associated with secondary triad chord harmony of the major and minor modes have been explained as being non-harmonic tones. The spelling of all secondary seventh chords also has been studied (Unit XIV).

Review the section on secondary harmony found in Units IX and X. Since the material was first studied with a somewhat more limited perspective, it now should take on added significance. Also, review the resolution of the (primary) dominant seventh chord (Unit XI). This resolution can serve as a standard with which to compare the root progression and the voice leading of each secondary seventh chord. All of this review will provide further background for better understanding the function of secondary seventh harmony.

348

1. Harmonic function.

   a. Basic resolutions of secondary seventh chords.

   When a secondary seventh chord resolves in its natural manner, that is, in the same relative manner as a dominant seventh chord, it moves to a chord whose root is technically a fifth lower in the scale—what we choose to call the *natural root progression* of music. The generally accepted voice leading—"the root to the root, or the root held as a common tone if in an upper voice; the leading tone (or 3rd degree) to the root; and the seventh to the third"— also is applicable to secondary seventh chords, just as it was to the secondary dominant chords. Study each example of secondary seventh progressions in the light of this description. Note, in particular, its application to music composed during the past three hundred years. In the given resolutions interpret the Arabic symbol "7" as referring to any possible seventh chord or inversion. Analyze each quoted musical example harmonically whenever this has not been completed.

   1) the supertonic seventh chord.

   Symbols ....

Major Mode		Minor Mode		Remarks
ii⁷	V	ii°⁷	V	—The *natural root progression* as spelled in the various scale forms. The first inversion supertonic seventh chord in both modes occurs most often.
		ii°⁷	v	
		ii⁷	V	
ii⁷	I⁶	ii°⁷	i⁶	—Note the scale-wise lower voice.

(a)   Wachet Auf   Bach

ii⁷

Freuet euch, ihr Christen   Bach

f: VI

2) the submediant seventh chord.

Symbols ....

Major Mode		Minor Mode		Remarks
vi⁷	ii	VI⁷	ii°	—The *natural root progression*.
		vi°⁷	vii°	—Both progressions involving the
		vi°⁷	V⁶	diminished submediant of the melodic minor are based upon the natural tendency of a diminished triad to contract, or move together.

Nun lob', mein' seel', den Herren   Bach

ii

3) the mediant seventh chord.

Symbols ....

Major Mode		Minor Mode		Remarks
iii⁷	vi	III⁺⁷	VI	—The *natural root progression*.
		III⁷	VI	—The *natural root progression* using the natural form of the minor scale.

"Fugue in D Major" (WTC I)   Bach

iii

4) the leading tone seventh chord.

    a) as a member of the dominant family (dominant function)

    Symbols ....

Major Mode	Minor Mode	Remarks
vii$^{7\circ}$ I	vii$^{\circ 7}$ i	—This progression, in which the diminished triad contracts, is the most important one involving the use of the leading tone seventh chord. In the progression this chord functions as a member of the dominant family, since its basic resolution is motivated by the (absent) dominant root. This fact was pointed out in Unit XIII and is mentioned here for the sake of completeness.

Was mein Gott will, das   Bach

vii$^{\circ 7}$ i^3

    b) as a secondary seventh chord.

    Symbols ....

Major Mode	Minor Mode	Remarks
vii$^{\circ 7}$ iii		—This *natural root progression* occurs quite often in harmonic sequences in the major mode.

VII⁷ III —The *natural root progression*. In the minor mode the mediant and leading tone chords from the natural minor scale often are used. While they are secondary to the minor tonic as a tonality, their (quasi V⁷ I) use suggests modulation to the area of the relative major tonality. Note the inverted form of the progression in the given chorale.

Wer nur den lieben Gott   Bach

Also, see the example given under the mediant seventh chord.

5) the subdominant seventh chord.

   a) as a primary triad (characteristic function).

   Symbols ....

Major Mode	Minor Mode	Remarks
IV⁷ V	iv⁷ V	—The common function of the seventh chords, built on the sub-
	iv⁷ v	dominant degree, is to move to the dominant chord by the con-
	IV⁷ V	trasting technique of no common tones.

Gott lebet Noch   Bach

Also, see the example under the leading tone seventh chord used as a member of the dominant family.

b) as a secondary seventh chord.

Symbols ....

Major Mode	*Minor Mode*	*Remarks*
IV⁷ vii°	iv⁷ VII	—The *natural root progression.* This progression, the subdominant seventh to the leading tone chord, also is found fairly frequently, most often in harmonic sequences based on a descending circle of fifths. The circle of fifths used does not always belong entirely to the key of origin.

Ballade in G Minor, Opus 118, No. 3   Brahms

Also, see the examples under the mediant seventh chord and under the leading tone seventh chord used as a secondary seventh chord.

6) the tonic seventh chord.

Symbols ....

Major Mode		Minor Mode		Remarks
I⁷	IV	i⁷	iv	—The *natural root progression.*

Because of its position as the most important chord of a key, the tonic seventh chord of the major and minor mode can progress to almost any other chord found in a tonality by the techniques of holding either one or more common tones or using small contrary motion movements to smooth the connections. Parallel fifths which may arise from this type of harmonic connection are not nearly as objectionable in musical effect as they were in the exposed connections of the simple triad chords. The example shown illustrates the natural root progression of the tonic seventh chord's moving to the subdominant chord.

March of the Men of Harleck

Welsh Air

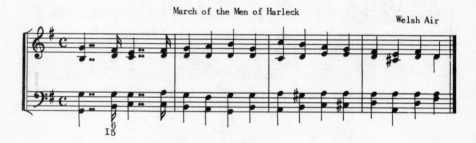

b. further suggestions regarding voice leading and resolution of secondary seventh chords.

1) whenever the movement or resolution is to a chord rooted other than a fifth lower, it may be possible to hold over one or more tones in common with the second chord. Further, one or possibly two voices may follow the natural tendency (such as the "third move up," or the "seventh move down") only to have the second chord appear in a different function from that implied by the voice movements. A clear example of this shift of function in the second chord is found in the resolution of the dominant seventh chord to the submediant chord—the familiar deceptive cadence. See three examples in the following excerpt.

Nun lob' mein' seel', den Herren

Bach

2) in the minor mode consider the natural tendency of
the raised 6th degree and leading tone to rise, as well
as the similar tendency of the lowered 6th and 7th
degrees of the natural minor scale to fall. Occasionally
these tendencies may seem to be almost contradictory,
but usually adequate harmonic and contrapuntal logic
will be available to explain any effective usage.

Singen wir aus Herten's Grund

Bach

2. Non-harmonic function.

In discussing the harmonic function of secondary seventh
chords, it was suggested that the root, 3rd, and 7th degrees of these chords frequently function in the manner of
their primary and secondary dominant counterparts. This

knowledge is of help in recognizing some of the subtlety of voice leading. Understanding the harmonic function will help to stress the importance of the non-harmonic function of these chords. Restudy the examples given under the discussion of the harmonic function of secondary seventh chords. Determine how many of the secondary seventh chords can be satisfactorily explained as being triads with non-harmonic 7th degrees.

Knowledge of harmonic rhythm, the returning tone, passing tone, escape tone, suspension, anticipation, appoggiatura, and the various forms of the six-four dissonance can be applied to the study of the non-harmonic function of secondary seventh chords. A procedure for the study of the non-harmonic functions may be as follows:

—work out the basic triadic analysis either in Roman numerals or by using the letter names of the roots of chord movements.

—account, as far as possible, for all unanalyzed tones as being non-harmonic tones, properly labelling each one whose name and non-harmonic function is obvious. Note that such analysis will frequently account for the 7th and 9th degrees of secondary chords.

—account, when logical, for a particular chord's being functional as a secondary seventh chord, that is, used in such a manner that a triadic and non-harmonic analysis seems inadequate.

II. ALTERED CHORDS.

A. The Neapolitan Chord—spelling.

From the Baroque period even to the present day, composers have been and are exploring ways to produce music displaying originality in their style of writing. One such development was the use of the Neapolitan chord,* which occurred so frequently in its first inversion that it became known as the Neapolitan Sixth Chord. The Neapolitan chord (designated by the functional symbol "N") and its positions and inversions will be indicated by Arabic numerals in the same manner as those of other chords. Apparently no firm relationship can be ascribed to its Italian name other than that of its frequent use by Italian composers, but even this characteristic is not unique.

The Neapolitan chord occurs in both modes as a major chord based on the lowered 2nd degree of the scale concerned. As explained in discussing the diminished seventh chord (Unit XIII), there are 18 major and/or minor keys, each of which has its own Neapolitan chord. Because of its frequent use, the first inversion form will be studied.

SUGGESTIONS FOR STUDY—Neapolitan chord (*Theory Skill* #38)
—the following steps are suggested for attaining proficiency in spelling the Neapolitan chord (symbolized by N, N6, N3, N5, N8, N7, etc., according to usage):
1. given the key, think its tonic degree.
2. think the lowered supertonic degree which lies a minor second above the tonic.
3. build a major chord on this lowered supertonic degree, naming its tones in 3, 5, 8 order to show an easy form of its first inversion.

—practice spelling the 18 Neapolitan chords associated with the 15 major and 15 minor keys, remembering that parallel major and minor keys share the same Neapolitan chord. Practice in writing the Neapolitan chord in it first inversion form is provided on Work Sheet #60.

SATISFACTORY ATTAINMENT: the correct spelling (in five minutes) of at least 12 Neapolitan first inversion chords in alternate treble and bass clefs using whole notes and accidentals, given either the major or minor tonic degree or the major or minor key signature.

B. The Augmented Sixth Chords—derivation and spelling.

The search for a more sonorous style of writing did not cease with the finding of the Neapolitan chord. At the same time the feeling for the authentic cadence, the full cadence, the half cadence, and especially the prominence of the dominant chord in each of these cadences, became fully established. Throughout the period of their use a principal function of the various augmented sixth chords* has been that of leading forcefully toward the dominant chord as a harmonic goal. Through the logic of their resolution to the dominant chord, the augmented sixth chords thus have been able to impart prominence to the dominant chord itself as well as to its immanent function at a cadential point.

The various chords of the augmented sixth are alike in that they include an augmented sixth interval in their structure. The approach to, and the handling of, this interval often suggest a melodic origin such as could arise from the use of two melodic lines in contrary motion. Such contrary motion is a valuable compositional technique, frequently found and used in both

harmony and counterpoint. The illustrations show the naturalness of such movement in two melodic lines.

This melodic figure can be expanded to give—

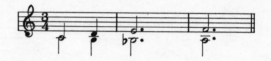

Further logical expansion will produce—

Note how easily the augmented sixth interval fits into the
melodic lines at "a" (above and below), and how logically the
octave follows at "b." After the letter "b" a cadence is logical.

In these simple steps a contrived musical phrase based on an
augmented sixth (chord) has been presented. Note how closely
this melodic pattern is exemplified in the subject of a fugue appropriately known as "The Wedge (fugue)," drawn from the
organ works of Bach.

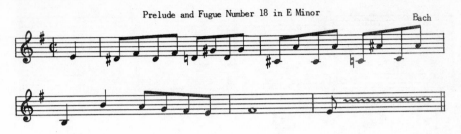

Prelude and Fugue Number 18 in E Minor

Bach

The interval of the augmented sixth, basic to the four common forms of the augmented sixth chord, is that interval whose upper and lower voices move a minor second in contrary motion to expand into a perfect octave, most often that of the dominant, as was shown in the musical phrases just presented. Therefore, the lower tone of the augmented sixth interval is a half step above the dominant degree—in harmonic minor the submediant degree, and in the major mode the lowered submediant degree.

The descriptive names usually attached to the forms of the augmented sixth chord will be used for this discussion. In the main, the augmented sixth chords sound like, but do not function like, a dominant seventh chord. This fact will prove useful in studying their application to advanced modulation in the final unit of this text. A description of the spelling of each type follows:

1. the Italian Sixth Chord (functional symbol, "It6").

The augmented sixth interval is filled in with a major third above the lower tone. This tone is always doubled in four part writing. Thus, the Italian sixth chord sounds like an incomplete dominant seventh chord without its 5th degree. *Remember*: ITALIAN–THIN–INCOMPLETE.

The Italian Sixth Chord is often referred to by theorists as the chord of the augmented sixth, or simply, the augmented *sixth* chord. The word "sixth" in the name "augmented sixth chord" refers to the chord's derivation from an altered first inversion chord. In the minor mode the Italian Sixth Chord is a first inversion subdominant chord with a raised root. In the major mode it is a first inversion subdominant chord with a lowered third and a raised root. The Roman/Arabic symbols associated with this chord in the major and minor modes are enclosed in brackets. Either of the types of symbols shown—the abbreviation, or the Roman/Arabic symbols for each mode—may be used, but both should be understood and learned.

2. the German Sixth Chord (Ge6) in the minor mode.

The augmented interval is filled in with a major third and a perfect fifth to form a complete major triad above its lower tone. The German sixth chord thus sounds like a complete dominant seventh chord. *Remember*: GERMAN–THICK–COMPLETE.

Theorists often called the German Sixth Chord the chord of the augmented six-five, or the augmented six-five chord. In the minor mode the German Sixth Chord is a first inversion subdominant seventh (minor/minor) chord with a raised root. The Roman/Arabic symbol is shown in brackets. Both types of symbols should be known.

3. The German Sixth Chord (Ge6) in the major mode.

The German sixth chord is indigenous to the minor, but it is also found in the major mode. The sound of the chord and its relation to the dominant is the same in both modes, but the spelling differs. In the major mode the German sixth chord is based on the lowered submediant degree. The interval of a perfect fifth above the lower tone of the augmented interval as found in the minor mode is usually spelled as a doubly augmented fourth interval in the major mode, since this makes better notational logic.

Walter Piston (*Harmony*) calls this form of the chord that of the doubly augmented fourth. Considered as an altered chord, the German sixth of the major mode becomes somewhat formidable, since it consists of a supertonic seventh (minor/minor) chord, whose root and 3rd degree have been raised and whose 5th degree has been lowered, each, of course, a half step! Both functional symbols given should be known and understood.

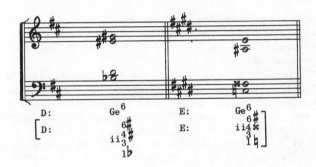

4. The French Sixth Chord (Fr6).

The augmented sixth interval (based upon the submediant in the minor mode, and upon the lowered submediant in the major mode) is in this case filled in with two major thirds, one up from its lower tone and the other down from its upper, to form the French sixth chord. This chord's sound— that of a dominant seventh chord with a lowered 5th degree— is found in the music of the Romantic period particularly, and can be characterized as being a pleasantly *different* sound.

Remember: FRENCH—EXOTIC!

Considered as an altered chord, the French sixth chord in the minor mode is a supertonic seventh (diminished/minor) chord in the second inversion with a raised 3rd degree. In the major mode this becomes a supertonic seventh (minor/minor) chord in the second inversion, with a raised 3rd and lowered 5th degree. Hence, the French sixth chord is often called that of the augmented six-four-three by theorists.

SUGGESTIONS FOR STUDY: The Augmented sixth chords (*Theory Skill* #39)

Proficiency in spelling the augmented sixth chords involves, principally, a thorough understanding of the augmented sixth interval and its relation to the dominant octave, and to the interval patterns of the four common forms.

The procedure for spelling augmented sixth chords is almost identical in both the major and minor modes. For this reason the 18 major and minor keys found on the tonic degrees between A♯ and C♭ will be used. Remember that A♯, D♯, and G♯ are only minor, and D♭, G♭, and C♭ only major keys, while the other 12 tones are the tonic degrees of keys found in both modes. There are two steps: after these are understood and can be applied, practice writing augmented sixth chords on Work Sheet #61.

Step 1. —Spell the basic augmented sixth interval.

> *a.* given the key, think a perfect octave on the dominant degree.
>
> *b.* from this octave think up a minor second from the lower tone and down a minor second from the upper tone to form the desired interval of the augmented sixth; then—

Step 2. —Select and complete spelling the desired augmented sixth chord—

> *a.* It6—add a major third above the lower tone, remembering to double it in four part writing. USABLE IN BOTH MODES.
>
> *b.* Ge6 (m)—add a major triad above the lower tone. USABLE ONLY IN THE MINOR MODE.
>
> *c.* Ge6 (M)—add a major triad above the lower tone, but remember to spell the perfect fifth interval of the triad as a doubly augmented fourth interval. USABLE ONLY IN THE MAJOR MODE.
>
> *d.* Fr6—add a major third interval up from the lower tone, and a major third down from the upper tone. USABLE IN BOTH MODES.

SATISFACTORY ATTAINMENT: the ability to spell correctly (in five minutes) at least 12 augmented sixth chords of the several types, using alternate treble and bass clefs, whole notes and accidentals, when given either the major or minor tonic degree or the major or minor key signature.

ASSIGNMENT #47: Harmonic and Non-harmonic Analysis—secondary triads, secondary seventh chords, secondary dominant chords, pivot modulation, the Neapolitan chord, and dominant prolongation.

This assignment, together with any further necessary explanations, is found on Work Sheet #62.

ASSIGNMENT #48: Harmonization—various types.

This assignment, together with any further necessary explanations, is found on Work Sheet #63.

ASSIGNMENT #49: Contrapuntal and Harmonic Analysis of Excerpts from the Motet Literature.

In Assignment #46 (Unit XIV) some attention was given to the melodic, harmonic, and non-harmonic shapes of the motives found in a Bach Invention. Such study leads directly to that of imitation, many examples of which were seen in the sight singing material of the same unit (pages 338-343). In analyzing imitation, one of the contrapuntal techniques, it is important to note two points, namely;

1) the interval distance at which one voice imitates the preceding voice, and

2) the rhythmic distance and position at which the imitation occurs.

One new contrapuntal concept—the point of imitation*—is given some illustration in the current assignment. Observe how this concept is used, and also note carefully how the succession of harmonies underlying each musical example gives it a sound and logical foundation.

This assignment and further instructions are found on Work Sheet #64.

MUSICIANSHIP

Pitch Ear Training

1. Review: practice singing, playing, hearing, and recognizing—

   a. the 25 scales based on all possible combinations of two tetrachords. The quaint sound of many of these combinations should prove to be quite interesting.

   b. the many voice distributions of the root and inverted positions of the dominant ninth chord (Unit XIII), and the dominant thirteenth chord (Unit XIV).

   c. the primary and secondary seventh chords. These are the several combinations of triads and seventh intervals which comprise the seventh chords found on each degree of the major and each form of the minor scales.

2. Altered chords.

    a. the Neapolitan chord.

        This chord has a major sound. This fact, coupled with the chord's position on the lowered second degree of the scale—most often in its first inversion—makes its recognition quite easy, especially if one understands its usual voice leading when resolving its tension.

        In the normal resolution of the supertonic function to that of the dominant, the basic formula V I (now becoming N V)— is applicable. One unique characteristic to note in the N to V resolution is that of the melodic interval of the diminished third (d3) occurring in one of the upper voices between the root of N and the leading tone of the V chord. Another is that of the cross relation between the root of the N chord and the 5th of the V chord (see D♭ and D, but in differing voices). Another that occurs quite often is that of doubling the 3rd degree of the N chord.

b. the Augmented Sixth Chords.

        The problem of distinguishing, or noting, the existence of the augmented sixth chords is primarily that of recognizing their function. Discerning the four types of these chords (three *basic* types) is a matter of recognizing the interval differences in their structure and correlating these differences with a knowledge of their usual resolutions. To achieve proficiency in this type of ear training, note carefully the unique characteristics of the resolution of each chord type.

        Remember that the resolution of the augmented sixth interval to a perfect octave on the dominant degree is a *general* characteristic of the four augmented sixth chords studied in this unit.

1) the Italian Sixth Chord.

The sound is that of an incomplete dominant seventh chord with its 3rd degree doubled and its 5th omitted. The resolution may be to the dominant chord of either mode, or to the dominant octave embellished with dissonant 6th and 4th degrees, which accordingly resolve in the usual manner.

2) the German Sixth Chord in the minor mode.

In this instance the sound is that of a complete dominant seventh chord. The usual resolution is to the tonic six-four chord of the minor mode, that is, to a dominant octave filled in with dissonant (minor) 6th and 4th degrees, which again resolve in the usual manner.

3) the German Sixth Chord in the major mode.

The sound is identical with that of the German sixth chord in the minor mode. However, the perfect fifth interval of the chord in the minor mode is now spelled as a doubly augmented fourth interval in order that the latter chord can be used conveniently in the major mode. In the resolution, note the dissonant (major) 6th and 4th degrees above the dominant root which move properly to tones of the dominant chord.

4) the French Sixth Chord.

The sound of the French sixth chord is pleasingly different from that of the other augmented sixth chords. One interpretation is that it sounds like a dominant seventh chord with a lowered 5th degree. As in the case of the Italian sixth chord, the usual resolution is to the dominant chord of either mode, or to this chord's root embellished with the dissonant 6th and 4th degrees of either mode treated in the usual manner.

Practice singing, playing, and recognizing the distinctive sound of each of the special sixth chords and its resolution. Learn the characteristics that differentiate each of them. Practice hearing these progressions. Record the analysis and the notation according to the key and the mode used.

Sight Singing: FORM EMPHASIS—the motet; anthem

In contrast to the instrumental forms studied in the last several sections on sight singing, the motet was originally a vocal composition. As a compositional form, its history covers the continuous period of five centuries between 1250 and 1750, with occasional appearances later. The motet was often transcribed for the lute, a guitar-like instrument of the Renaissance and Baroque periods. Further, the motet style of writing was used in whole or in part as the basis for many movements of the larger choral forms such as cantatas, oratorios, and operas.

Because of its extended period of use, a comprehensive description of the motet as a musical composition is difficult to formulate. Important considerations are, however, the use of a sacred text, a polyphonic and contrapuntal texture, a varying number of voice parts, and in particular, the use of points of imitation. Many motets consist of a succession of such "points," and in them several ways for using the technique of imitation can be found. Occasionally homophonic sections (see homophony) are interspersed for contrast between contrapuntal sections of the motet form. The motets of the Renaissance period are largely modal in harmony and melody, and are thus more closely related to plainsong, while those of the late Baroque period are understood in terms of present day traditional harmony, and harmonically oriented counterpoint. The motets written since the time of Bach seem to have derived much from the harmonic and contrapuntal features of his style.

The anthem* and the verse anthem* used in the liturgy* of the Episcopal Church are the English counterpart of the Latin motet. Its notable composers include Byrd, Gibbons, Purcell, and Handel.

In the study and practice of the sight singing examples, note the use of imitation between pairs of voices and the occurrence of points of imitation. Learn each voice part.

1. *Sicut Cervus*   Palestrina

Each voice flows freely within a simple scale with fairly frequent crossing of the parts. The first 13 measures contain the first point of imitation.

2. *Dona Nobis Pacem*   Byrd

Each point of imitation is canonic.

3. *Erravi Sicut Oves*   Clemens non Papa

Carefully study the free imitation used in this excerpt, and the
resulting harmony which is somewhat modal in style.

4. *Mass in B Minor*   Bach

Bach uses this movement twice in the B Minor Mass. Consult the
complete score to determine how the excerpt fits into the over-all
texture of the composition.

5. *We Praise Thee, O Father*   Gibbons

   Note the omission of bar lines in this example. Bar lines are a
relatively modern means for helping the musician organize his rhythmic thinking. Much music of the past was free in its rhythmic
organization. This freedom of rhythmic organization is also a characteristic of many present day compositions. Determine how bar
lines logically can be placed in the following excerpt, using tied
values to replace long notes whenever a bar line should be inserted.
If necessary, bar individual voices independently.

5. We Praise Thee, O Father   Gibbens

Keyboard Emphasis

Keyboard Skill #16—Two Altered Chords: the Neapolitan chord and the Italian sixth chord.

Perhaps the most important use of the Neapolitan chord and the Italian sixth chord is that of preceding the dominant chord. Often this occurs with telling effect at the point of a cadence.

SATISFACTORY ATTAINMENT: the ability to perform each of the following cadence patterns at the highest possible level.

"Minimum" level—each cadence pattern in any two major and any two minor keys.

"Above-average"—each cadence pattern in any four major and any four minor keys.

"Superior" level—each cadence pattern in any four requested major and any four requested minor keys.

Dictation

1. Melodic.

These musical phrases and sentences are drawn from the motet and anthem literature. In taking this dictation, evaluate the proficiency achieved as done previously.

2. Contrapuntal.

In the last five units attention has been given to listening to one voice of a four voiced texture. The type of selective listening demanded by such dictation can now be applied to practicing the copying of two parts simultaneously. The necessary techniques are those of recognizing and recording the scale patterns, rhythms, and intervals identified as belonging to each of the two distinct voices. Judge your proficiency.

(1) Chorale melody, *"Die goldne sonne, voll freud' und wenne"*   Bach

This dictation should be given in three four-measure phrases.

(2) *Gelobt sei Gott*   Vulpius

(3) *Then Round about the Starry Throne*   Handel

(4) *A German Requiem,* Opus 45   Brahms

(5) *Praise Jehovah* (Psalm 149)   Dvorak

3. Harmonic.

    The harmonic dictations include secondary seventh chords, the Neapolitan chord, and the Italian form of the augmented sixth chord. The response may be in either Roman/Arabic symbols, letter-name/Arabic symbols, or, either one of these with the appropriate notation. Determine the proficiency achieved.

(1)   (2)

(3)   (4)

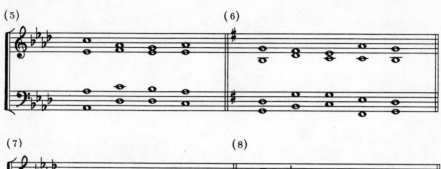

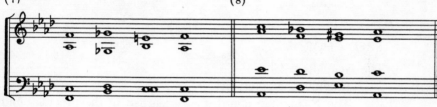

UNIT 16

HARMONY

I. ALTERED CHORDS

 A. The Neapolitan Chord.

  1. Harmonic characteristics.

   The Neapolitan chord, as we learned in the previous unit, is based on the lowered supertonic scale degree of the major and minor scales. The familiarity gained with its spelling will serve as excellent background for understanding its harmonic function. Note the characteristic quality and color of this chord in the Chopin illustration. Note also that the Neapolitan chord can be identified as the supertonic triad of the Phrygian modal scale on the parallel tonic degree.

Waltzes, Op. 34, No. 2

Chopin

 We see thus that the Neapolitan color may result from the influence of the Phrygian mode upon the major-minor system of scales. In all instances, when evaluating this influence, be aware of the contrast which exists between any major or minor scale and its associated Neapolitan supertonic chord.

For example, in the C minor scale, whose signature is three flats, the D♭ major chord, which implies a signature of five flats, is two accidentals flatter than the tonality which it colors. This contrasting tonal effect is intensified by the natural resolution of the supertonic chord to the dominant function. In this progression, the root movement from the lowered supertonic degree to the dominant degree (actual, or implied when inverted), is either the tritone interval of an augmented fourth up, or that of a diminished fifth down. Observe these Neapolitan contrasts in the minor mode in the two illustrations.

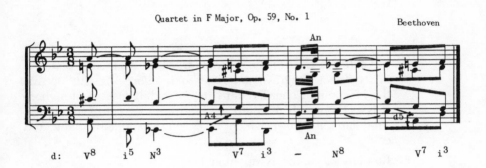

Quartet in F Major, Op. 59, No. 1   Beethoven

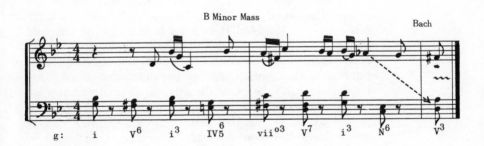

B Minor Mass   Bach

For further illustration, in a major key the color effect resulting from the use of the Neapolitan chord is still more contrasting, since it is now five accidentals flatter than the tonality with which it is associated. In the major as in the minor mode, the effect is heightened by the tritone interval of the root movement, actual or implied. Observe the Nea-

politan contrast in the major mode in the illustration from
Mozart. The Neapolitan chord is preceded by its dominant.

Clarinet Quintet in A, K. 581

Mozart

A: vii°⁷   I⁴⁻³   V/N   N⁶   V⁷   I⁸

Another aspect of the Neapolitan chord contrast is revealed
in its direct progression to the tonic chord. As this occurs,
the Neapolitan chord retains its color, but loses its function.
It is as though its own 3rd degree were the root of an altered
subdominant chord which takes on Neapolitan shape and
color.

2. Resolutions of the Neapolitan chord.

   a. to the dominant chord in either mode.

      The 3rd degree, and to some extent the root of the
Neapolitan chord, easily can be doubled, but, when the
5th degree is doubled the chord is less easy to manage.
When resolved to the dominant chord one root of the
Neapolitan chord traditionally moves a diminished third
interval to the leading tone of the dominant chord. Such
resolutions can take place directly, or, as is often the case,
one or more tones or chords (which also can be interpreted as being non-harmonic tones or chords) can be
interpolated between a given Neapolitan chord and its
significant chord of resolution. Stated in another way, the
Neapolitan chord, in moving to the dominant or to the
tonic chord, can connect with any chord which of itself
can also resolve to either the dominant or to the tonic
chord.

      Study each of the given resolutions and its analysis. In
the examples containing interpolations, either non-harmonic or chordal, note the logic of each of the analyses
offered. Each example might well be found in the minor
mode, and all but Nos. 6 and 9 in the major mode.

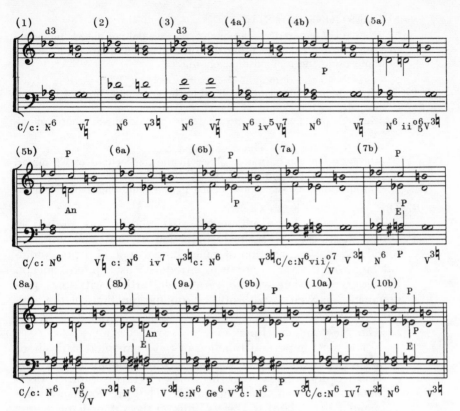

b. to the tonic chord in either mode.

Occasionally the Neapolitan chord is found resolving directly to the tonic rather than following its natural progression to the dominant chord. When this kind of resolution occurs, the Neapolitan chord relinquishes its function to the subdominant root, which is the 3rd degree of the Neapolitan chord. In the Beethoven excerpt, the Neapolitan chord is first shown resolving to the tonic, whereas, a few measures later, another form of the chord resolves to the dominant function.

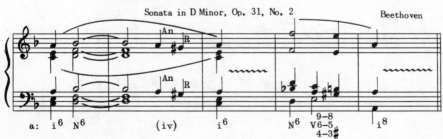

Sonata in D Minor, Op. 31, No. 2   Beethoven

SUGGESTIONS FOR STUDY

Write the suggested resolutions of the Neapolitan chord, including in each key one example using the first inversion chord, and another example using the root position chord.

—directly to the dominant chord of F major.
—through one non-harmonic chord to the dominant chord of B minor.
—directly to the dominant chord of E major.
—through one non-harmonic chord to the dominant chord of Ab major.
—directly to the tonic chord of A major.
—through one non-harmonic chord to the tonic chord of F♯ minor.
—directly to the tonic chord of C♯ minor.
—through one non-harmonic chord to the tonic chord of D major.

B. The Augmented Sixth Chords.

The spelling of the augmented sixth chords was studied in Unit XV. In the "Musicianship" section of the same unit, the sound of a basic resolution of each chordal type of a pre-dominant augmented sixth chord was introduced as a pitch concept. Now our discussion will concern itself further with the "pre-dominant," as well as with other harmonic functions of the augmented sixth chords.

1. The pre-dominant function.

The most important function of the augmented sixth chord is that of preceding, or leading to the dominant chord. This is especially noticeable in the works of Haydn, Mozart, Beethoven and their contemporaries. The pre-dominant augmented sixth chord is always built on the submediant degree of the minor mode, or the lowered submediant degree of the major mode. The augmented sixth chord sound has much in common with that of the dominant seventh chord. When a minor seventh interval functions like an enharmonic augmented sixth interval and expands into the dominant octave, the characteristic effect of the pre-dominant augmented sixth chord has been achieved. The examples illustrate the Italian, German, and French sixth chords used as pre-dominant augmented sixth chords.

Sonata in C Major, Op. 2, No. 3   Beethoven

Sonata in C Minor, Op. 13 — Beethoven

In the examples just studied, the augmented sixth chord is clearly defined. However, this same chord can be found decorated with non-harmonic motives such as the melodic movements 4-3 and 6-5. The harmonic and non-harmonic shape of the chord filling out the dominant octave depends in part upon the type of augmented sixth chord used. Usually the German sixth chord of either mode leads to a dominant octave filled in with the 6/4 dissonance to avoid the occurrence of parallel fifths between the two chords concerned. A rare contradiction of this principle, however, is found in the excerpt from Beethoven's Op. 57—the first perfect fifth being spelled as a doubly augmented fourth interval. In his Op. 2, No. 1, note how Beethoven avoids such parallel fifths in another way, that is, by resolving the augmented sixth chord to an incomplete dominant chord. The first illustration shows non-harmonic dissonance added to both the augmented sixth and dominant chords.

Sonata in D Major, Op. 10, No. 3 — Beethoven

Sonata in F Minor, Op. 57

Beethoven

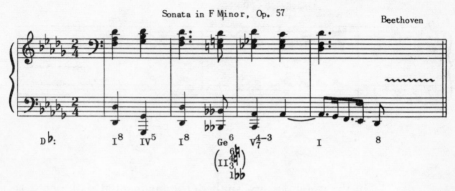

Sonata in F Minor Op. 2, No. 1

Beethoven

The pre-dominant augmented sixth chord also can be found resolving to the dominant function through one or more intermediary chords which enhance, but do not alter, the eventual effect of the resolution. Three illustrations are cited.

Sonata in C Minor, Op. 111

Beethoven

A German Requiem, Opus 45

Brahms

In this third illustration note the deceptive cadence in the third measure. In the fifth bar the use of the German augmented sixth chord following the dominant seventh chord produces, in effect, an intensified deceptive cadence, which, together with an intermediary chord, defers the final full cadence until the seventh measure.

Sonata in C Minor, Op. 10, No. 1

Beethoven

While the pre-dominant augmented sixth chords can occur anywhere within the formal structure of a musical composition, perhaps their most typical use is that of lending
emphasis to the dominant chord at or approaching the cadence points. The emphasis thus imparted to the dominant
chord—with or without modifying contrapuntal dissonances
—further strengthens the dominant chord's ability to form
an effective cadence. Although the augmented chord is most
often encountered in its fundamental position, inverted forms
do occur. In such cases the augmented sixth interval can be
replaced by its inversion, the diminished third or the diminished tenth, which in turn contracts to the unison or
octave. The first illustration shows a diminished tenth interval emphasizing a dominant octave; the other—in five vocal
parts—uses both intervals, including the diminished third contracting to a unison.

Quartet in A Minor, Opus 29

Schubert

Otello

Verdi

Occasionally the pre-dominant type of augmented sixth chord is used to lend emphasis to scale functions other than the dominant. The first of the illustrations shows a pre-subdominant augmented sixth chord which serves to introduce harmony quite foreign to the basic tonality. (What occurs just after this point is discussed under "Enharmonic Modulation" on page 397). The second illustration uses a misspelled pre-mediant augmented sixth chord to emphasize the mediant octave in a iii ii V I cadence. The third illustration shows both pre-dominant and pre-tonic augmented sixth chords used in the context of an interesting coda section.

Thirty Three Variations ..... Diabelli, Opus 120

Beethoven

Quartet in F Major, Op. 18, No. 1

Beethoven

Sonata in C Major, Op. 2, No. 3

Beethoven

2. The chromatic function.

The chromatic augmented sixth chord is seldom notated in a "theoretically" correct manner, but its general sound and use are unmistakable once they are understood. Since the function of this chord is essentially a non-harmonic one of bridging a gap, the notation is made to accord logically with the key concerned. In the three examples note how readily the sound of this chromatic progression becomes familiar. Sing the following melody.

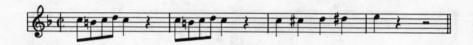

Now sing the melody a second time and play the dominant seventh chord to provide a logical harmonic foundation.

Next, note how the chromatic melody of the last two bars can be harmonized by using these same chromatic tones in

retrograde* order as the lower voice. Chords numbered 2
and 4 are the chromatic augmented sixth chords.

One typical chromatic augmented sixth chord progression
thus is used to bridge the harmonic gap between a V 6/5 and
a V⁷, or the inverse, by using chromatic lines in contrary
motion. This is not the only type of chromatic augmented
sixth chord progression found, but the study of this formula
emphasizes several characteristics. Mention of these will
conclude our discussion.

   —the progression, in its entirety, sounds like dominant har-
     mony supporting two opposing chromatic voice lines.
   —one or more of the chromatic chords may sound and
     function like an augmented sixth chord expanding into
     an octave, or continuing past an octave. (See how chord
     2 expands into the octave of chord 3, and further note
     how chord 4 moves to chord 5 in relation to chord 3 in
     the preceding example.)
   —the entire progression from chord 5 through chord 1
     can be played backwards from chord 5 down to chord 1
     in a constantly contracting manner with an effective result.

Study the next illustration, which is typical of this type
of chromatic harmonic progression. Note how the fifth chord
in the Brahms excerpt momentarily acts like an inverted
dominant seventh (E²) resolving to its first inversion tonic
chord (A⁶) before continuing chromatically to the final dominant seventh and tonic chords of the proper key, namely
F♯ minor.

Symphony No. 2 in D Major, Opus 73

Brahms

SUGGESTIONS FOR STUDY: The Augmented sixth chord.

Gain familarity with the forms of the augmented sixth chord by writing the following resolutions.

  a. The pre-dominant augmented sixth chord functions.

    1) F: It⁶ V I

    2) e: It⁶ V 6-5 i
                4-3

    3) D: Ge⁶ V 6-5 I
                4-3

    4) c♯: Ge⁶ V (incomplete) i

    5) B: Fr⁶ V 6-5 I
                4-3

    6) a flat: Fr⁶ V7 i

  b. Other "pre-" type augmented sixth chord functions.

    1) F♯: (pre-tonic) Ge⁶ I IV I

    2) E♭: (pre-mediant Ge⁶ iii V I

    3) D♭ (pre-tonic) Fr⁶ I

    4) C: (pre-subdominant) It⁶ IV V 4/3 I

  c. The chromatic augmented sixth chord function.

    1) G: fill in the harmonic gap between V 6/5 and V 7. Use the opposing chromatic voice lines in the outer voices.

    2) E: fill in the harmonic gap between V 7 and V 6/5. Use the opposing chromatic voices in contrary motion in the bass and tenor parts in four-part writing.

C. Modulation: conclusion.

Previous discussions dealt with diatonic modulation (Unit XII) and certain aspects of chromatic modulation (Unit XIV).

Diatonic modulation involving direct pivot chords was shown to be possible whenever two keys do not differ by more than two accidentals. Similarly, chromatic modulation involving the secondary dominant chord as an indirect pivot proved to be possible if two keys do not differ by more than five accidentals. Now we shall see that the possible ambiguous interpretations of the Neapolitan and the augmented sixth chords can be used to provide pivots between keys differing by as much as seven accidentals. A discussion of the use of the Neapolitan chord as a chromatic pivot chord in one key will complete our study of chromatic modulation.

1. Chromatic modulation using the Neapolitan chord.

We know that the Neapolitan chord is a major chord, either two or five accidentals flatter than the tonality (depending upon the mode) within which it is found. Being a major chord, it can function like a primary or secondary triad in a key which is sufficiently remote. Therefore, a chord which functions like a Neapolitan chord in the first key can serve as a pivot for modulation if it is made to assume a different function in the second key, or vice versa. Some type of ambiguity of function has been true of all pivot chords, direct and indirect. Since the Neapolitan chord of any key is an altered chord in that key, modulations involving this chord are therefore identified as a form of chromatic modulation.

Consider, for example, the Neapolitan chord of C major/minor, the D♭ major triad. In the major mode a D♭ major triad can be—

—the subdominant chord of A♭ major (4 flats).

—the tonic chord of D♭ major (5 flats).

—the dominant chord of G♭ major (6 flats).

—the secondary dominant of the dominant chord of C♭ major (7 flats).

By similar reasoning, a D♭ major chord can be identified with the following functions in the minor mode—

—the major submediant chord of F minor (4 flats).

—the major mediant chord of B♭ minor (5 flats).

—the major leading tone chord of E♭ minor (6 flats).

—the major subdominant chord of A♭ minor (7 flats).

The determination of pivotal possibilities is first and foremost a matter of knowing the major and minor scales, and thus being aware of precisely which chords are available in all keys of both modes. If this knowledge can become functional, one of the principal problems encountered in understanding modulation has been solved.

With the use of the Neapolitan chord and its ambiguous relationship to the simpler triadic functions of harmony, a means for achieving remote modulations can be understood. The composers of the Baroque, Classic, and Romantic eras used such modulations with or without a change of mode, the latter perhaps more frequently. These possible pivotal connections also have provided composers with interesting ways for writing the less distant modulations.

The first example shows the Neapolitan chord of the minor tonality assuming the function of a temporary major tonality of its own. This type of modulation is found quite frequently.

Quartet in F Minor, Opus 95

Beethoven

In the second example the subdominant chord of a major key assumes a Neapolitan function in relation to the minor tonality a major third higher.

Sonata in C Major, Opus 1

Brahms

The third example portrays the opposite situation in that the Neapolitan chord of the first key assumes the subdominant function of the new key. It is interesting to note that the tonic chord of this new key becomes the Neapolitan chord of the final tonality, that of E major.

Sonata in E Major, Op. 14, No. 1

Beethoven

SUGGESTIONS FOR STUDY (Chromatic Modulation).

Review the material on chromatic modulation to answer the following questions.

—What is the Neapolitan chord in the key of D major? D minor?

—What are the three major keys in which this chord can function as each of the three primary triads?

—What are the three minor keys in which this chord can function as the mediant, submediant, or leading tone chord?

—In what key is the tonic chord of C major the Neapolitan function?

—In what key is the mediant chord of E minor the Neapolitan function?

—In what key is the subdominant chord of F♯ major the Neapolitan function?

—In what key is the dominant chord of A major the Neapolitan function?

—In what key is the submediant chord of C minor the Neapolitan function?

—In what key is the leading tone chord of B minor the Neapolitan function?

2. Enharmonic Modulation.

We stated previously that it is not necessary to consider signature differences of more than seven accidentals in modulating between two keys. This is true because such differences will never exceed seven accidentals if one key is considered enharmonically.

> *e.g.*: The key of C♯ major has seven sharps, and the key of C♭ has seven flats, making an apparent total difference of *14* accidentals. However, the key of B major, which has five sharps, is enharmonic to the key of C♭. Comparing C♯ and B as major keys reveals that a difference of only two accidentals exists; hence, there must be two possible enharmonic pivot chords by which the modulation from C♯ major to C♭ major —the latter key considered enharmonic to B major— can be made.

The use of the augmented sixth chord as an enharmonic pivot introduces a new concept, whose understanding is essential to success in dealing with enharmonic modulation.* This concept is—GIVEN THE IDENTICAL, OR NEARLY IDENTICAL, SOUND OF THE AUGMENTED SIXTH AND THE DOMINANT SEVENTH CHORDS, THEIR ENHARMONIC SPELLING REVEALS THE INTENDED PIVOTAL FUNCTION. The Italian and German sixth chords sound precisely the same as, but do not function like, the dominant seventh chord. The augmented sixth interval usually expands to the dominant or other octave, whereas the *enharmonic* minor seventh interval follows the well-known tendency of dominant chords. Instances will be found in which a composer has, for other than theoretical reasons, misspelled a chord, but again an *enharmonic* interpretation will usually reveal the ambiguity that is basic to the pivotal function.

In general, it is possible for an augmented sixth chord to enharmonically become a functioning dominant seventh chord, either primary or secondary. Note in the first of the examples that the Italian sixth chord in the third measure helps to establish the A major tonality, whereas, in the seventh and eighth bars its enharmonic form becomes the dominant seventh of the temporary B♭ major key, which has a Neapolitan relationship to the original key. This example thus portrays both the Italian sixth-dominant seventh am-

biguity and the Neapolitan chord becoming the tonic chord
of a short section in the related Neapolitan tonal area.

Sonata in A Major, Op. 2., No. 2

Beethoven

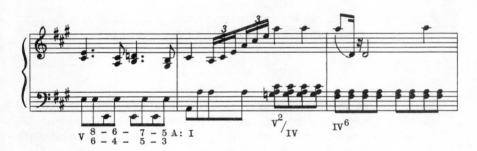

The "Allegretto" from Beethoven's Op. 14, No. 1 begins
in C major. In the second full measure the listener could assume that F major is being suggested by the C dominant
seventh sound, but its treatment as a C Italian sixth chord
soon accomplishes the modulation to the mediant key of E
minor, which is, in fact, the basic tonality of the movement.

Sonata in E Major, Op. 14, No. 1

Beethoven

In the next example the D♭ major chord pivots from a temporary tonic function to that of a somewhat obscure D♭ German sixth chord which resolves to the dominant with six-four dissonance in F major.

Fantasy in F Minor, Opus 49

Chopin

Number 15 of the Diabelli Variations of Beethoven illustrates how the G♭ Italian sixth chord in C major is introduced as a pre-subdominant augmented sixth chord, but its pivot function is that of leading into a chromatic series of chords embellishing the E♭ dominant seventh chord. The tonality of A♭ is hinted at but is never reached; it is avoided by the use of the diminished chord in bar 12. This chord in turn provides an approach to the D♭ German sixth chord, functioning as a pre-tonic augmented sixth chord in the original key of C major, which is then established by the final plagal cadence.

Thirty Three Variations ..... Diabelli, Opus 120

Beethoven

The Verdi example includes a Neapolitan sixth chord in its first measure and in its second measure a descending series of chromatic minor thirds within the C tonic minor function. The fourth bar shows a French sixth chord which expands into the dominant octave with a six-four dissonance approached by contrary motion. The augmented sixth chord returns in enharmonic German form as the third inversion of the dominant seventh of the Neapolitan chord, to which it resolves in measure five. At this point an over-all Neapolitan, dominant, tonic cadence by the first beat of the sixth bar becomes obvious, but an interesting momentary diversion occurs on the 2nd and 3rd beats of the fifth measure —two transient modulations occur based on the possible ambiguous interpretations of the Neapolitan or a major chord.

Looking ahead from the first beat of measure five, the D♭ first inversion chord must be considered as a dominant of the dominant chord to sustain analytical logic until the C♭ major chord becomes a momentary tonic. The two forte "G's" which follow clearly suggest the dominant of C major/minor to reaffirm the orginal tonality. But how can the C minor tonality follow that of C♭ major? It can do so because the Neapolitan chord in C♭ major would be D♭♭ major, which is, enharmonically, C major. Thus the two "G's" pivot backwards as the dominant of the enharmonic Neapolitan chord of C♭ major, while performing the ordinary dominant function to the C minor tonality. Perhaps there are other solutions to this problem? Study the example thoroughly.

SUGGESTIONS FOR STUDY (Enharmonic Modulation).

Review the augmented sixth-dominant seventh enharmonic relationships by completing these statements—

—the pre-dominant Italian sixth chord of E major is the enharmonic dominant seventh chord of ———————.

—the pre-dominant German sixth chord of F minor is the enharmonic dominant seventh chord of ———————.

—the pre-dominant German sixth chord of G major is the enharmonic dominant seventh chord of ———————.

—the subdominant German sixth chord of D major is the enharmonic dominant seventh chord of ———————.

—the pre-dominant German sixth chord of Ab major is the enharmonic subdominant augmented sixth chord of ———————.

—the dominant seventh chord of Gb major is the pre-dominant German sixth chord of ———————.

—the dominant seventh chord of Eb major is the pre-tonic Italian sixth chord of ———————.

ASSIGNMENT #50—Harmonic and Non-harmonic Analysis, including the Neapolitan chord, the augmented sixth chords, secondary dominant chords, primary and secondary triad chords, primary dominant, chromatic modulations, enharmonic modulation, and non-harmonic tones.

This assignment, together with further instructions, is found on Work Sheet #65.

ASSIGNMENT #51—Part-writing and Harmonization, including the augmented sixth chords.

During the Baroque period, when realizing a figured bass line was a daily practical art for the musician, it was customary to use only the Arabic numerals below the notated bass line to suggest the harmonic change and flow. Later, as the study of harmony and harmonic analysis became specialized academic pursuits, it became customary to use both the Roman and the Arabic numerals.

In this assignment the choral excerpt from Haydn's *Creation* offers a creative opportunity for realizing a figured bass. The given Roman and Arabic figures provide a harmonic analysis of the choral portion of this excerpt.

The second example is a ground bass,* which serves as an ostinato in the "Crucifixus" from Bach's *B Minor Mass*. In the original score this ostinato bass is played 13 times, and considerable variation is found in the harmony realized above it. This realization—in effect, a passacaglia*—serves as the accompaniment for the choral setting which is in an imitative contrapuntal style. No Roman numerals are used in the figured bass.

It will prove interesting and enlightening to "compete" with the masters and then compare the results achieved, since the scores are so readily available.

This assignment, together with further instructions, is found on Work Sheet #66.

MUSICIANSHIP

Pitch Ear Training

Since all necessary pitch skills have now been introduced, the emphasis in this last unit is one of reviewing the more important harmonic concepts beginning with the dominant seventh chord. Complete each analysis as it has been started. Practice singing, playing, recognizing, and hearing each example until its harmonic logic and actual sound are combined into a meaningful unit.

1. Melodic resolutions of the root position and inverted dominant seventh chord in the major and minor modes.

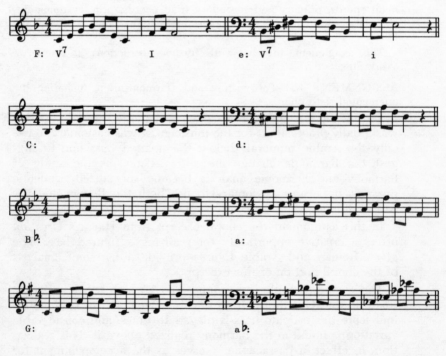

2. Melodic resolutions of the root position and inverted dominant ninth chord in the major and minor modes.

3. Melodic resolutions of the root position and inverted diminished seventh chord in the major and the minor modes. Note the use of both the half diminished and full diminished seventh chord in the major mode.

4. Melodic resolutions of the root position and inverted dominant thirteenth chord in the major and the minor modes.

5. Melodic resolutions of the Neapolitan chord in first inversion and root position in the major and minor modes.

6. Melodic resolutions of the various augmented sixth chords used in either the major, minor, or both modes, as appropriate.

7. Melodic examples of the sound of the several forms of the
   secondary seventh chords. Resolutions are not included because there are a number of possible ones.

Sight Singing: FORM EMPHASIS—the variation forms

The use of some form of repetition is one of the basic means of extending as well as unifying a musical composition. The repetition may involve motives or small segments of melody, or entire sections of a composition. In the variation forms, the basic idea repeated is either an ostinato or a melody, such as is found in many sets of piano and other instrumental variations.* Perhaps the most familiar type of variation is that in which a melody, or some skeletal form of one, is obvious as the basis of a section written in rapid notes.

The ostinato, also called "basso ostinato" or ground bass, was used as the basis for many compositions of the Baroque period. The ground bass patterns used in Purcell's opera, *Dido and Aeneas,* and the similar kind of pattern found repeated some 13 times as the ostinato of the "Crucifixus" of Bach's *Mass in B Minor,* illustrate the variety of usage the repetition of such a bass figure permits. In examining the music of these compositions, note how the melodic phrases in the upper parts are not always bound by the phrase length of the ostinato. Further, note that the former selection is quite homophonic in nature, and that the latter is decidedly contrapuntal. Each of these diversities gives to the ostinato form a type of continually contrasting effect while still being bound by the unity of the repeated bass pattern.

Compositions of these types differ from the passacaglia in that the latter usually consists of a set of variations, each of which is inspired by, and essentially coincides in length with, the initial bass theme. Instead of the bass theme, which usually is not confined to the bass voice, the relatively constant factor may be a series of chords, or chord roots. Sometimes a composition based on this type of harmonic ostinato is called a chaconne* (cf., Bach "Chaconne for Unaccompanied Violin in D Minor" in the contrapuntal dictation section following). However, another equally impressive example based on a similar compositional technique has been called a passacaglia (cf. Brahms, *Symphony No. 4 in E Minor*, "4th movement").

Despite the lack of clarity in the use of the terms passacaglia and chaconne, there is no doubt that the strong harmonic ostinato heard in both of the mentioned compositions was intended as a unifying force. This feeling is reinforced by the fact that each variation is the same length as the basic theme, notwithstanding the various devices of overlapping, which keep the continuity from lagging.

Ground bass (Two examples from Purcell)

(1)

(2)

Ostinato, Passacaglia, and Chaconne
"Crucifixus," Mass in B Minor   Bach

(3)

Passacaglia and Fugue in C Minor (Organ)

(4)   Bach

"Passacaglia," Symphony No. 4 in E Minor

(5)   Brahms

Chaconne with 60 Variations in G Major   Handel

(The bass part of the first two variations is an adaptation of the given harmony. The third variation is quoted verbatim.)

(6)

(7)

Symphonic Etudes, Opus 13

Schumann

(9) Andante M. M. [♩ = 52]

Legatissimo

Symphonic Études, Opus 13   Schumann
(Note that this variation is in canon.)

Variations on a Theme by Paganini, Opus 35   Brahms
(The theme and one variation are quoted.)

Keyboard Emphasis

Keyboard Skill #17—Altered Chords: the German sixth chord in the major and minor modes, and the French sixth chord.

In studying the German and French augmented sixth chords, we have stressed their prominent use in preceding the dominant chord in approaching a cadence. The use of the German augmented sixth chord on the subdominant of the major mode, and also the use of the French sixth chord on the lowered supertonic degree are mentioned in this unit. The following keyboard skills include examples of each of these uses.

SATISFACTORY ATTAINMENT: the ability to perform each of the following keyboard skills at the highest possible level.

"Minimum" level—each keyboard skill in any two keys, major or minor, as appropriate.

"Above-average" level—each keyboard skill in any four keys, major or minor, as appropriate.

"Superior" level—each keyboard skill in any three requested keys, major or minor, as appropriate.

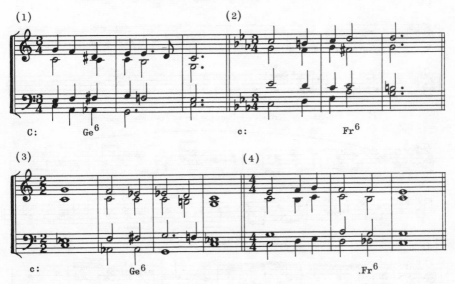

Dictation

1. Melodic

   The following examples of pitch dictation are phrases and sentences drawn from the several variation forms found in musical literature. Evaluate your proficiency in hearing these dictations.

a. ground bass and ostinato.

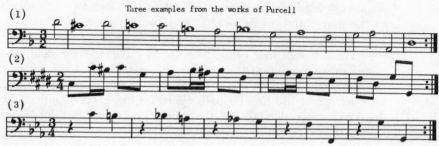

Three examples from the works of Purcell

(1)

(2)

(3)

b. theme and variations.

(1)

Variations on a Theme by Haydn, Opus 56a (orchestra)

Brahms

Andante

"Variation 3," ..... on a Theme by Haydn, Opus 56a

Brahms

(2)

Sonata in A♭ Major, Opus 26

Beethoven

(3)

2. Contrapuntal

These examples are likewise drawn from the variation literature, three being from the famous "Chaconne for Un-accompanied Violin in D Minor" by Bach. This composition is the last movement of a larger work entitled *Partita* in D Minor for Unaccompanied Violin*. Evaluate your proficiency in hearing two simultaneous voices.

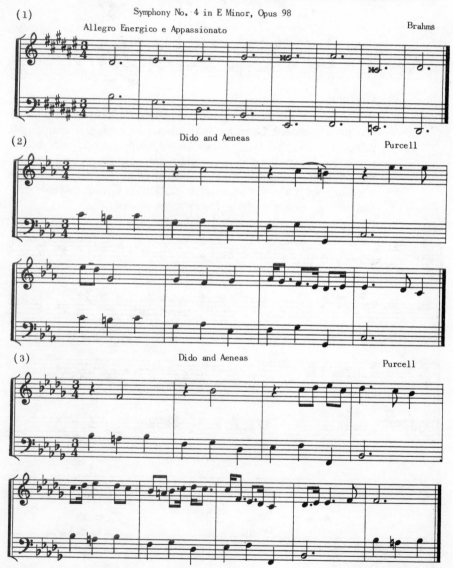

(1) Symphony No. 4 in E Minor, Opus 98 Brahms
Allegro Energico e Appassionato

(2) Dido and Aeneas Purcell

(3) Dido and Aeneas Purcell

3. Harmonic.

The exercises in harmonic dictation include examples of the pre-dominant German sixth chord in both the major and minor modes, the Neapolitan chord, and modulations based upon the Neapolitan and German sixth chords. The response may be in either Roman/Arabic symbols or such symbols together with the correct music notation. Evaluate your proficiency in hearing these harmonic concepts.

SUPPLEMENTARY UNIT I

ACOUSTICS AND MUSIC[1]

The term "acoustics"* originally was derived from certain Greek words meaning "to hear" or "pertaining to hearing." In modern terminology we have come to put the emphasis mainly on the physical aspects of sound when using the word "acoustics."

In the various sciences, acoustics is defined in its relationships to the particular science. Referring to music, we may suggest that acoustics is concerned to a large extent with the physical idea of sound, but also must be concerned with our hearing faculty—the partnership of our ear and our brain. Thus musical acoustics has its physical aspect dealing with the production of musical sounds and its psychological aspect dealing with our aural perception, including our reaction to these sounds.

Since the study of harmony, fundamentals, and musicianship gives an understanding of the association of musical sound with notation, we can consider acoustics to be an auxiliary science which contributes a certain broadness to this understanding. It forms one facet or part of the total musical picture. It is in this light that certain of the more simple acoustical concepts and principles will be introduced.

THE NATURE OF MUSICAL SOUND

Sound is produced by the vibratory motion of some physical body. Since we can hear sounds produced by objects separated in distance from us, it becomes clear that some medium for transmitting these vibrations must exist. Such a medium is air; one need only recall how the sound of an electric bell diminishes as air is exhausted from the jar in which a bell is ringing.

All sounds share four characteristics. They are duration*, amplitude*, timbre*, and pitch. It is this fourth characteristic, however, that distinguishes musical sound or tone from what we refer to as noise or non-

[1]Permission to quote freely from certain materials originally written by Dr. William Wing, Division of Fine Arts, Central College, Pella, Iowa, is hereby gratefully acknowledged.

musical sound. Tones (musical sounds) are based upon relatively simple, regular or periodic vibrations, which produce tones whose pitch can be understood and is generally pleasing to the ear. The pitch of non-musical sounds results from a complex of irregular vibrations which do not appeal to the ear in the same aesthetic manner as do musical tones. Regular vibration will result in a tone recognizable as a musical pitch if the rate of vibration falls roughly within the limits of 16 to 16,000 vibrations per second (vps).

A mental picture of a pure tone can be formed by converting the vibration of a tuning fork into an elongated tracing of its motion. This can be done by drawing a vibrating fork in a straight line across a smoked glass plate at a uniform rate of speed. The line traced is a mathematical sine wave or curve. Examined against a light it will be found to have a regular form, each crest coming at the same distance from its neighbors. It is also smooth, having no very sudden changes in its flow.

e.g.:

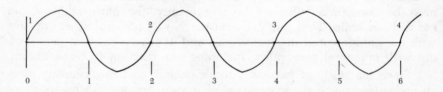

—*duration* has been converted into length of line.

—*loudness* of the tone is represented by the height of wave and the depth of the trough, or, in other words, by its amplitude. This will be obvious to anyone who has intently watched a vibrating string, tuning fork, or other object whose vibrations are clearly visible. The louder the tone, the fuzzier the vibrating object becomes and the broader its vibrations.

—*pitch* of the tone has been converted into a given number of waves per unit of measured distance; for example, one complete double vibration per each two unit measures in the foregoing example. If a higher pitched tuning fork is used, a similar tracing procedure will produce a greater number of waves per inch, since it vibrates faster. The following illustration shows twice as many waves per unit of distance, and hence represents the octave above the pitch of the tone whose wave is shown in example "1."

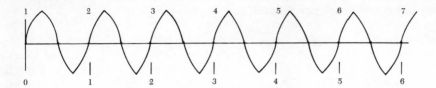

Since the octave above a given sound has twice as many waves, or vibrations, the same relationship holds with the next octave, which then has four times as many as the first octave, etc. It soon becomes apparent that these frequencies are not based on addition (arithmetical progression), but on multiplication (geometric progression). Applying this same type of reasoning, one finds that the note an octave below a given tone has a frequency*one-half that of the first, and the note two octaves below has one-fourth the frequency of the first. The wave shown following is an octave lower than the wave shown in example "1."

 e.g.:

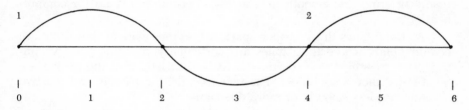

The same principle holds within each octave, but the reasoning becomes less obvious and more mathematical. Suffice it to say that in the tuning of the equal tempered scale the octave is divided into 12 half steps, each of which has the same relative sound and must therefore be based upon the same mathematical pitch ratio.

Converting a tone into visible form provides a means of understanding why it is that two notes slightly out of tune with each other seem to pulse or to produce beats* as they are sounded. This is because the waves reinforce each other at one moment and cancel each other at the next, as their crests or troughs either coincide or oppose. Study the two waves next illustrated. Note that they reinforce each other at the points marked "x," but that at the mid-point between these marks they are in almost complete opposition. The points of reinforcement will sound with the combined volume of the two tones, giving a pulse or throb at each such occurrence. The result is that if two waves differ by one vibration per second in their rates, there will be one corresponding pulse or "beat" per second.

e.g.:

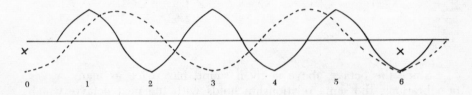

INTERVALS AND SCALES

Two notes nearly but not quite in tune, sounded together, are faintly discordant, producing clearly defined beats as their waves now enforce, now detract, from each other's power. As the pitches of the notes draw closer together, the beats are, of course, slower. As the pitches draw away from each other, the beats become more and more rapid, finally blurring into smooth tone as they become too rapid for comprehension.

As the pitches draw farther apart, it becomes evident that there are certain points where their tones are particularly pleasing. The two intervals of the third, the fourth, the fifth, the sixth, and the octave are notable for their smoothness. The two seconds, the tritone, and the two sevenths are less smooth, or more dissonant.

Much argument has arisen over the comparative dissonance* or consonance* of the 12 musical intervals. The reason is that in music, dissonance or consonance are relative matters which depend upon such diverse factors as context, melodic shape, and harmonic background, rather than on only the mathematical ratio and psychological effect of the tones of the particular interval. The mathematical ratio for each interval is helpful, however, in terms of understanding the production of different pitches by the several classes of instruments. The accompanying table gives these ratios, based upon the relations found in the harmonic series.* The occidental scales have been built on this mathematical basis.

(1) minor second 15:16
(2) major second 8:9
(3) minor third 5:6
(4) major third 4:5
(5) perfect fourth 3:4
(6) tritone 32:45
(7) perfect fifth 2:3
(8) minor sixth 5:8
(9) major sixth 3:5
(10) minor seventh 5:9
(11) major seventh 8:15
(12) perfect octave 1:2

Although the intervals as tabulated provide the best possibilities for producing pleasing melodies, it happens that they are not the best possible ratios from which to build chords in harmonic writing. In harmony it often is necessary to pass rapidly from one key to another, as well as convenient not to be limited to only a few starting keys. If one follows the scale of just intonation* (as represented in the foregoing ratios), or any other scale based on purely physical laws, the seemingly simple scale becomes a mathematical strait-jacket, which defies anything more than limited usage. The reason is simply that the steps of this pleasing, melodic scale are of relatively unequal size. For instance, the distance between the 1st and 2nd degrees of a major scale in just intonation is not in the same ratio as the distance between the 2nd and the 3rd degrees, even though both intervals are called major seconds. As long as the key preserving the original pattern of steps is used the result remains pleasing, but if a beginning is made on some other tone—hence in another key—the original pattern is no longer correct. The very inequalities which made the original scale pattern pleasing will make any other scale differing by more than one or two flats or sharps in its signature quite out of tune.

Performers on keyboard instruments therefore have gradually accepted a compromise which began having some favor in the Baroque period, during Bach's lifetime. There is now general agreement that the octave can best be divided into 12 relatively equal half steps. This means that no one of the intervals, except the perfect octave of this equal tempered scale, is as well in tune as it could be, but, on the other hand, every key is equally pleasing. Hence, with our modern equal tempered scale a performer can pass from one key to another at will, always knowing that his intervals and chords will be acceptable, even though not as beautiful as a single scale tuned in a more pure intonation.

VIBRATING STRINGS AND THE PARTIAL SERIES

A brief description has been given of the sound wave produced by the pure tone of the tuning fork. The tones produced by musical instruments are not pure, that is, single pitch sounds, but rather each one is a family of sounds. Such a family of sounds is mathematically related and physically subsidiary to the basic pitch sound being produced; in fact, it requires some aural acuteness to detect any pitch other than the basic or lowest sound being produced.

We can use the vibrating string to provide a convenient introduction to complex tones because it is a relatively simple instrument, and lends itself to demonstration. The facts regarding the pitch of strings were stated by Mersenne in the seventeenth century as:

—other factors being equal, the period of vibration is proportional to the length.

—other factors being equal, the frequency of vibration is proportional to the square root of the tension.

—other factors being equal, the period of vibration is proportional to the square root of the weight of the string.

These laws govern the primary or fundamental tone of the string. However, it becomes evident to the carefully listening ear that a vibrating string produces other tones higher in pitch than this fundamental tone. If we should reinforce these weaker tones by means of resonators*, we would discover that a string plucked at any point other than the mid-point has a long series of overtones*, each with a frequency a whole number of times greater than that of the fundamental tone.

The following illustration shows the use of "great C"* as a fundamental tone, together with its first 15 overtones. Stated in another manner, the fundamental tone and its first 15 overtones are the partial tones* numbered "1" through "16." Such a family of partial tones often is referred to as a partial series.

—partials 7 and 14 are unacceptably flat.

—partial 11 is flatter than F♯, but higher than F.

—partial 13 is flatter than A, but higher than A♭.

The eye ordinarily cannot detect the specific motion of the vibrating string producing these partials, since it is slight in comparison with that which produces the fundamental tone. These tones are produced by the vibration of the segments or parts of the string, which vibrates in halves, thirds, fourths, etc., all, of course, simultaneously. These partials give the string the characteristic timbre which makes its sound distinct in quality from those of the pure tone of the tuning fork, or the relatively pure tone of the flute.

In the tone of a particular musical instrument, some of the partials which constitute the family of pitch sounds in a given complex tone will be stronger than others, and in another instrument still other members of the partial series will predominate. The pattern of the prominence of partials in a musical sound is called its formant* and it is this formant which enables us to distinguish the timbre or sound of one instrument from that of another. It however is essential to remember that the exact percentage-wise composition of the partial prominence in a formant varies from tone to tone, from one instrument to another, and, in general, from one performer to another in other than keyboard instruments.

Violin tone, like piano tone, runs the full gamut of partials, all those possible being present up to a relatively high number. The violinist can cause the string to vibrate in such a way as to produce no fundamental tone whatsoever. This is done by lightly touching the string at a point where a node*, or point of no vibratory motion, will naturally fall. For example, this might be done one-fifth of the length of the string from the bridge, and this would cause the string to vibrate in five segments producing the fifth partial tone (or the fourth overtone) possible on the string. Such tones, called "harmonic tones" by violinists, have a high, piercing timbre.

The fact that the bow has a certain width brings about the suppression of some of the more unpleasant overtones which the string would otherwise produce. In addition the fact that the violin body brings out certain chosen overtones—making them more prominent by sympathetic response—further modifies the tones which the sounding strings produce. The tone of the violin considered as a complete instrument is thus quite different from that produced by a single vibrating string.

Piano tone, although another variety of string tone, also has its peculiar timbre. Some of the more unpleasant overtones have been carefully suppressed by making the hammers strike the wires at certain nodal points, and by using broad, soft felts. Other overtones have been made prominent by the design of the sounding board. The timbre of the piano thus is such that one does not confuse piano tone with that of other musical instruments.

In general, the remarks made regarding the violin apply to all the orchestral string instruments. The four instruments in this group are the violin, viola, violoncello, and the double bass, each of which has four strings played by a bow. The tuning pattern for each of these instruments is shown. Notice that all except the bass are tuned in ascending perfect fifth intervals from the lowest through the highest string, but that the bass is tuned similarly in perfect fourth intervals.

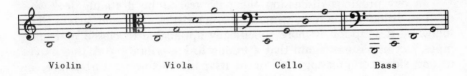

Violin   Viola   Cello   Bass

Due to the richness of their tone, individually and in ensemble, each instrument has an extensive solo repertory, and there are a large number of compositions written by the finest composers for various types of string ensembles, with or without piano accompaniment. Perhaps the most elegant of string ensembles is the string quartet, consisting of two violins, a viola, and a violoncello (or simply, cello). Almost every composer of note has lavished his best talent on compositions for this queen among ensembles.

SUGGESTIONS FOR STUDY

Consult a standard music dictionary or encyclopedia for further discussion of the subjects listed.

1. acoustics
2. intervals
3. scales
4. just intonation
5. Pythagorian intonation
6. tone
7. harmonic (or, harmonic tone)
8. partial tone
9. equal temperament
10. decibel
11. formant
12. timbre

ASSIGNMENT #52: Writing partial series.

This assignment is found on Work Sheet #67.

OPEN AND CLOSED PIPES

The various brass and woodwind instruments are based upon either the closed* or open* pipe principle. In some instances the vibrating medium is a reed, in others the lips of the performer, and in still others, the air itself. Instruments using reeds can be either open or closed pipes, as also can those in which the air itself is the medium of vibration. All of the instruments using cup mouthpieces are open pipes. It makes no difference whether a buzz is produced by vibrating lips or whether a rapidly moving current of air forms eddies or puffs as it splits about some obstacle, such as the edge of a flute mouthpiece—in each instance, the open or closed pipe acts as a resonator and transforms as well as amplifies the basic sound into a musical tone.

In our previous discussion the path traced by a tuning fork was cited to bring out certain general characteristics of sound waves. The following description is more specifically applicable to closed and open pipes. Let us assume again that a tuning fork is vibrating. A tine moves to one side, compressing the air in its path to form a turbulence, or condensation. It then moves back to the center as the turbulence moves on away from the tuning fork in all directions. Next, the tine moves to the opposite side and back to the center, creating a second condensation, which follows behind the first. This verbally describes one complete motion called a double vibration*, with two turbulences, condensations, or "crests." Successive vibrations follow each other out from the exciting medium in ever-widening concentric circles, much like the ripple that is seen in the waves spreading out from the point where a tossed stone strikes the water of a quiet pool. It is obvious to an observer that the water in a given area moves only up and down, contributing to, but quite apart from, the horizontal wave motion that is seen. Thus the motion of a sound wave results from the transfer of energy from one particle to the next, rather than from the continuous movement of the medium—usually air.

Two important facts must be kept in mind at this point. First, properly proportioned pipes, open or closed, vibrate in sympathy with, or reinforce, those sound waves whose lengths form certain ratios with the lengths of the pipes. That is, a pipe will resonate waves whose lengths are even subdivisions or multiples of the pipe's length. Second, in any given pipe, open or closed, an area of turbulence can exist only at its open end. The next statements develop these principles.

1. an open pipe can house one-half of a complete sound wave, since an area of turbulence, or a condensation, will exist at the two open ends. The lowest tone an open pipe can produce must therefore be one whose wave length is twice that of the length of the pipe.

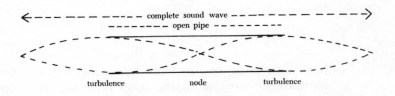

2. juggling condensations and rarifactions shows that the next smaller sound wave that fits into an open pipe is a complete double vibration. Since the pipe length has not changed, the length of this wave must be one-half of the one above, and therefore, the pitch of the new wave must sound one octave higher than that of the fundamental pitch. This tone is called the second partial, and also is correctly described as the first overtone. Further filling of the combinations of condensations and rarifactions of

sound waves would establish the fact that the open pipe
resonates to the *entire series* of partial tones generated
by the fundamental pitch compatible with its length.

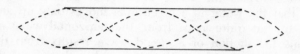

b. this principle of the open pipe applies to all brass instruments, to all reed instruments except the clarinet, and to
the open pipes of the organ, such as the "diapason."

2. a closed pipe is able to house only a quarter of a complete
sound wave in its simplest period of resonance, since the area
of turbulence must be at its open end. The length of this
wave therefore must be four times that of the length of the
closed pipe.

turbulence

It is interesting to conclude, by comparing the foregoing
illustration with that of the open pipe, that a closed pipe
produces a fundamental tone sounding one octave lower than
that produced by an open pipe of the same length. Roll a
piece of paper into a pipe about one-and-one-quarter inches
in diameter and listen to the sound produced by lightly clap-
ping on one end while, with the other hand, alternately closing and opening the other end.

a. the next smaller wave that will fit into a closed pipe is
three-quarters of a full wave. Reasoning will show that
this wave is only one-third as long as the fundamental
wave, and must, therefore, have a frequency three times
that of the fundamental. This is the third partial (second
overtone). Further investigation will bear out the fact

that only the *odd-numbered* partials can be reinforced by a *closed pipe*.

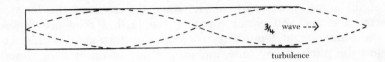

$\frac{3}{4}$ wave --->

turbulence

 b. the closed pipe principle applies to the clarinet and to the various closed pipes of the organ.

THE BRASS INSTRUMENTS

 The instruments in this category include those with three valves, namely, the cornet, trumpet, mellophone, French horn, baritone horn, and tuba, as well as the quite different slide trombone. As stated before, each of these instruments functions like an open pipe, which means that in each instrument consecutive series of partial tones are available. Actually most of the brass instruments derive their scale from the partials numbered one through eight (and somewhat higher in certain instances). The *exception* is the French horn, whose great length of tube, coupled with a small bore and mouthpiece, makes possible the use of the additional partials through number sixteen.

 The application of the open pipe principle to the brass instruments is most easily understood through the slide trombone. When the slide is closed, that is, in "first position," the following series of partials can be sounded as possible musical tones.

By extending the slide about three inches, the same series of intervals, or partials, transposed down a half step to a beginning "A" fundamental tone, can be produced. Note that lengthening the open pipe of the trombone by approximately six inches lowers the pitch of the series of tones one half step.

This process can be continued down the successive half steps through "E," whose partial series is called "seventh position." It is apparent that these seven series of partial tones cover the entire chromatic scale, with more than one slide position possible for some tones. This is true of the upper tones particularly, since the notes of the harmonic series crowd closer and closer together the farther they are removed from the fundamental tone. The trombonist is fortunate in that he can adjust the pitch of any tone, including those in the first or closed position in certain specially built instruments. He also shares with the other brass instrument performers the possibility of making some pitch adjustment through what is known as "lipping up" or "lipping down" a given tone, as the need may require.

The valved brass instruments also utilize the seven series of partial tones to form their scale. These seven series result from using the several possible valve combinations to lengthen the sounding and resonating tube appropriately.

Trombone slide positions	*Equivalent valve combination*
1st (closed)	none (open)
2nd	2nd
3rd	1st
4th	1st and 2nd (or 3rd)
5th	2nd and 3rd
6th	1st and 3rd
7th	1st, 2nd, and 3rd

THE REED INSTRUMENTS

The flute, oboe, bassoon, English horn, and saxophone are considered to be open pipes, since their acoustical behavior is founded upon this principle. The flute acts like an open pipe because a second area of turbulence is induced at the edge of the side hole across which the player blows, the other area being at the open far end of the instrument. Each of the double reed instruments, as well as the saxophone, acts like an open pipe because of the conical bore, which tends to emphasize the production of consecutive partials. Further, each of these instruments repeats, or overblows at the octave, the second partial.

On each instrument a series of holes and keys which can be manipulated by the fingers of the performer enable him, in effect, to shorten or lengthen the resonating tube length at will. Thus, all the semi-tones in the lower octave, that is, those which do not repeat the fingering of a tone an octave lower, are fundamental tones. Since the fingerings of the second octave repeat those of the tones an octave lower, these, in general, are second partials. Above the second octave cross-fingerings are used. These are in reality higher partials, whose basic fingering is altered (often quite considerably) for the better intonation of each individual tone.

The lone representative in the class of closed pipes is the clarinet, which uses a single reed like the saxophone. As was true in the case of the flute, the clarinetist also can change the effective length of his instrument by the appropriate use of keys and holes. Since his instrument, being a closed pipe, overblows at the twelfth instead of the octave, several additional keys are needed to bridge this extra tonal gap with chromatic steps. These are the so-called "throat tones" of the clarinet, and often they tend to sound somewhat weak. Part of the technique of this instrument consists in striving for clarity and strength in these throat tones. All the tones above the "break," from middle line "B" to "C" two lines above the staff, are third partials of the corresponding fundamental tones. Above these there lies an additional octave of high tones, each of which can be shown to be a cross-fingered variant of certain fifth, seventh, and ninth partials above the underlying fundamental tones.

HEARING OF MUSICAL SOUND

Although extremely sensitive to changes in atmospheric pressure, the ear is a mechanical instrument with measurable limitations, both as to dynamic level and pitch. The ear cannot detect sounds of extreme softness, indeed, it presents a definite threshold of mechanical inertia, below which all sounds pass unheard. At the other extreme, the ear is unable to withstand extremely loud sounds, and its tympanic membrane even can be broken by them. The ear is not particularly sensitive in its perception of changes in dynamics. A tone must be increased by about 25 per cent of its original volume in order to present a perceptible change to the ear. One rather unexpected consequence of the comparative insensitiveness of the ear to changes in volume is brought out by the following scale of relative sound intensities:

1	unit of energy gives a sound intensity of 0 decibels*
2	units of energy give a sound intensity of 3 decibels
4	units of energy give a sound intensity of 6 decibels
8	units of energy give a sound intensity of 9 decibels
10	units of energy give a sound intensity of 10 decibels
100	units of energy give a sound intensity of 20 decibels
1000	units of energy give a sound intensity of 30 decibels

This would mean, for instance, that a chorus of one hundred singers *actually sound* only twice as loud as a group of ten singers! Possibly the eye assists in creating the illusion that the sound seems to be of greater volume than is really the case.

When two tones are sounded together, other tones are produced by their interaction. It appears that the original sound waves blend or fuse together in forming two other distinct wave patterns, one the sum and the other the difference between the original waves, but the process does not stop here. The new tones further combine with the original waves, forming over-all a series of "difference"* and "summation"* tones. All the new tones are at successively lower dynamic levels than the original sounds, but often can be heard. For example, if two clarinets play, respectively, the concert pitches $d^{|2}$ and f^2 (fourth and fifth lines of treble clef), the difference tone, concert B♭, pitched two octaves and a third lower will be clearly audible. One may conclude that ensemble intonation will suffer if the variance of pitch on the given tone is great, not only because of the discepancy between the original pitches, but also because of the blurring caused by the out-of-tune summation and difference tones.

One of the unbelievable tricks that our ears play on us is the combining of the upper partials or overtones of a musical note into a semblance of the fundamental pitch of the implied harmonic series, even when many of the lower partials are removed. Manufacturers of radios and phonographs take advantage of this principle by giving us loud speakers which are physically incapable of producing the low tones of the larger musical instruments. The speaker faithfully reproduces several of the important partials which our ear then obligingly re-combines into a satisfactory sounding bass tone. The mechanism of the inner ear is not fully understood, but it can be likened to an imaginary harp with thousands of strings, each capable of vibrating in sympathy with one frequency, and passing on to its own nerve a report of that frequency.

ACOUSTICAL CHARACTERISTICS OF THE CONCERT HALL

Although the ear is more sensitive to treble sounds than to bass sounds, the average concert hall favors bass sounds so much that they are likely to predominate. In part, this is because the long waves of the bass sounds are able to travel around obstacles better than can the short waves of treble sounds, which are often scattered by reflection. In addition, the building materials frequently used in concert rooms have a greater coefficient of absorption for high than for low sounds.

This last point is particularly important because of the way in which a sound wave travels in a closed space. It travels straight to the hearer's ear, of course, but also to the walls and ceiling from which it is in turn reflected to the ear—some sounds being reflected many times before finally arriving at the ear. If a tone is half absorbed each time it bounces from a surface, it is obvious that it will quickly be reduced below the threshold of audibility by soft sound-absorbing surfaces. An open window (or open space out-of-doors) is the most perfect sound absorber. However, an audience, porous building materials, cloth, carpets, and drapes all absorb a large percentage of a sound's energy. An unpainted room absorbs much more sound than does one that has been painted.

The ear seems to desire a certain amount of reverberation in a room, more for hearing music than for speech, and more in a large room than in a small one. In a concert hall, sound may reverberate for about two or a fraction more seconds without causing unpleasant blurring. This amount of reverberation is necessary in a hall of any size if the musical tone is not to seem cold and small. For good speech the sound should not reverberate more than a second or so in the average sized hall. A room of given size will react best when a certain optimum number of performers is used for such ensemble groups as a band, chorus, or orchestra.

SUGGESTIONS FOR STUDY

Read further information regarding the listed subjects in an appropriate standard reference.

1. architectural acoustics	7. difference tone	13. the physical ear
2. baritone horn	8. English horn	14. saxophone
3. bassoon	9. flute	15. summation tone
4. clarinet	10. French horn	16. trumpet
5. closed pipe	11. oboe	17. tuba
6. cornet	12. open pipe	

ASSIGNMENT #53: Acoustics and instruments.

This assignment is found on Work Sheet #68.

SUPPLEMENTARY UNIT II

VOCAL AND INSTRUMENTAL TRANSPOSITION

The teacher of instrumental music often is confronted with the task of providing playable, correctly written parts for instruments of small or large ensembles. Occasionally, the singer finds it necessary to change the key of a vocal composition to a level more suitable for the voice. In both cases the problem is that of understanding transposition. The basic principles of transposition were discussed in Unit II in connection with making practical applications of the knowledge of scales. It is suggested that these principles be reviewed.

The material presented in this supplementary unit will concern only the matter of learning the correct pitch and clef transposition for each voice and for a number of instruments. The usual pitch range of each voice and instrument, its basic key, and its needed interval of transposition, if any, should become familiar knowledge. Such understanding is essential for the study of vocal arranging, instrumentation, and orchestration.

A. Vocal transposition.

    1. Usual range.

    2. Voices and clefs.

        The soprano and alto voices sing parts written in the treble clef, and the bass voice sings those in the bass clef, all at concert pitch. All voice parts are written in the given concert key.

        The tenor voice usually sings from the treble clef (a), sounding an octave lower than the indicated notation. To indicate this usage, it is common in musicological publications to subpend an "8" to the treble clef sign, as shown following (b). Sometimes a C clef sign is placed on the third space (c) to indicate the tenor's middle C. On still other occasions the tenor part is written in the bass clef (d), in which case the notation is at concert pitch.

3. Simple scoring for mixed voices—S A T B.

Notice how easily the given examples can be written in open score* for mixed voices. (See "a" and "b" following.)

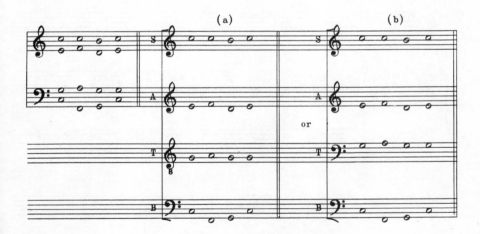

4. Simple scoring for male quartet.

The illustration in open score shows how the four given chords are scored for the standard male quartet— T1 T2 B1 B2.

5. Transposition of vocal solo and accompaniment.

The following illustration shows the first measures of "Still as the Night" by Bohm, transposed from E♭ major to D♭ major. Note that such a transposition lowers the needed range of the vocal soloist a whole step. Further note that the harmonic and non-harmonic analysis is and must be identical in the two keys.

6. Vocal music in the less used clefs.

Occasionally music written in the soprano, alto, and tenor clefs is encountered. Note the transposition from the open clef score to the modern SATB score and to the equivalent keyboard score. Each clef is sung in the concert key and at concert pitch.

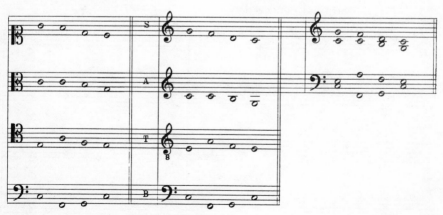

B. Instrumental Transposition—introduction to basic principles.

    1. Orchestral string instruments.

        Parts for these instruments are written in the concert key and at concert pitch, except that the string bass tones are notated an octave higher than concert pitch to lessen the use of ledger lines. The violinist reads the treble clef, the violist the alto clef with some treble clef, the cellist the bass clef with some tenor and treble clef, and the string bass the bass clef. In our study the string bass will be assigned only the task of doubling the bass part an octave lower than the cello.

    2. The woodwind quartet—flute, oboe, clarinet, and bassoon.

        Parts for all but the clarinet are written in concert key and at concert pitch. The B♭ (soprano) clarinet part is written in treble clef notated in the key a major second higher. The new key will contain two less flats or two more sharps than the original concert key.

ASSIGNMENT #54: Vocal and instrumental transpositions.

This assignment is found on Work Sheet #69.

As has been pointed out, only the part written for one instrument—the B♭ (soprano) clarinet—required a key other than the given concert key. The necessary change required writing each note a major second above the concert pitch, changing the key signature to one with two less flats or two more sharps. This transposition is explained by the fact that the B♭ clarinet produces tones a major second below the given concert key and pitch (note that B♭ is a major second lower than C), and therefore, to compensate, its part must be written in that key which lies a major second above the given concert key.

Using the principle concerning the interval of transposition which we derive from considering that of the clarinet, we can deduce two other general statements concerning instrumental transposition. Each of these statements is presented in outline form to extend its application to certain other of the band and orchestral instruments.

> C. Instrumental Transposition—intervals of transposition.
>
> 1. All instruments whose parts are written in the treble clef sound the concert pitch of their key name (*e.g.*: B♭ cornet) when their written C is played.
>
>   *a.* those instruments pitched in C.
>
>   1) the *violin, flute, oboe,* and the *trumpet in C* produce only concert pitches.

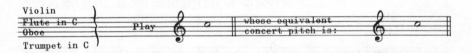

> 2) the *piccolo in C* plays in the concert key. It however is notated an octave lower than its sound to decrease the use of ledger lines.

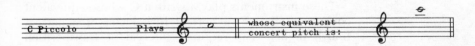

> *b.* those instruments pitched in "other-than-C," known as transposing instruments.*
>
>   The interval found between each instrument's written C, and this note's equivalent sound in concert pitch is the pitch difference, up or down, for which adjustment must

be made. Measured in the opposite direction from the desired concert key, this pitch discrepancy becomes the required interval of transposition.

1) the *B♭ clarinet, B♭ trumpet* or *cornet,* and *B♭ soprano saxophone* have an interval of transposition which is the major second up.

Each instrument in this group plays a written C whose equivalent concert pitch is B♭, a major second lower. The required interval of transposition therefore is the major second up, in a key containing two less flats or two more sharps than the given concert key.

2) the *B♭ tenor saxophone* and the *B♭ bass clarinet* have an interval of transposition which is the major second plus the octave up.

These instruments play a written C whose equivalent concert pitch is B♭, a major second plus an octave lower. The required interval of transposition therefore is the major ninth up to the key which contains two less flats or two more sharps than the given concert key.

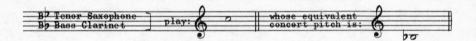

3) the *French horn, English horn,* and *F trumpet* have an interval of transposition which is either the perfect fifth up or the perfect fourth down.

These instruments play a written C whose equivalent concert pitch is F, a perfect fifth lower or a perfect fourth higher. The required interval of transposition therefore is a perfect fifth up or a perfect fourth down to the key containing one less flat or one more sharp than the given concert key.

The part for the French horn is often notated for other than the F pitched instrument. Some commonly-used horn transpositions are those for the "horn in E, in E♭, and in D." The instrumentalist performs these parts on the F horn by transposing each one down, respectively, a minor second, a major second, or a minor third.

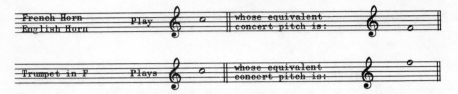

4) the Eb *clarinet*, Eb *alto saxophone*, and Eb *alto clarinet* have an interval of transposition which is either the minor third down or the major sixth up.

   a) the Eb clarinet plays a written C whose equivalent concert pitch is Eb a minor third higher. The required interval of transposition therefore, is the minor third down, in the key requiring three less flats or three more sharps than the given concert key.

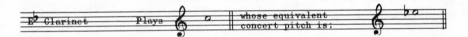

   b) the Eb alto saxophone and the Eb alto clarinet play a written C whose equivalent concert pitch is Eb a major sixth lower. The required interval of transposition therefore is the major sixth up to the key containing three less flats or three more sharps than the given concert key.

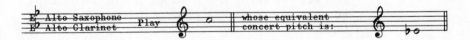

5) the Eb *baritone saxophone* and the Eb *contrabass clarinet* have an interval of transposition which is the major sixth plus the octave up.

   These two instruments play a written C whose concert equivalent is Eb, a major sixth plus an octave lower. The required interval of transposition therefore is an octave and a major sixth higher to the key con-

taining three less flats or three more sharps than the
given concert key.

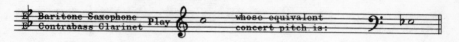

6) the *piccolo in Db* has an interval of transposition which
is a minor second plus an octave down.

The Db piccolo plays a written C whose concert
equivalent is Db a minor second played an octave
higher. The required interval of transposition therefore is a minor second plus an octave down (*i.e.*, a
minor ninth down) in the key containing five less
flats or five more sharps than the original concert
key. As in the case of the C piccolo, the octave transposition lessens the need for ledger lines.

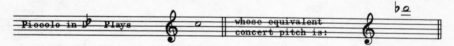

7) the *A clarinet* has an interval of transposition which
is a minor third up.

This instrument plays a written C whose equivalent
concert pitch is A a minor third lower. The required
interval of transposition therefore is a minor third
up to a key containing three more flats or three less
sharps than the original concert key.

When necessary, the part for the A clarinet is played
on the Bb clarinet by transposing down a minor second
to a key containing five less flats or five more sharps,
however, this gives it a rather different tone color or
timbre.

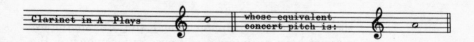

8) the *D trumpet* has an interval of transposition which
is a major second down.

This instrument plays a written C whose equivalent
concert pitch is D a major second higher. The re-

quired interval of transposition therefore is a major second down to the key containing two more flats or two less sharps.

When the D trumpet is not available, its part can be played on the C trumpet in the key a major second higher containing two less flats or two more sharps, or with yet more difficulty on the B♭ trumpet—the most common instrument—in the key a major third higher containing four less flats or four more sharps.

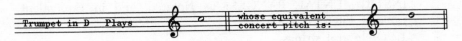

2. All instruments whose parts are usually written in other than the treble clef produce only concert pitches.

  a. those instruments pitched in C.

   The *bassoon, cello, viola, string bass,* and *contrabassoon* produce only concert pitches. The parts for the bassoon and cello are usually written in the bass clef; that for the viola in the alto clef; those for the string bass and contrabassoon are also in the bass clef, but are notated an octave higher than their sound.

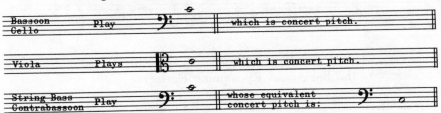

  b. those instruments pitched in B♭ or E♭.

   The *trombone* and *baritone horn* in B♭, the *tuba in B♭,* as well as the *tuba in E♭,* do not require transposition when their parts are written in the bass clef, and are therefore known as non-transposing instruments.* This is because the compensation for their B♭-C or E♭-C pitch discrepancy is made in the assignment of slide positions and fingerings used for directly producing the desired concert pitches.

D. Instrumental Transposition—ranges of instruments.

After one knows an instrument's required interval of transposition, it is still necessary to be aware of its range in order to score a part for it. The following instructions, shown in family groups, give the minimum essentials concerning the usable range of these instruments. Further help in scoring can be obtained by consulting a standard textbook on instrumentation or orchestration to get information on each instrument's peculiar characteristics.

INSTRUMENTAL RANGES: as Notated, and in Equivalent Concert Pitch Notation.

1. Orchestral strings.

2. Flute and piccolo.

3. Clarinet family.

    a. the B♭, A and E♭ soprano clarinets.

    b. the E♭ alto, B♭ bass, and E♭ contrabass clarinets.

(shorter range)

4. Double reeds.

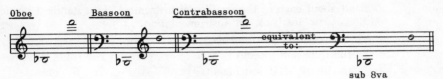

5. The Saxophone family.

6. Trumpet and cornet.

7. The French horn in F.

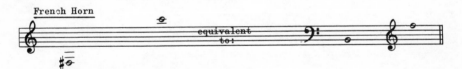

8. The lower brasses.

a. the trombone and baritone horn in B♭.

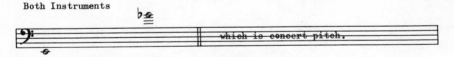

b. the E♭ tuba and B♭ tuba.

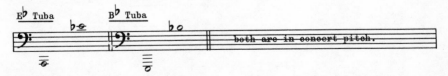

SUGGESTIONS FOR STUDY

Read about each of the families of instruments in a standard music dictionary or textbook on instrumentation.

—the woodwind instruments
  —the flute and piccolo
  —the single reed instruments
  —the double reed instruments
—the brass instruments
—the orchestral string instruments
—the percussion instruments

While percussion instruments were not included in the scope of this discussion, it will be interesting and worthwhile to learn about the more important members of this family, such as the tympani and the several sizes of drums.

ASSIGNMENT #55: Scoring for the brass sextet, the saxophone quartet, the band, and the orchestra.

This assignment is found on Work Sheet #70.

GLOSSARY OF MUSICAL TERMS

A-C-S-O-G—an acrostic formed from the first letters of the movements found in many of Bach's Suites. The movements are: the allemande, courante, sarabande, optional (group of dances), and the gigue.

ACCENT—emphasis given a musical tone. The accent can result from the rhythmic position within a measure, from duration, or from a specific instruction, such as "marcato," "sforzando," or the sign ">."

ACCIDENTAL—an inflexion of a given tone that is not accounted for by the key signature. Its effect is limited to that particular degree and to the measure within which it occurs.

ACOUSTICS—that branch of physics dealing with the phenomenon of sound, its generation, behavior, transmission, and to some extent, its reception.

ADAGIO—slow, but not as slow as largo; often used as the name of a movement.

AEOLIAN MODE—a modal scale consisting of the minor and Phrygian tetrachords disjunct by a whole step. It is identical with the natural minor scale.

ALLEGRO—fast, brisk, lively; often used as the name of a movement.

ALLEMANDE—originally a slow German dance. In the Bach Suites the allemande has a moderate tempo in common meter. It has a highly ornate melody including a short upbeat or anacrusis for each of its two sections, the first of which is in open form.

AMPLITUDE—an acoustical term used to describe the relative volume of a sound by means of observing certain characteristics of its sound wave.

ANACRUSIS—the notes, one or more, which precede the first full measure of a melody. Often called "pick up."

ANDANTE—moderately slow but flowing; often used as the name of a movement.

ANSWER—the form which the subject of a fugue generally takes upon its entrance in the second voice, in "answer" to the subject given by the first voice.

ANTECEDENT—the first of two phrases which differ only in their final cadence and together form a sentence.

Anthem—a choral composition used in the service of the Anglican and Protestant churches. It is written to words from the Scriptures or other sacred texts.

N H ANTICIPATION (tone)—a non-harmonic tone which is approached by step and left by repetition. Its name is derived from the fact that a tone of the second chord is sounded prematurely, that is, during the duration of the first chord.

N H APPOGGIATURA—a non-harmonic tone which is approached by leap and left by step. Its most characteristic form is accented, although it also occurs unaccented. (For a restricted use of the unaccented appoggiatura, see "cambiata").

ARIA—a musical composition for voice or instrument, accompanied by other voices or instruments.

ARPEGGIO—harplike; the notes of a chord played in succession, usually upward. The direction of arpeggiation often is indicated in contemporary scores by means of an appropriate arrow.

ARTICULATION—the act of achieving distinctness in the execution of musical tones either instrumental or vocal.

AUGMENTATION—a fugue subject or other contrapuntal concept sounded in rhythmic values which are twice their original values.

AUGMENTED SIXTH CHORD—a chord which generally sounds, but is not spelled or does not function like, a dominant seventh chord. It is most often (but is not limited to this) found on the submediant of the minor mode, or on the lowered submediant of the major mode.

AUTHENTIC CADENCE—the harmonic progression of the dominant chord to the tonic chord within any major or minor key.

AUTHENTIC MODES—the four basic ecclesiastical or church modes: the Dorian, Phrygian, Lydian, and Mixolydian. They are the basis of most of the church music written in the first 1600 years, A.D.

AUXILIARY TONE—synonymous with returning tone (q.v.).

BAR LINE—the vertical line used to indicate the end of one measure and the beginning of the next.

BEATS—the pulsation caused by the periodic reinforcement and lessening of the volume of sound produced by two tones with different pitches. It is most easily observed when the pitches of the two tones differ in rate by only a few vibrations.

BOURRÉE—a French dance of the seventeenth century in quick duple meter, usually beginning with a quarter note upbeat. It is often found in the optional dances of the Bach Suites.

BREVE—a double whole note. In the music of the Ars Nova and the Renaissance periods, the breve was somewhat comparable to our quarter note. Both the longa and maxima, now obsolete, were of longer duration.

CADENCE—a harmonic or melodic progression which occurs at the end of a musical phrase, sentence, or composition to give the impression of a momentary or a permanent conclusion.

CADENCE RHYME—a type of similarity in endings (except for key) of the last several measures of each section of the two part open form q.v.). It is analogous to poetic rhyme.

CAMBIATA—an unaccented non-harmonic tone which is approached by a leap of a third and resolved by a step movement in the opposite direction. It also can be called the unaccented appoggiatura.

CANON—a musical composition whose entire effect—melodic, harmonic, and contrapuntal—is produced by the use of a single melodic line or theme, which is announced by one voice (dux) and imitated, usually exactly, by one or more other voices (comes), entering at specified rhythmic intervals.

CANTATA—a musical composition based upon a story. It is set for voices accompanied by instruments.

CAROL—a type of folk song usually celebrating Christmas, but sometimes honoring another festive occasion. Carols are commonly associated with the country of their origin.

CATCH—an English round of the seventeenth and eighteenth centuries, written for the popular male singing clubs of the day.

CHACONNE—a set of variations based upon a series of chords related by a well defined harmonic rhythm, usually in a slow triple meter. The form was very popular during the Baroque period, and has been used occasionally since that time.

CHOIR—an ensemble of voices or a group of homogeneous instruments, such as the string choir, the woodwind choir, or the brass choir.

CHORALE—the name given to the hymn tunes of the German Protestant church. They were especially important in the German music of the Baroque period, and particularly in that of J. S. Bach (1685-1750).

CHORD—a combination of tones (usually three or more) sounding simultaneously. The particular interval arrangement determines the quality of the chord.

CHROMATIC MODULATION—modulation effected by the use of one or more chords containing tones which are foreign to one of the keys concerned. Most chromatic shifts involve movements of a half step.

CHROMATIC SCALE—the scale of half steps comprising the 12 tones available in each octave.

CHROMATICISM—the use of various accidental tones which are foreign to the scale degrees indicated by the key signature or tonal context of a musical composition.

CIRCLE OF FIFTHS—a succession of descending perfect fifth (or the equivalent ascending perfect fourth) intervals, in which each one is the dominant (or 5th degree) of the one that follows. The 21 tone circle of fifths is B♯, E♯, A♯, D♯, G♯, C♯, F♯, B, E, A, D, G, C, F, B♭, E♭, A♭, D♭, G♭, C♭, and F♭. Note that the 15 tone major circle of fifths, as well as the 15 tone minor circle of fifths, lie within this 21 tone circle. (See the "21 Tones," Flashcard Set #3).

CLASSIC PERIOD—usually understood to mean the period of "Viennese Classicism" (1770-1830), including Haydn, Mozart, Beethoven, and their contemporaries.

CLEF—the fixed relationship of the musical alphabet to the staff, indicated by the appropriate clef sign.

CLOSED PIPE—a term denoting a pipe which is acoustically closed at one end, with the result that it can produce only the odd-numbered partials.

CLOSED POSITION—that distribution of chord tones which includes the three upper voices within the interval of an octave, and the bass and tenor voices separated by an interval ranging from a unison to a twelfth.

CODA—a musical section of varying length added to a composition to give it a musically effective close. In its shortest form it may consist of simply an added or repeated cadence.

COMES—see "canon."

COMMON TONE—a tone whose sound and spelling occur in the same voice in two successive chords.

COMPOUND INTERVAL—an interval whose span is greater than an octave.

COMPOUND METER—any meter whose numerator is 5 or larger.

CONCERT PITCH—usually defined as International Concert Pitch whose A (a¹, second space of treble clef) is tuned to 440 vibrations per second. The pitch and transposition for any given instrument are reckoned from this standard pitch.

CONSECUTIVE FIFTH (or octave)—the effect produced by the duplication of the melodic movement of a part by another part at the distance of a fifth (or octave). This movement can be that of parallel fifths (or octaves) moving identical distances in the same direction at approximately the same rhythmic movement, or it can be that of moving by opposite motion to an interval of the twelfth (or the fifteenth). In the first instance consecutive fifths (or octaves) by parallel motion are formed; in the latter, consecutive fifths (or octaves) by contrary motion.

CONSEQUENT—the second of two phrases which differ only in their final cadence and together form a sentence.

CONSONANCE—a stable interval, hence one whose degree of tension does not require further resolution.

CONTRAPUNTAL (writing)—music, especially polyphony (music with two or more independent parts or voices), written with emphasis upon the horizontal, rather than on the vertical (harmonic) point of view.

CONTRAPUNTAL INTERCHANGE—synonymous with "interchangeable counterpoint" (q.v.).

CONTRARY MOTION—the movement of two voices in opposite directions.

CORELLI CLASH—that use of the anticipation—usually in a cadence—in which the tonic degree as a non-harmonic tone is made to sound against the leading tone of the dominant chord.

COUNTERPOINT—the study of the writing of music from the horizontal rather than the vertical (harmonic) point of view.

COUNTERSUBJECT—the name given to a contrapuntal part which is sounded as a counterpoint to the subject or answer each time either is used. Occasionally more than one countersubject is used.

COURANTE—a French dance in triple meter (3/2 or 6/4) distinguished by a predominance of dotted notes and the use of hemiola throughout the composition, but especially in the cadence area of each section. It is written in two part open form. The Italian form of this dance is termed "corrente" and consists chiefly of running passages in fairly rapid tempo, usually in two voices, and always in two part open form.

CRAB CANON—canon canzicrans, that is, a canon whose last half is the first half played backwards.

CROSS-RHYTHM—the effect obtained by the use of irregular rhythmic groupings, as opposed to that resulting from a regular metric pulse.

DA CAPO—a direction to return to the beginning of a movement or a composition; often abbreviated as "D. C." (See "fine.")

DECEPTIVE CADENCE—the cadence movement of a dominant chord to any chord other than the tonic; but the movement of the dominant chord to the submediant chord is *the* deceptive cadence of traditional harmony.

DECIBEL—an acoustical unit for measuring the intensity or loudness of sound.

DENOMINATOR—the lower number in a meter signature whose function is to indicate the note value which is the unit of measurement in a given meter.

DEVELOPMENT SECTION—the middle of the three parts in a sonata form (exposition, development, and recapitulation) in which the composer presents the themes in varied form and in several keys. This manipulation is known as thematic development.

DIATONIC MODULATION—the technique of moving from one key to another through a pivot consisting of one or more common tones or chords.

DIATONIC SCALE—the natural scale which is major in quality starting from any C, including the tones C, D, E, F, G, A, B, and C. In this scale the intervals between adjacent tones are whole steps, except for those between E and F and B and C which are half steps.

DIFFERENCE TONE—an acoustical phenomenon in which two sounding tones give rise to another weaker tone, whose frequency is the difference between their rates of vibration.

DIMINISHED SEVENTH CHORD—(in the major mode) a chord composed of a diminished triad and an added major third, often called "half diminished;" (in the minor mode) a chord composed of three successive minor thirds. This latter form, often called "full diminished," is useful in both the major and minor modes.

DIMINUTION—a fugue subject or other contrapuntal concept sounded in rhythmic values one-half their original value.

DIRECT PIVOT CHORD (or area)—in modulation that chord, group of chords, two tones, or single tone which can be related to both the initial key and the key of destination. Its function is to smooth the transition between the keys or tonalities concerned.

DISJUNCT—literally unjoined. The tetrachords including degrees 1, 2, 3, 4 and 5, 6, 7, 8 are disjunct by a step; whereas, the tetrachords including degrees 1, 2, 3, 4 and 4, 5, 6, 7 are conjunct, that is, they have one tone in common.

DISSONANCE—an unstable interval, hence one whose degree of tension requires resolution.

DOMINANT—the 5th degree of the major or minor scale, or, in harmony, the triad built upon this degree. The affinity of the dominant for the tonic is a harmonic fact of primary importance.

DOMINANT FAMILY—the group of chords composed of the root position and inversions of the dominant triad, seventh, ninth, eleventh, and thirteenth chords, together with the forms of the triad and seventh chord built on the leading tone degree of the major and harmonic minor scales.

DOMINANT ELEVENTH CHORD—a chord which, in its ideal form, consists of a dominant root, a leading tone, a seventh, and a dissonant 11th degree.

DOMINANT PROLONGATION—a purposeful delay in the resolution of dominant tension, accomplished by the use of a succession of harmonies governed by the dominant root. (See also, pedal point.)

DORIAN MODE—the ecclesiastical mode whose gamut runs from D to D in the diatonic scale. Technically, it consists of two minor tetrachords, disjunct by a whole step.

DOUBLE FLAT—the sign (♭♭) used to indicate that a given tone is to be played 2 half steps below its natural pitch. To cancel the effect of one of the flats on the same tone within the same measure, the sign (♮♭), or just a single flat, can be used.

DOUBLE PERIOD—a section of music consisting of two sentences, each of which may include two or more phrases.

DOUBLE SHARP—the sign (x) used to indicate that a given tone is to be played 2 half steps above its natural pitch. To cancel the effect of one of the sharps on the same tone within the same measure the sign (♮♯), or just a single sharp, can be used.

DOUBLE VIBRATION—the motions of any vibrating medium to both sides of a center point together constitute one complete double vibration.

DOUBLING—the simultaneous sounding of a chord tone of one chord, or some octave thereof, by two voices.

DUPLE ORGANIZATION—the grouping of equal rhythmic pulses in two's.

DUPLE SUBDIVISION—the note whose value is one-half that of the denominator of any given meter. The denominator value thus divides into two duple subdivisions of the first order, four of the second order, etc.

DUPLET—a group of two notes of equal rhythmic value.

DURATION—the length of a tone measured in some unit of time, either absolute or relative.

DUX—see "canon."

ECCLESIASTICAL MODES—see "authentic modes."

ENGLISH SUITES—the name familiarly given to Bach's six keyboard suites for harpsichord composed around 1725. Perhaps the inclusion of "preludes" before the suites proper (somewhat in the English tradition) gave rise to their present description as "English Suites."

ENHARMONIC (often "enharmonic tone" or "enharmonic equivalent")—the term used to indicate that two notes share the same sound but differ in spelling (i.e., have different letter names).

ENHARMONIC INTERVALS—two intervals that share the same sound but differ in spelling, name, and function are enharmonic to each other.

ENHARMONIC MODULATION—modulation accomplished by a pivot chord whose function and interpretation can be made more clear through the use of enharmonic spelling in one or the other of the keys concerned.

EPISODE (as relating to fugue)—any portion of a fugue in which the entire subject does not appear. Often an episode is based upon a motive from the subject or countersubject.

Equal tempered scale—the type of tuning which has been used for keyboard instruments for the past 150 years. The division of the octave into 12 equal semitones makes it possible to play acceptably tuned chords using any of the 12 degrees as the tonic.

ESCAPE TONE—a non-harmonic tone whose initial movement is traditionally a step in the direction opposite to the normal step movement leading to the following chord tone. It is appoached by step and left by leap. A liberal interpretation allows the step and leap to be in either direction.

EXACT IMITATION—the repetition of a figure, motive, subject, phrase, or part of a melody by a second voice on the same or different level, maintaining an identical interval relationship throughout.

EXPOSITION—the first of three parts of the sonata form (exposition, development, and recapitulation) in which the composer introduces his themes for the movement.

FIGURED BASS—a bass part provided with numerals (figures) which indicate the harmonies.

FINE—"to the end;" often employed to indicate the end of the repetition initiated by the "da capo" sign.

FLAT SIGN—the sign (♭) used to indicate the lowering of a given note by one half step. The flat can occur in a key signature or before the note it modifies.

FORMANT—the particular combination and intensity of partial tones that lend the characteristic timbre to any given musical tone.

FREE VOICED—music written for keyboard instruments without adherence to a set number of voices or parts.

FRENCH SUITES—the name given to six keyboard suits of Bach, which were written in the "French manner." These are not preceded by preludes, as are the so-called "English Suites."

FREQUENCY—the acoustical term used to show the highness or lowness of pitch by indicating the number of cycles, or complete double vibrations per second, necessary to produce a given tone.

FUGUE—a polyphonic musical composition of two to five voices based on the use, imitation, and development of a short, usually terse, theme called the subject, handled in a characteristically stylistic manner.

FULL CADENCE—an authentic cadence preceded by one or two chords which contribute to its "fullness" and closing effect. There are several standard formulas, *e.g.*: IV V I; ii V I; and vi V I, as expressed in Roman symbols of the major mode.

FULL SCORE—a term used to describe a conductor's score in which each part or voice of the ensemble is assigned a separate staff. The antonym is "condensed score" in which the gist of all the parts is combined on two or at the most three staffs.

GAMUT—the octave range of a scale or the range of a voice or instrument.

GAVOTTE—a French dance of the seventeenth century in moderate 4/4 meter, beginning with an upbeat of two quarter notes. It is often found in the optional dances of the Bach Suites.

GIGUE—an old Italian dance written in a lively triple meter, or in duple meter with triple subdivisions, normally used as the final movement of the suite. It is a two part open form, and has a predominantly fugue-like texture in which the theme of the first section usually appears freely inverted at the beginning of the second section.

GREAT C—the name given to the C on the second added ledger line below the bass clef staff—"C" as shown on the pitch identification chart, page 1.

GREAT STAFF—the term used for the treble and bass clefs joined by a brace, upon which keyboard music is written.

GROUND BASS—a short melodic phrase whose manifold repetition served as the bass voice of a composition called a "ground." The interest in this type of composition derived from the variety of melody, harmony, and counterpoint that the composer was able to bring out in the upper voices.

HALF CADENCE—the inconclusive termination of a phrase, whether melodic harmonic, or both. The harmonic half cadence frequently ends on the dominant chord, less often on the subdominant or other chord.

HARMONIC FUNCTION—the relationship of a chord to the tonality within which it is found, *e.g.*, the C major triad, when considered as a principal triad can be the tonic of C major, the subdominant of G major, and the dominant of F major.

HARMONIC MINOR SCALE—one of the three forms included in the minor mode. Compared with the major, the harmonic minor scale has lowered 3rd and 6th degrees, with a 7th degree identical with that of the major mode, except that, due to the difference in signatures between major and minor scales, the latter occurs as an accidental.

HARMONIC RHYTHM—the relative duration of a series of harmonies whose pattern of rhythm is derived by noting the changes in chord roots as they occur. The over-all vitality of music is determined to a considerable extent by the underlying pattern of chord changes.

HARMONIC SERIES—the composite of tone sounded by a freely vibrating string, included by its vibrating as a whole, in two parts, in three parts, etc., or the series of tones which can be induced to sound by overblowing an open pipe.

HARMONIC TETRACHORD—an altered diatonic four-tone pattern spanning a perfect fourth interval. It includes half steps between its 1st and 2nd, and 3rd and 4th degrees and forms the upper half, or second tetrachord, of the harmonic minor scale, hence the name.

HARMONY—the science of chord progression based upon the observation, evaluation, and application of the tensions and tendencies generated by a succession of chord roots.

HEARING—the ability to discern the quality of a pitch concept and to associate this concept with its notation. This association of pitch concept with notation distinguishes hearing from recognition (q.v.).

HEMIOLA—the cross-rhythm which results when the prevailing organization of the triple meter is replaced by that of a meter of the same size but of opposite organization, or by that of a meter of similar organization, but either one-half or twice the size.

HOMOPHONY—music whose principal interest lies in its melody or tune. The other voices are entirely subservient and tend to be chordal in texture.

HYMN TUNE—the melody which is used with or composed for a religious poem as distinguished from the Psalms, which are often set to music.

HYPO-MODES—synonymous with the term "plagal modes" (q.v.).

IMITATION—the repetition of a rhythmic or melodic figure, motive, or subject within a given voice, or in other voices, either exactly or freely at the same or (most often) different levels of pitch. Imitation is a basic unifying device in musical composition.

INDIRECT PIVOT CHORD—a chord which is dominant to parallel major and minor chords, each of which is related to one of the two keys concerned in a modulation.

INTERCHANGEABLE COUNTERPOINT—counterpoint in which any of the voices can effectively and functionally serve as the bass for the other parts.

INTERVAL—the difference in pitch between two tones, measured in terms of the number of diatonic degrees included in their span.

INTONATION—the state of "in-tuneness," good or bad, of a musical performance, either individual or group.

INVENTION—the name given to short two- or three-part contrapuntal keyboard compositions usually in two-part open form (q.v.). Bach entitled his three voiced examples "Sinfonia," but the name "invention" tends to prevail today.

INVERSION (of an interval)—the transposition of the lower tone of an interval to an octave higher; or the upper tone to an octave lower.

INVERSION (of a chord)—any chord position in which the root is not in the bass voice.

INVERTED CHORD—synonymous with "inversion (of a chord)" (q.v.).

INVERTIBLE COUNTERPOINT—synonymous with "interchangeable counterpoint" (q.v.).

IONIAN MODE—a modal scale consisting of two major tetrachords disjunct by a whole step. It is identical with the major scale.

IRREGULAR METER—any meter whose numerator is not divisible by either two or three. However, a regular duple or triple meter can be made to function like an irregular meter through the use of pulse groupings which conflict with the implied pulse.

Just intonation—a means of tuning the scale in which all intervals are those derived from the harmonic series. Since two sizes of major seconds result, the scale will be of only limited use in modulation, or in keys other than the basic one.

Key signature—the group of flat or sharp symbols—each with its characteristic order of appearance—placed immediately to the right of the clef sign to indicate the key which may be major, minor, or modal.

Largo—very slow, broad, and stately.

Leading tone—the 7th degree of the major or minor scale, the name being especially applicable when the interval between the 7th and 8th degrees is a half step.

Ledger lines (sometimes "leger")—the short lines added above or below a staff to make possible the representation of pitches higher or lower than those notated on the staff.

Lento—slow; sometimes used as the name of a movement.

Lied—an artistic German song or ballad which was very important during the nineteenth century.

Liturgy—a set form for conducting a public worship service.

Lydian mode—that ecclesiastical mode whose gamut in the diatonic scale extends from F to F. Technically it consists of a lydian and a major tetrachord disjunct by a half step.

Lydian tetrachord—a diatonic four tone pattern made up of three successive whole steps spanning the interval of an augmented fourth.

Major interval—the span of a second, third, sixth, and seventh contained between the 1st degree, and respectively, the 2nd, 3rd, 6th, and 7th degrees of the major scale. Measured in half steps the major second, third, sixth, and seventh contain in order, 2, 4, 9, and 11.

Major mode—the mode used in writing music whose principal harmonies show derivation from the major scale.

Major second—the interval of a whole step, such as is found between the 1st and 2nd degrees of a every major scale.

Major tetrachord—a four tone pattern spanning the interval of a perfect fourth. It includes two major seconds and a minor second, in that order, in its sequence of intervals. The major scale is composed of two major tetrachords a whole step apart.

Masking—the tendency of a composite of sounding voices to obscure the sound of any given voice.

Mass—the most solemn service of the Roman Catholic Church ritual. It represents the commemoration of Christ's sacrifice on the cross. In its full form it is known as High Mass or Missa Solemnis.

MEASURE—synonymous with bar, hence, measures are marked off by bar lines. A group of notes (units of musical time), the first of which bears an accent.

MEDIANT—the 3rd degree of a major or minor scale, or, in harmony, the chord built upon that degree.

MELODIC MINOR SCALE—one of the three forms included in the minor mode. In the ascending form the melodic minor has only a lowered 3rd degree compared with the major scale, but its descending form includes lowered 3rd, 6th, and 7th degrees.

MELODIC RHYTHM—the particular succession of note values underpinning the musical tones or pitches of a given melody or tune.

MELODY—a succession of musical tones organized by such factors as rhythm, line, nuance, and harmony.

METER—a characteristic pattern of rhythmic organization, marked off by bar lines, and indicated by the appropriate meter signature.

METER SIGNATURE—the numerical symbol, such as 3/4 or 9/8, placed immediately to the right of the key signature, used to indicate the meter. It often is called the time signature.

METRICAL RHYTHM—rhythms characteristic of a given meter.

METRONOMIC TEMPO—a means of designating the fastness or slowness of a composition by indicating the number of rhythmic units to occur in one minute.

MINOR INTERVALS—seconds, thirds, sixths, and sevenths whose span is one-half step less than their major counterparts. Specifically, the minor second, third, sixth, and seventh include respectively 1, 3, 8, and 10 half steps or semitones.

MINOR MODE—the mode used in music whose principal harmonies show derivation from the three minor scales, singly or in combination.

MINOR SECOND—the interval of a half step, such as is found between the 3rd and 4th or the 7th and 8th degrees of every major scale.

MINOR TETRACHORD—a diatonic four-tone pattern spanning a perfect fourth interval, which includes a major second, a minor second, and another major second in its sequence of intervals. The first four notes of each form of minor scale comprise a minor tetrachord.

MINUET (or "menuet")—a stately French dance often found in the optional dances of the Bach Suites. Uniquely among the dances of the Baroque suite, it found further use in the symphonies of Haydn, Mozart, and other composers.

MIXED POSITIONS—positions of chords (other than root position triads) in which a combination of adjacent and non-adjacent chord tones is possible; or, possibly, root position chords using the doubled 5th or 3rd degree. Mixed position chords combine the characteristics of closed and open position chords.

MIXOLYDIAN MODE—that ecclesiastical mode whose gamut in the diatonic scale extends from G to G. Technically, it consists of a major and a minor tetrachord disjunct by a whole step.

MODAL DEGREE—the 3rd, 6th, 7th, and to a lesser extent the 2nd degree of the major, minor, or modal scales. They are so named because, in the case of the first three degrees, their inflexion determines the major and minor modes, and in the latter instance the Phrygian church mode.

MODAL INTERCHANGE—the harmonization of a musical passage in the parallel mode for variety and contrast. Modal interchange can also refer to the use of selected harmonies from one mode in its parallel mode.

MODERATO—moderate speed, i.e., between andante and allegro.

MODERN PERIOD—the period since 1900, characterized by a weakening of the influence of tonality of the type associated with tertian harmony, and a counterbalancing growth in rhythmic development with emphasis on the contrapuntal line.

MODULATING SEQUENCE—a musical pattern usually consisting of a melodic phrase and its harmony, repeated in successive keys, each different from the last.

MODULATION—the musical process of moving from one key to another by means of suitable harmonic connections and progressions.

MOTET—an important form of early polyphonic music which underwent many changes. Generally speaking, the motet is an unaccompanied (though there has been some deviation from this) contrapuntal choral composition based on a sacred text, intended to be used in the Catholic service. Since its principal history covers more than five centuries (ca. 1250 to ca. 1750), there are many types of motets. (See also "point of imitation.")

MOTIVE—a brief musical idea whose melodic, rhythmic, or harmonic content serve as the basis for either a part of or for an entire musical composition.

MOVEMENT—one of the several subdivisions of a large scale musical work such as a sonata or a symphony. Movements are usually designated by titles such as "allegro," "scherzo," or other appropriate name.

MUSICAL FORM—the physical shape of a musical composition as heard, considered in terms of themes, harmony, counterpoint, and rhythm.

MUSICIANSHIP—those qualities, such as sensitivity to pitch, rhythm, melody, harmony, and nuance, which contribute to the over-all proficiency of a musician.

NATURAL MINOR SCALE—one of the three forms in the minor mode. Compared with the major scale, its 3rd, 6th, and 7th degrees are lowered

NEAPOLITAN CHORD—a major chord built on the lowered second degree of the major and minor scales. Its characteristic color derives from the fact that its sound is respectively five or two accidentals more flat than the harmonic context with which it is associated in any given major or minor key.

NINTH CHORD—basically a five-tone chord consisting of the 1st, 3rd, 5th, 7th, and 9th degrees over any given root. Its use, either as a chord or, considered contrapuntally, on a non-harmonic basis, adds much of the enrichment considered characteristic of music from Beethoven through Franck.

NODE—a point of acoustical rest around which the vibrations of a sounding string or pipe occur.

NON-HARMONIC TONES—embellishing tones which are introduced as ornaments, but are not essential parts of the harmony, that is, not tones of the constituent triads.

NON-TRANSPOSING INSTRUMENTS—those instruments which do not require transposition. All instruments pitched in C, as well as all brass instruments reading the bass clef, automatically produce concert pitches and therefore are included in this category.

NOTE—the symbol for indicating the pitch and duration of a musical tone.

NUMERATOR—the upper number of the meter signature. Its function is to suggest the basic rhythmic organization of a given meter.

OPEN PIPE—a term denoting the acoustical functioning of certain organ pipes or of other musical instruments. Instruments based on the open pipe principle theoretically are capable of producing each numbered partial.

OPEN POSITION—that distribution of chord tones in which the upper three voices, considered as a unit, span an interval greater than an octave, and the tenor and bass voices are separated by an interval ranging from a unison to a twelfth.

OPEN SCORE—a term used to describe, in particular, but not only, vocal scores whose voice parts each are assigned a separate staff for clarity of detail.

OPERA—a drama with scenery, costumes, and acting, in which vocal and instrumental music contribute a most important part.

OPTIONAL GROUP—in the Bach Suites, any of the dances occurring between the sarabande and the gigue. These include dances such as the minuet, gavotte, bourrée, air, loure, polonaise, passepied, and the anglaise. Generally these dances are more free in form than are the four constant dances of the suite.

ORATORIO—similar to the cantata, but of broader scope. Sometimes thought of as an opera without scenery, costumes, or acting.

ORNAMENTAL TONES—synonymous with "non-harmonic tones" (q.v.).

OSTINATO—a distinct melodic phrase which is repeated persistently, often in immediate succession, throughout a musical composition or a section thereof.

OVERTONE—see "partial tone."

PARALLEL SCALES—scales of differing types built upon the same tonic degree; for example, the C harmonic minor and the C major scales are parallel.

PART WRITING—a term applied to the writing of practice exercises in either harmony or counterpoint.

PARTIAL TONE—the fundamental tone, or any of the tones which can be induced by overblowing an open pipe, or subdividing a string into integral parts. The first partial is the fundamental tone of any harmonic series, and the second partial is the first overtone of the series, etc.

PARTITA—a Baroque term used to indicate either a set of variations or a suite.

PASSACAGLIA—a set of variations based upon a "basso ostinato," which theme also occasionally may move into the upper voices. Like the term "chaconne," the passacaglia is indigenous to the Baroque period.

PASSEPIED (en rondeau)—the passepied was a gay French dance of the early Baroque period usually in either 3/8 or 6/8 meter. The added description "en rondeau" signifies that the first section alternated with contrasting sections in the pattern— a, b, a, c, a, etc.

PASSING TONE—a non-harmonic tone which is both approached and left by step, each movement being in the same direction.

PEDAL POINT (tone)—a single bass tone—usually the dominant or the tonic degree—which is sustained while harmonic activity continues in the other voices. If the sustained tone is in other than the lowest voice, the pedal is said to be inverted.

PERFECT INTERVALS—the span of a unison, fourth, fifth, and octave contained between the 1st degree, and respectively, the 1st, 4th, 5th, and 8th degrees of the major scale. Measured in half steps the perfect unison, fourth, fifth, and octave contain respectively, 0, 5, 7, and 12.

PHRASE—a short melodic idea from two to six measures in length, marked off by a feeling of cadence at its end. This cadential feeling may be final, but is more often inconclusive. At times one, but usually two or more phrases form a complete musical thought called the sentence.

PHRYGIAN HALF CADENCE (or, Phrygian cadence)—in the minor mode
    that cadence—common to the Baroque period—in which the first
    inversion of the subdominant chord precedes a major root position
    dominant chord. In the major mode that cadence whose final chord
    is a major chord on the mediant degree.

PHRYGIAN MODE—that ecclesiastical mode whose gamut extends from
    E to E in the diatonic scale. Technically it consists of two Phrygian
    tetrachords disjunct by a whole step.

PHRYGIAN TETRACHORD—a diatonic four-tone pattern spanning a perfect
    fourth interval, which includes a minor second followed by two
    major seconds. A Phrygian tetrachord is found on the 3rd and 7th
    degrees of each major scale.

PICARDY 3RD—a major 3rd degree used to give a major quality to the
    final tonic chord of a cadence in the minor mode. The Picardy 3rd
    found great favor during the Baroque period.

PLAGAL CADENCE—the harmonic progression of the subdominant chord
    to the tonic chord within any major or minor key. A well-known
    example is the "Amen" which often is sung following a hymn.

PLAGAL MODES—the four hypo- forms of the ecclesiastical modes: the
    hypo-Dorian, hypo-Phrygian, hypo-Lydian, and hypo-Mixolydian,
    whose octave gamuts are a perfect fourth lower than those of their
    authentic namesakes.

PLAINSONG (or plainchant)—a general title for the ancient style of
    monophonic and rhythmically free melody, which is the common
    possession of the Western ritualistic churches.

POINT OF IMITATION—a section of a polyphonic composition in which a
    musical subject is composed for a given line or phrase of text, and
    then is imitated in contrapuntal fashion in the other voices. The
    motet, at least since Josquin (1450-1521), thus becomes a succession
    of such points, one often dovetailing into the next, the whole
    occasionally relieved by a more homophonic section. (See also
    "homophony").

POLYPHONY—many voiced music, implying melodic interest in more than
    one voice, in contrast to homophony (q.v.).

PRELUDE—a first movement of many musical compositions, often written
    in a free formal style.

PRESTO—quickly; at a rapid pace. Often used as the name of a movement.

PRIMARY TRIADS—those triads built on the tonic, subdominant, and domi-
    nant degrees of the major and minor scales. They are also known
    as the three principal triads.

PROGRESSION—the term used to denote the harmonic movement of one
    chord to another, described by the root movements of the chords
    involved.

PROGRESSIVE (movement of a chord)—a term used to describe root motions following the circle of fifths, or in more specific terms, those of a fifth down or a fourth up between two successive chords. The effect of a series of progressive movements is that of a feeling of continual resolution, or release of tension.

PULSE UNIT—the basic note value for reading rhythm in a given meter. Its size varies in accordance with the combination of meter and tempo used.

REAL IMITATION—synonymous with exact imitation (q.v.).

REALIZATION—the translation of a figured bass, or figured melody, into appropriately organized musical sound, or into appropriate musical notation.

RECOGNITION—the ability to discern the quality of a pitch concept.

RELATIVE SCALES—scales of differing types employing the same key signature; for example, the C minor scale and the E♭ major scale are related, or relative scales.

RESOLUTION—the melodic or harmonic motion which produces a feeling of stability in an unstable interval or chord. Chords which are not stable in sound, whatever the reason, require a satisfactory continuance to relieve the tension they generate.

RESONATOR—an object which because of its size, weight, shape, or some combination of all of these factors, tends to respond to a particular rate of vibration. This sympathetic response reinforces the volume of the pitch with which it is in resonance.

REST—the symbol used to represent the duration of silence in a musical score.

RETARDATION—the name often applied to an upward suspension (q.v.).

RETROGRADE (motion)—a term used to denote the backward reading of a melody, that is, starting with the last note and ending with the first one.

RETROGRESSIVE (movement of a chord)—a term used to describe root motions following the circle of fifths backwards, or in more specific terms, those of a fifth up or a fourth down between two successive chords. The effect of a retrogressive movement or of a series of them is that of increasing the state of harmonic tension.

RETURNING TONE—a non-harmonic tone which is entered by step and left by step in the opposite direction. This decoration of a given or single tone is common in music literature. (Piston calls the returning tone an "auxiliary tone," and Sessions calls it a "neighboring tone." Acknowledgement for the term "returning tone"—a name clearly descriptive of its function—and its related and consequent uses is hereby made to a Dr. Thomas Turner, The State University of Iowa. See Turner, "A Proposal for a Stabilized Non-Chord Tone Nomenclature," *American Music Teacher*, March-April 1954, page 6.)

RHYTHM—the actual sequence of sounds, silences, and stresses occurring in any given unit of a musical composition. This unit may comprise a portion of one measure, or the entire composition.

RIDDLE CANON—the name given to the canons of the Renaissance and Baroque periods whose rule for the entry of voices was purposely stated in an obscure manner.

RITARDANDO—growing gradually slower.

ROMANTIC PERIOD—the period following the Classical period, occupying the last three quarters of the nineteenth century. Music of this period (Schumann, Chopin, Brahms, and others) is characterized by its direct emotional appeal.

ROOT—the note upon which a triad or chord is built.

ROUND—the common name for a circle or infinite canon, in which each voice repeats the subject either without pause, or after a brief pause.

SARABANDE—a graceful dance, once popular in England, France, and Spain, whose origin may possibly have been in Mexico. As the slow movement of a suite, it is usually in triple meter, of square construction, telling beauty, and highly ornamented melody, giving it a homophonic texture and effect.

SCHERZO—a spritely, playful musical composition, often found as the third movement of a symphony, an inner movement of a sonata, or as an independent composition. Its predecessor was the more stately minuet.

SECONDARY DOMINANT—that major chord (usually in the dominant seventh form) which stands in a dominant relation (V I, either mode) to the major or minor chord found on any but the first or tonic degree of any scale.

SECONDARY SEVENTH CHORD—a seventh chord based upon the six degrees of the scale other than the dominant, whose seventh chord normally is known as the primary dominant seventh.

SECONDARY TRIADS—the non-primary triads, hence, those built on the supertonic, mediant, submediant, and leading tone degrees.

SECTION—a term of convenience—useful in discussing any desired portion of a musical composition.

SENTENCE—two or more phrases forming a complete musical thought.

SEQUENCE—a series or progression of similar chord patterns in succession; a melodic phrase or passage successively repeated on higher or lower levels.

SEVENTH CHORD—a four voiced chord formed by adding another interval of a third to a triad. The name derives from the fact that the added tone lies a seventh above the root of the basic triad concerned.

SHARP SIGN—the sign (♯) used to indicate the raising of a given tone by a half step. The sharp sign can occur in a key signature or before the note it modifies.

SIMPLE INTERVAL—any interval whose span does not exceed an octave.

SIMPLE METER—any meter whose numerator is four (4) or less. The size of the denominator affects only the size of the measure, not its organization.

SIX-FOUR DISSONANCE—the dissonance created by momentarily displacing by one upward step the 5th and 3rd degrees of a chord.

SIXTH CHORD—the name given to a chord whose 3rd degree is in the bass voice; also known as a first inversion chord.

SLUR—a curved line used to group together two or more notes on different degrees of the staff to indicate a legato articulation.

———— also, a similar but longer curved line often used to show the phrasing of a musical passage.

Brahms

SOLMIZATION—using the syllables (do, re, mi, fa, so, la, ti, do) to sing the tones of the major scale. Appropriate modifications of these symbols are used to indicate either the raising or lowering of each of these symbols a half step.

SONATA—a musical composition written for a solo instrument, or for an instrument and piano, consisting of three or four movements.

SONATA FORM—the formal title given to movements which include an exposition, development, and recapitulation; also known as sonata-allegro form, first movement form, or sonata-movement form.

SONG CYCLE—a unified series of songs inspired by, and based upon, successive stanzas of a poem.

SONORITY—the resonance, fullness, richness or other descriptive quality of a musical sound or composite of sounds.

SOPRANO CLEF—the highest pitched of the C clefs, having middle C (c¹) as its bottom line. Its use has been exclusively vocal.

SPACING—the interval between any two voices of a musical score.

STACCATO—a detached articulation of musical tones, usually indicated
by either a dot or the sign (▼), placed at the pitch end of a note.
e.g.:

STRETTO—a means of building contrapuntal tension in a fugue by allowing the subject to appear in canon with itself. The canonic entrances
can occur in more than one voice and may be at other pitch levels
than that of the subject.

SUBDOMINANT—the 4th degree of the major or minor scale, or, in harmony,
the chord built upon that degree.

SUBJECT—the theme of a fugue, usually from two to five (at times
more) measures in length. It usually is based on one or more distinctive melodic, rhythmic, and harmonic factors.

SUBMEDIANT—the 6th degree of the major or minor scale, or, in harmony,
the triad built upon that degree.

SUBORDINATE THEME GROUP—the second theme or group of themes found
in the exposition of the sonata form in contrast to the first occurring,
or principal, theme group.

SUMMATION TONE—an acoustical phenomenon in which two sounding
tones give rise to another weaker tone, whose frequency is the
sum· of their rates of vibration. Both difference and summation
tones can and do occur simultaneously.

SUPERTONIC—the 2nd degree of the major or minor scale, or, in harmony,
the triad built upon that degree.

SUPERTONIC SIX-FIVE CHORD—the first inversion of the supertonic seventh
chord. Its normal function is *pre*-dominant, that is, to precede the
dominant, but it may be *pre*-tonic.

N H SUSPENSION—a non-harmonic tone whose effect is produced either by
prolongation or by repetition and whose resolution is by step, either
up or down, as is appropriate.

SYNCOPATION—the effect produced when rhythmic emphasis upsets the
prevailing pulse and meter.

SYNTHETIC SCALE—an invented scale, that is, one based on a step pattern
different from those found in any of the familiar scales.

TEMPO—the rate at which pulse units occur under a given meter signature.

TENSION—the term used to denote the stability, or instability of an interval or chord.

TERTIAN HARMONY—harmony based on the use of triads and other advanced forms of chords built in superimposed thirds.

TESSITURA—the actual pitch range required for an instrument or voice in a given musical situation.

TEXTURE—the composite of voices used at any given moment in a musical composition.

THEME—a short melody or phrase serving as the subject of a musical composition.

THIRTEENTH CHORD—a seven-tone chord including the 1st, 3rd, 5th, 7th, 9th, 11th, and 13th degrees above a given root. Its most usual form —that on the dominant degree—includes the dissonant 13th (or 6th scale) degree, the leading tone, and the 7th degree above the dominant root.

TIMBRE—the distinctive quality of tone associated with each instrument, voice, or musical medium, whatever its type.

TONAL ARCH—the group of tonal areas outlining the main points of harmonic emphasis in a section of music.

TONAL AREA—a succession of chords whose function is guided by one main chord, or chord root.

TONAL DEGREES—the 1st, 4th, 5th, and 8th degrees of the major or minor scale. They are so named because progressions using the chords built upon them tend to define the tonality. The quality of these chords, in turn affected by the modal degrees, will tend to determine the modality, or the major, minor, or modal feeling of a particular tonality.

TONAL IMITATION— like exact imitation, the repetition of a figure, motive, subject, phrase, or part of a melody by a second voice at the same or different level, but with some latitude as to the choice of size and quality of the intervals used.

TONALITY—the state of being in a key, whether it is major, minor, modal, or ambiguous.

TONIC—the 1st degree of a major or minor scale, or, in harmony, the triad built upon that degree.

TRANSPOSING INSTRUMENTS—those instruments requiring transposition. Any instrument not pitched in C, except brass instruments reading the bass clef, must have its part transposed to suit its basic pitch. They therefore are called "transposing instruments."

TRANSPOSITION—the writing or performing of a musical composition in some other than the given key.

TRIAD—a chord consisting of three tones.

TRIO—originally a composition for three instruments; the contrasting middle section of the complete minuet or scherzo.

TRIPLE ORGANIZATION—the grouping of equal rhythmic pulses in threes.

TRIPLE SUBDIVISION—the division of any simple note or rest into three notes of the next smaller denomination, indicated by either a bracket or beams together with the numeral three (3).

TRITONE—an interval whose span is three whole steps. It is spelled either as an augmented fourth or as a diminished fifth, depending upon its function. Uniquely among intervals, the tritone and its inversion have the same basic size and quality of sound.

TURN—an ornamental figure, usually consisting of a five-note upper and lower returning tone decoration of a single tone. It is found in music of the Baroque and, in freer form, in that of the Romantic period. The turn sign graphically suggests the shape of the embellishment.

TUTTI—a direction indicating that every performer is to participate in a given section of a composition.

TWO PART OPEN FORM (or, open two part form)—a musical composition consisting of two sections, the first of which ends in a related key. This ending, (usually) on the dominant when in the major mode and (usually) in the relative major when in the minor mode, is called "open form," since it is not an ending in the tonic key. The last section completes the form satisfactorily by ending in the tonic key.

VARIATION—a musical form in which the theme or basic idea is presented in a succession of diverse sections, each of which is a varied form of the basic theme or idea.

VERSE ANTHEM—a choral composition like the "anthem," except that it includes sections for solo voices. This form was used by the English composers of the Baroque period.

VOICE DISTRIBUTION—the particular sequence of spacing between voices of a chord which distinguishes one chord position from another.

WHOLE TONE SCALE—a seven tone scale consisting of six whole steps and an octave. The scale consists of two Lydian tetrachords conjunct on the enharmonic form of the center tone of the scale. The use of this scale is a characteristic of the music of Debussy and other Impressionistic composers.

APPENDIX B

OUTLINE SUMMARIES

CHORDS

I. Prerequisites.

    A. Scales—major, and natural, harmonic, and melodic minor.

    B. Triads—major, minor, augmented, and diminished.

    C. Modes—pertinent chord qualities.

        1. Major

	Tonic	*Subdominant*	*Dominant*
a. primary chords.......... in major scale	major	major	major

b. secondary chords in major scale	*Supertonic* minor	*Mediant* minor	*Submediant* minor	*Leading tone* diminished

        2. Minor

a. primary chords	*Tonic*	*Subdominant*	*Dominant*
1) natural scale	minor	minor	minor
2) harmonic scale	minor	minor	major
3) melodic scale	minor	major	major

b. secondary triads	*Supertonic*	*Mediant*	*Submediant*	*Leading tone*
1) natural scale	diminished	major	major	major
2) harmonic scale ..	diminished	augmented	major	diminished
3) melodic scale	minor	augmented	diminished	diminished

II. Primary and secondary triadic connections—strict or free with appropriate attention to voice leading.

    A. Root position chord connections based on—

        1. One common tone.

        2. No common tones.

        3. Two common tones.

    B. First inversion chord connections—freer voice leading and doubling possible.

    C. Second inversion chords—often better connected after being interpreted as a form of six-four dissonance.

III. Primary dominant chords—the "dominant family" of each key.

    A. Triad and first inversion.

    B. Dominant seventh and its inversions.

    C. Leading tone triad (especially its first inversion form).

    D. Dominant ninth and its inversions.

    E. Leading tone seventh chord and its inversions (half and full diminished forms).

    F. Dominant eleventh chord—usually better interpreted as a dominant seventh with non-harmonic dissonances.

    G. Dominant thirteenth and its inversions.

IV. Secondary dominant chords—those chords which are dominant in function to any degree *other than* the tonic. Their use is possible in both modes as indicated:

    A. Major—the dominant family of each degree except the leading tone, whose diminished quality does not permit it to function like a tonic, primary, or secondary.

    B. Minor—the dominant family of each degree as found in the natural minor scale including that of the leading tone, noting that the secondary dominant of the supertonic is related to the melodic form of minor scale.

V. Secondary seventh chords—chords built on only the unaltered scale degrees available in the major mode, and, in the minor mode, those chords available from the three scale forms, omitting, however, the dominant seventh chord which is primary in both modes.

M—major; m—minor; d—diminished; A—augmented
T—tonic; ST—supertonic; M—mediant; SD—subdominant; D—dominant; SM—submediant; LT—leading tone

	$\frac{M}{M}$	$\frac{m}{M}$	$\frac{M}{m}$	$\frac{m}{m}$	$\frac{m}{d}$	$\frac{d}{d}$	$\frac{M}{A}$
A. Major mode	T	D			ST	LT	
	SD				M		
					SM		

B. Minor mode ......

1. natural ....M	LT		T	ST		
SM			SD			
			D			
2. harmonic ....SM	D	T	SD	ST	LT	M
3. melodic	SD	T	ST	SM		M
	D			LT		

VI. Altered chords.

A. Chords altered for use in the opposite mode.

It often is desirable to use a chord quality belonging to one mode in a comparable position in the opposite mode. This adaptation can be accomplished by making the necessary alterations in spelling and quality, and is called modal interchange. The use of such chords can vary from that of a single chord to that of translating an entire phrase, sentence, or section from one mode to the other. Examples of modal interchange are:

1. Other-than-dominant chords.

   a. major tonic chord in minor mode—Picardy third.

   b. minor subdominant chord in the major mode.

   c. diminished submediant chord in the major mode.

   d. diminished supertonic chord in the major mode.

   e. lowered mediant major chord in the major mode.

   f. lowered submediant major chord in the major mode.

2. Chords of the dominant family.

   a. leading tone seventh of minor in the major mode.

   b. dominant minor ninth of minor in the major mode.

   c. dominant minor thirteenth of minor in the major mode.

B. Neapolitan chord—in both modes a major chord built on the lowered second scale degree; used most frequently in first inversion.

C. Augmented sixth chords—an altered chord based on an interval of the augmented sixth which tends to resolve by expanding into an octave interval based on the degree designated.

1. Pre-dominant types.

   a. Italian sixth chord—

      1) minor mode—a subdominant sixth chord with a raised root.

      2) major mode—a subdominant sixth chord with a raised root and a lowered 3rd degree.

   b. German sixth chord—
    1) minor mode—a subdominant six-five chord with a raised root. $\widehat{IV}\ _{6}^{5}$
    2) major mode—a supertonic four-three chord with a raised root, a raised 3rd, and lowered fifth degrees.
   c. French sixth chord—
    1) minor mode—a supertonic four-three chord with a raised 3rd degree.
    2) major mode—a supertonic four-three chord with a raised 3rd, and lowered 5th degree.
  2. Pre-tonic (or, pre-other degree) types—based on the use of chords whose augmented sixth interval tends to expand into octave interval of the degree designated.
   a. pre-tonic in both modes—
    1) Italian sixth chord—a leading tone first inversion triad with a lowered 3rd degree.
    2) French sixth chord—a dominant four-three chord with a lowered 5th degree.
   b. pre-mediant in the *major* mode.
    1) Italian sixth chord—a supertonic sixth chord with a raised root.
    2) German sixth chord—a supertonic six-five chord with a raised root.
  3. Chromatic type—an augmented sixth chord whose principal function is to serve as a passing embellishment between the root position and the first inversion of the dominant seventh chord.

VII. Modulation.
  A. Direct pivot—
   1. by a pivot chord between—
    a. relative major and minor keys—no signature change.
    b. major and minor keys differing by two or less accidentals.
   2. by two common tone pivot
   3. by one common tone pivot
  B. Chromatic—
   1. by alteration of chords—changing their quality, hence, their function and allegiance.
   2. by indirect pivot chord—a dominant chord related to parallel major and minor chords whose function is primary, secondary, or some combination of these to the tonalities concerned.

3. by the Neapolitan chord—whose function in one or the other of the keys can be primary in the major mode or secondary in the minor mode.

C. Enharmonic—by the augmented sixth chord (especially the Italian and German forms)—in which the augmented sixth chord can assume the function of either a primary or a secondary dominant seventh chord in one or the other of the keys concerned.

CADENCES

I. Classes of cadences.

A. conclusive—cadences that end with finality, hence on the tonic chord of either mode.

1. *Authentic*—the dominant followed by the tonic chord in either mode.

2. *Plagal*—the subdominant followed by the tonic chord in either mode.

3. *Full*—an authentic cadence "filled out" by adding one, or at times two chords before the dominant-tonic progression ending the cadence. There are four frequently occurring formulas—

   a. supertonic, dominant, tonic in either mode.

   b. subdominant, dominant, tonic in either mode.

   c. submediant, dominant, tonic in either mode.

   d. a second inversion tonic (or better named, a dominant with six-four dissonance), dominant, tonic in either mode.

B. Inconclusive—cadences that end with lack of finality, hence on other than the tonic chord of either mode.

1. *Half*—a cadence closing a phrase whose last chord may be the dominant, its first inversion, the subdominant, its first inversion, or a first inversion tonic chord. The most usual form is that ending on the dominant chord of either mode.

2. *Phrygian*—a form of half cadence popular in the Baroque period.

   a. minor mode—a first inversion subdominant chord followed by a dominant (major) chord.

   b. major mode—one possible form is a supertonic root position chord with the third in the soprano followed by a root position major chord on the mediant degree whose root is doubled in the soprano voice.

3. *Deceptive*—in its most usual form characterized by the progression of the dominant to the submediant chord in either mode.

II. Characteristics of cadences.

A. Conclusive cadences.

1. Descriptive names—authentic, plagal, full—are associated with the particular chord progression involved.

2. Perfection—a cadence is *perfect* whenever the last two chords are in root position with the root doubled in the soprano voice of the last chord. Any other voice leading results in an imperfect cadence.

3. Rhythmic gender—a cadence whose final tonic chord occurs on the first beat of any measure, or on the third beat of a four beat measure, is *masculine*. Any other rhythmic position of the final chord results in a feminine cadence.

B. Inconclusive cadences.

1. Descriptive names—half, Phrygian, deceptive—are associated with the particular chord progression involved.

2. The terms perfect, imperfect, masculine, and feminine are not used to describe the inconclusive cadences, since their general effect tends to be imperfect and feminine in most cases.

III. Other cadence progressions.

A number of other cadence progressions, or cadences, are possible, but have been used less frequently. One very interesting series occurs in the closing 18 measures of the Berlioz *Requiem* (*q.v.*). Following a form of the full cadence, a succession of six cadences, including four of the less used cadence progressions, is found. Considered in the closing key of G major, there are—

A. a subdominant chord followed by the tonic chord—a plagal cadence,

B. a mediant chord followed by the tonic chord—a "mediant" cadence,

C. a supertonic chord followed by the tonic chord—a "supertonic" cadence,

D. a raised (major) submediant chord followed by the tonic—an "altered submediant" cadence,

E. the Neapolitan chord followed by the tonic chord—a "Neapolitan" cadence, and

F. the dominant chord followed by the tonic chord—a final authentic cadence.

NON-HARMONIC TONES

I. Basic information.

   A. Definitions.

      Notes of chords are *chord tones.* Those not belonging to, but sounded with, a chord, are *non-harmonic tones,* also called *non-chord tones.* Most non-harmonic tones are one step above or below a chord tone, which is either a root, 3rd, or 5th degree. A non-harmonic tone and the adjacent and related chord tone seldom occur together. One or more non-harmonic tones thus momentarily displace one or more chord tones. The examples show such displacement of each degree of root position and first inversion chords. The horizontal combinations involved include the 2-1, 2-3, 4-3, 4-5, 6-5, 7-6, and 7-8.

   B. Descriptive names.

      In general, the descriptive name of each non-harmonic tone is assigned as a result of noting the approach to, or *preparation* of, the dissonant tone. An unprepared dissonance, as well as one approached by a leap, is called an appoggiatura (see 4 and 5). The returning tone, suspension, passing tone, and appoggiatura clearly differ in their distinctive manner of approaching the dissonant tone.

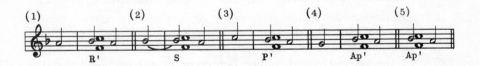

   C. Accent.

      1. The returning tone, passing tone, suspension, and appoggiatura can be accented or unaccented, depending upon the rhythmic position of the dissonant tone. They are:

a. *accented*—when the dissonant tone occurs over a change of harmony or chord position or on a relatively strong beat, with or without a change of harmony or chord position.

b. *unaccented*—when the dissonant tone occurs after a change of harmony, or on a weak beat without a change of harmony or chord position.

2. The cambiata is unaccented since it is a weak form of the appoggiatura.

3. The escape tone and the anticipation are unaccented since their dissonant tone occurs in a weak rhythmic position.

II. The common non-harmonic tones.

A. Returning tone—occurs as a half or whole step decoration—down and up or up and down—of any sustained or repeated tone *common* to two chords (or chord positions) with or without an accompanying change of harmony.

B. Suspension—occurs at a point of step motion between two chords (or chord position) when a tone of the first chord is sustained or repeated over the change of chord or position, and is then resolved by step, up or down, as appropriate.

C. Passing tone—includes at least three scalewise diatonic or chromatic tones, the middle one being the dissonant passing tone.

D. Escape tone—occurs at a point of step motion between two chords (or chord positions) when a tone of the first chord moves a step to a dissonant tone—traditionally in the direction opposite to the implied resolution—and then leaps a third to the second chord tone. A liberalized interpretation allows the initial step and leap to be in the same direction and the size of the leap to exceed a third.

E. Anticipation—occurs at a point of step motion between two chords (or chord positions) when a tone of the first chord moves to its resolution as a part of the second chord *before* the harmonic rhythm of the second chord has become effective.

F. *Appoggiatura*—occurs at a point of stepwise or larger motion between two chords (or chord positions) when a tone of the first chord *leaps* to a dissonant tone a step above or below a tone of the second chord, either *before* or *at the moment* that the harmonic rhythm of the second chord becomes effective. The resolution is by step motion—usually opposite to the direction of the leap—to the chord tone displaced.

G. Cambiata—the form of appoggiatura in which the rhythmic position of the dissonant tone is weak.

III. Less common non-harmonic tones.

A. Free tone—a dissonant tone whose preparation and resolution are both by leap, with or without accent of harmonic change in the chords involved.

B. Pedal point—an extended dissonant tone whose preparation and resolution—considered for each successive pair of chords—are both by prolongation.

NOTE: The existence and use of non-harmonic tones is granted by all theorists; however, there is some disagreement concerning the assignment of descriptive names. The student is urged to consult other sources so he can be aware of the differences in interpretation.

SUGGESTED STANDARDS FOR PROFICIENCY AND SKILLS

These "Suggested Standards" are given as a help to the student in self-evaluation. By constantly striving for his highest level of attainment, he will be increasing his proficiency in the use of the basic skills. By ascertaining the areas in which more drill and study are needed, the student will be aiding himself in making his fundamental knowledge functional.

I. Theory Skills.

A. Clefs—SATISFACTORY ATTAINMENT: the correct notation of 24 items on the staff in—
   1. Minimum ....2 minutes
   2. Above-average.... 1½ minutes
   3. Superior ....1 minute

B. Scale Tests—all types, except the melodic minor as a separate test. SATISFACTORY ATTAINMENT: the correct notation of the indicated number of scales in five minutes—
   1. Minimum 8
   2. Above-average 12
   3. Superior 16

C. Melodic Minor Scale—for all scale tests in which the melodic minor is included with other scales write its upward form only. For *Theory Skill* #22—SATISFACTORY ATTAINMENT: the correct notation of the indicated number of scales in five minutes—
   1. Minimum 6
   2. Above-average 9
   3. Superior 12

D. Whole and Half Steps,
   Closed Chord Positions,
   Open Chord Positions, and
   Five Tetrachords—SATISFACTORY ATTAINMENT: the cor-
   rect notation of the indicated number of groups, chords, or
   patterns in five minutes—

   1. Minimum 16
   2. Above-average 28
   3. Superior 40

E. Four Triads, and each of the
   Interval Tests, except the Whole and Half Step Test—SATIS-
   FACTORY ATTAINMENT: the correct notation of the indicated
   number of triads or two note interval groups in five minutes—

   1. Minimum 20
   2. Above-average 35
   3. Superior 50

F. Three Primary Triads in *either* mode, and
   Four Secondary Triads in *either* mode—SATISFACTORY AT-
   TAINMENT: use the standards for the foregoing "Scale Tests,"
   considering the three primary triads, or the four secondary triads
   in a key as the equivalent of one scale..

G. The Dominant Seventh Chord,
   Diminished Seventh Chord,
   Secondary Dominant Seventh Chord,
   Secondary Seventh Chord,
   Neapolitan Chord, and
   The Augmented Sixth Chords—SATISFACTORY ATTAIN-
   MENT: the correct notation of the indicated number of chords
   in five minutes—

   1. Minimum 12
   2. Above-average 21
   3. Superior 30

II. Performance Skills.

   A. Keyboard Skills—(unless other standards are provided), and
   B. Rhythm Skills—SATISFACTORY ATTAINMENT:

      1. Superior—the ability to perform any given skill with little, if
         any, hesitation, and with no major errors.
      2. Above-average—the ability to perform at a high level of skill,
         but with an occasional hesitation and error, usually noticed
         by the student.

3. Minimum—evidence of understanding the basic principles, but with some hesitation and occasional errors.

III. Dictation—the following steps are suggested—

A. Compute the PROFICIENCY PERCENTAGE by following the directions given or referred to in each instance.

B. Note the types of errors for guidance in further study.

C. Evaluate the attained PROFICIENCY PERCENTAGE in terms of the following standards: (this is one possible scale for use)

1. Superior 95%-100%
2. Above-average 85%- 94%
3. Minimum 75%- 84%

The above process often is suggested in the dictation sections found in the manual by such phrases as "evaluate," or "determine the PROFICIENCY PERCENTAGE and evaluate." This general type of evaluation gives a useful assessment of status in all pitch skills, pitch achievement, rhythm achievement, melodic dictation, and harmonic dictation which can serve as a guide to the serious student.

REFERENCE INDEX OF
MUSICAL ILLUSTRATIONS

MUSICAL SOURCES

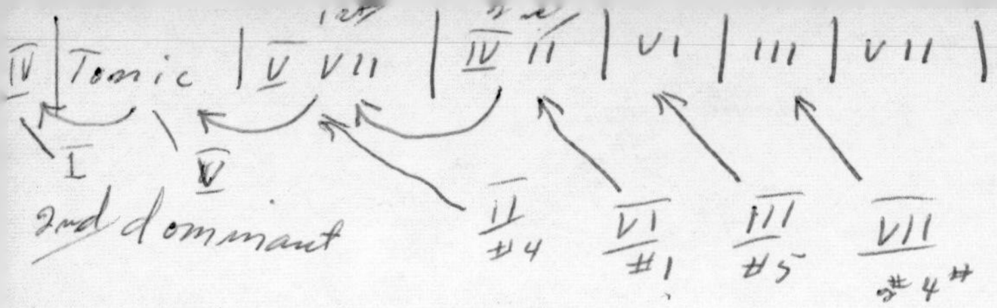

IV | Tonic | V VII | IV II | VI | III | VII)

I   V

2nd dominant

$\overline{II}$ $\overline{VI}$ $\overline{III}$ $\overline{VII}$
#4   #1   #5   #4#